Inter-organizational information exchange, supply chain compliance and performance

Inter-organizational information exchange, supply chain compliance and performance

Guangqian Peng

Wageningen Academic
P u b l i s h e r s

ISBN: 978-90-8686-178-1
e-ISBN: 978-90-8686-736-3
DOI: 10.3921/978-90-8686-736-3

First published, 2011

© Wageningen Academic Publishers
The Netherlands, 2011

Wageningen Academic Publishers
P.O. Box 220
6700 AE Wageningen
the Netherlands
www.WageningenAcademic.com
copyright@WageningenAcademic.com

Dedicated to my parents,

my husband Junfeng and

my sweet daughter Anna

Table of contentes

List of tables

List of figures

Abbreviations

EDI	Electronic data interchange
IOC	Inter-organizational communication; inter-organizational information exchange
IOIS	Inter-organizational information systems
PLS modeling	Partial least squares modeling
RCT	Relational contracting theory
SCM	Supply chain management
SEM	Structural equation modeling
TSI	Transaction specific investments

Acknowledgements (致谢)

During the last five years I have had the privilege to work in a stimulating and supportive work environment. This book could not have become true without the contribution and encouragement of so many around me. I would like to take this opportunity to thank them.

First of all, I would like to thank my supervisors, Onno Omta and Jacques Trienekens, for their support and interest in this research. Onno, thank you for the pragmatic guidance over the years and for constantly pushing me to improve my work and to get the best out of my intelligence. You always point out the key issues directly and clearly. And Jacques, thank you for always spending so much time reading and discussing my work in details and helping me through the 'pessimistic moments' during my PhD research. I am deeply impressed by your logical and meticulous way of thinking and writing. From you I have learnt how to write project proposals and express my academic ideas briefly and to the point. You supervise me in such a wise way that I have great freedom to design and conduct the research in the way I like on the one hand, but never have shortage of inspiring and highly-qualified supervision on the other hand. I enjoyed similar wonderful experience when cooperating with Emiel Wubben during 2003-2004 for my MSc thesis. I am so lucky to have both you as my daily supervisors during my study in the Netherlands. Enthusiastic Emiel and steady Jacques, thank you also particularly for encouraging me to apply for the PhD position.

Special thanks also go to Wensheng Wang 王文生, the supervisor during my field research in China. Thank you for being supportive of my application for the PhD position and for your introduction into your network of agricultural technology and information experts for interviews and surveys. Many appreciations also go to Jikun Huang 黄季昆. Thank you for your open-mindedness and encouraging me to pursue the PhD research. In addition, I especially acknowledge the encouragement I have received from 袁易明 to extend my academic background to *economics and business administration*. It turned out to be a significant shift in my academic background, which I truly appreciate. Furthermore, I am indebted to 方子节，Harrie ver Hoeven, 金道超，Ronnie Vernooy, 桑维君， 宋一清， 孙中魁， 徐成云， 徐涵， 熊清华 for influencing and facilitating my career development in *economics and business administration* in one way or another.

Working at the Business Administration Department of Wageningen University has been an inspiring and enjoyable experience. I acknowledge my (former) colleagues and friends: Abebe, Anna, Andre, Danny, Derk-Jan, Djala, Domenico, Ekaterina, Etriya, Frances, Geoffrey, Hanieh, Harry, Hons, Hualiang, Ina, Janne, Jeanette, Jiqin, Joanna, Jose-Jaime, Katja, Lilly, Maarten, Mark, Mersiha, Nel, Paul, Peter, Rannia, Rita, Stefanie, Verena, Vincent, Wijnand, Willeke, and Zhen – for your valuable support in one way or another. I do enjoy our academic and cultural communication, monthly staff meeting, coffee breaks, the-end-of-the-month drinks, group lunches and dinners, group trips and PhD Friday drinks over the past years.

Special thanks go to Jos Bijman and your warm family, Jacqueline, Lu, Jip and Abe. Thank you for accompanying and looking after Anna during my intensive period. Thank you, Annie Royer, my wise and sweet officemate. The daily conversation involving broad issues during the working break is always pleasant and inspiring. Thank you, Leonie, your knowledge and contribution have greatly facilitated the budget management of my research project and the arrangement of my family life. My thanks also go to Anthony, Ineke, Marion, Richard, and Eveline for facilitating the progress of the research project in one way or another. Thank you all sincerely!

I would have never completed my research project without the support from so many in the survey areas. Numerous experts, officers, managers and practitioners have been involved. Thank you all for your contributions. A special word of appreciation goes to Ben Kamphuis, 柴晓冲, 胡定寰, 李东, 卢海, 吕新业, 龙祖上, 秦富, 王秀香, 王耀球, 薛飞, 岳福菊, 袁浩宗, 杨青松, 杨兴洪, 云鹏, 朱法江, 赵薇.

I would like to thank Ron Kemp, 王惠文, 吴喜之, 易丹辉 for assistance in solving my doubt in data analysis. I am also grateful to Janne Denolf for translating the English summary into Dutch. In particular I want to thank Hanieh Khodaei and you to be my paranymphs. My sincere thanks also go to Sandra and 吉昌 for proofreading the book.

In addition, I would like to thank the members of my dissertation committee; i.e. Adrie Beulens, Olaf van Kooten, B.M.J. van der Meulen, and Aad van Tilburg for your willingness to review this book and to participate in the public defence. I am also indebted to 高平, Shirley Gregor, Detmar Straub, Jack van der Vorst, and the anonymous reviewers for the valuable comments on my work.

My special gratitude goes to Gerda, 老关, 何倩, 春明, 雷颖, 万希, 禾青, 雪芹, Xiaoyong, 克强 and your family for friendship and hospitality. I also sincerely appreciate my friends especially Cathy, Gert Jan Hofstede, 季晨, 贾立, 刘畅, 梁丹, 书秦, 李元, Nicolien, Paul, Margherita Poto, Tanita, Jelena Vlajic, 涓文, 阎云, 张磊, 丽锦, 曾源. Your friendship and insights will be with me forever. Thanks also go to Zhenwei Ye for providing the idea for cover design.

Last but not least, I thank my great family for their encouragement. Special thanks goes to my father 彭新明 for his unconditional support and encouragement in pursuing my study. Appreciation also goes to my uncle 傅树湘 and my cousin 傅敏. My sweet Anna, thank you for being with mom in Spain and the Netherlands. My most special thanks go to my husband Junfeng. You shared the frustrations and the happiness during my career and private life. Your continuous support and encouragement have been with me along the way. Thank you for your support, patience, and most of all, love.

Guangqian
Wageningen / Beijing, May 2011

Chapter 1

Introduction

1.1 Research background

To obtain competitive advantages in the late nineteenth century and early twentieth century, companies optimized the productivity of labor through time and motion studies, and analysis of the worker-machine interfaces (Skinner, 1985). In the final third of the twentieth century, companies build competitive advantage by organizing, simplifying, and integrating factory flows using just-in-time and lean production (Womack *et al.*, 1990). Recently, facing intensified global competition, companies are seeking to gain competitive edge through supply chain collaboration, which leverages the resources, information sharing, and knowledge creation of customers and suppliers, and coordinates and integrates the flow of products and information across the supply chain (Verwaal and Hesselmans, 2004; Cao *et al.*, 2010). Nowadays, 'one of the most significant changes in the paradigm of modern business management is that individual businesses no longer compete as solely autonomous entities, but rather as supply chains' (Lambert *et al.*, 1998).

Supply chain collaboration can bring with substantial benefits and advantages for companies (Mentzer *et al.*, 2000; Cao *et al.*, 2010). It helps companies to guard against risks (Kogut, 1988), obtain complementary resources (Park *et al.*, 2004), improve technological capabilities (Powell *et al.*, 1996), reduce logistical costs (Stank *et al.*, 2001), reduce transaction costs, enhance productivity (Kalwani and Narayandas, 1995), and enhance profit performance and competitive advantage over time (Dyer and Singh, 1998).

A basic enabler for tight supply chain collaboration is inter-organizational communication. Communication is looked as the glue that holds supply chain partners together (Mohr and Nevin, 1990), the heart (Lamming, 1996), lifeblood (Stuart and McCutcheon, 1996), nerve center (Chopra and Meindl, 2007), essential ingredient (Min *et al.*, 2005), key requirement (Sheu *et al.*, 2006), and foundation (Lee and Whang, 2001) of chain collaboration. Effective and efficient communication is vital to on-going channel relationships and successful inter-firm exchange (Paulraj *et al.*, 2008). Inter-organizational communication and collaboration has been largely facilitated by modern information tools. Correspondingly, communication difficulties are a prime cause of collaboration failures. Miscommunication could cause conflicts and misunderstanding among supply chain partners (Paulraj *et al.*, 2008; Cao *et al.*, 2010).

In more details, the benefits derived from information exchange include: the elimination of order verification, better service, support for procurement, Pareto improvement in chain level performance, reductions in inventory and costs, quality and on-time delivery; lower demand uncertainty that leads to lower costs, higher order fulfillment rates, shorter order cycle time; agility and flexibility, together with improved stability and performance of the individuals and of the whole supply chains. Nowadays, 'the debate is not about whether or not information should be exchanged through supply chains, but about how to share the right information at the right time in the right format by the right people under the right environment to maximize mutual benefits of the supply chain as a whole as well as the individual business players.' (Schiefer, 2004).

Effective and efficient information exchange is especially important for the food sector, because of agri-product market globalization, unstable production and supply, shelf life constraints, increasing food safety demands, and so on. These characteristics bring critical needs for fast, real-time and reliable communication of information flows in supply chains and networks.

Food supply chains comprise organizations responsible for production and distribution of food products. The nature of perishable food brings specific characteristics to food supply chains (developed based on Van der Vorst, 2000; Van der Vorst *et al.*, 2005), including:

- unstable supply time and yield, due to reasons such as animal diseases;
- seasonality and geographic localization (regarding specific varieties) in production, which require global (year-round) sourcing, increasing cross-border flows of meat products, while creating various types of international cooperation;
- high volume, increasing but still low variety production systems;
- long production throughput time;
- production often involves by-products, co-products and waste products;
- quality variation amongst lots of products;
- long distance to markets;
- perishable nature and shelf-life constraints, which demand short throughput times, and limit the possibility of using stock as a tool to balance supply and demand, while specific stock and transportation means are required (such as temperature adjustable facilities);
- increasing sanitary, environmental and animal-friendly demands;
- traceability is demanded by (EU) regulations and obtains higher and higher attention from consumers;
- different criteria regarding quality and safety are required by different countries.

These characteristics mentioned above bring challenges to supply chain management: balancing food supply and demand, measuring food quality, shortening lead times while lowering cost, guaranteeing freshness and safety in stock and transportation, planning of meat by-products or waste products; traceability systems, obtaining quality qualifications related to different regulations in different parts of the international market.

Until the early 1980s, diets with daily consumption of meat were the privilege of a small number of wealthy citizens in China. For most Chinese people, meat, milk and eggs were an unaffordable luxury, consumed only on rare occasions. However, huge developments have taken place in the meat sector since the government removed state procurement quotas and price controls in 1985 (Han, 2009). The changing composition of the meat sector and its expansion in the last 23 years from 1985 is depicted in Table 1.1. It reflects that the share of poultry have gradually increased in total output of livestock products, though pork still dominates the meat scene in China.

Table 1.2 presents the per capita possession of meat from 1990. It is shown that per capital possession of meat have gradually increased during the last 18 years, including per capital possession of poultry and pork.

Different from the highly integrated poultry chains in the West, fragmentation and integration coexist in the Chinese poultry chain. Table 1.3 shows poultry production scale and the total number of poultry produced in 2008. It is shown that small-scale, medium-size, and large-scale poultry farms coexist.

Table 1.1. The output of poultry and other meat in selected years in China (10,000 tonnes) (China Statistical Yearbook of Animal Husbandry 2009).

	1985		1995		2005		2008	
	Output	**%**	**Output**	**%**	**Output**	**%**	**Output**	**%**
Poultry	160.2	8.3	724.3	17.8	1,344.2	19.4	1,533.7	21.1
Pork	1,654.7	85.9	2,853.5	71.0	4,555.3	65.6	4,620.5	63.5
Other meat	111.6	5.8	496.6	12.2	1,039.4	15.0	1,124.5	15.4
Total meat output	1,926.5	100.0	4,074.4	100.0	6,938.9	100.0	7,278.7	100.0

Table 1.2. Per capita meat possession in selected years in China (kilograms per person; Chinese Yearbook of Meat 2008).

	1990	**1995**	**2000**	**2005**	**2008**
Poultry	2.8	6.1	9.4	11.2	11.5
Pork	20	24.2	31.4	38.3	34.8
Total meat	25.1	34.5	47.8	59.2	54.8

Table 1.3. Poultry production scale for 2008 in China (China Statistical Yearbook of Animal Husbandry, 2009).

Poultry production scale (Number of poultry / year)	**Number of poultry at the end of the year (10,000 heads)**	**Percentage of the total poultry**
Below 2000	144,668.9	18.4
2000 ~ 49,999	440,699.9	55.9
50,000 ~ 499,999	132,208.7	16.8
500,000 ~ 999,999	21,804.3	2.8
More than 1,000,000	48,640.8	6.2
Total	788,022.6	100.0

Meanwhile, different sizes of slaughterhouses and processors also coexist. Usually, small and medium-sized slaughterhouses and processors sell their poultry products as fresh meat immediately in nearby rural or urban markets. The medium-sized and large-scale slaughterhouses and processors account for about 20% of total production, and provide their poultry products mainly for the national markets.

Meat products reach final consumers via many different channels. In general, we distinguish three main types of meat chains in China: (1) the wet market chain; (2) the supermarket/restaurant chain; and (3) the international chain. Figure 1.1 illustrates the configuration of the meat chains in China.

The wet market chain is the traditional meat chain. Wet markets are the main places where local farmers and traders supply agri-food products to consumers. A typical wet market is located in the open air, with wooden or cement tables. They are often situated inside or nearby residence areas. Nowadays, many of such wet markets have moved indoors, and are called *Nongmao* (agri-trade) markets. Chinese consumers have the tradition to buy living poultry. The wet markets located in small towns or medium-sized cities provide consumers fresh poultry meat alongside living poultry. Those located in large cities provide only fresh poultry, and living poultry transactions are forbidden. Comparatively, the wet chain is characterized by without or less facilities, lower transaction costs and lower quality standards. But because it matches with the income level and purchasing habits of most consumers, it will probably prevail for the next decade in China.

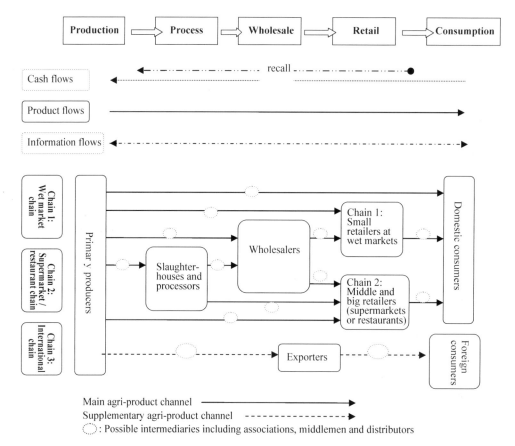

Figure 1.1. Configuration of the meat supply chains in China.

The supermarket chain is the modern chain in China. Supermarkets first appeared in the richer areas of Southeast China more than a decade ago, and then rapidly extended to other parts of China. They are often located in downtowns or nearby residence areas. Fresh produce first appeared in supermarkets around 1996, when several international chains started their business in China (Hu *et al.*, 2003). These chains have more investments in facilities and higher quality standards. Most supermarkets rely on three different chains for sourcing meat products, including: (1) poultry processors, such as Huadu (chicken), Dafa (chicken) and Jinxing (duck); (2) wholesale markets; (3) and specialized poultry bases/villages.

The international chain provides poultry products to international markets according to relevant international food standards and requirements, such as HCCAP. The poultry sector was the biggest foreign-capital-earning sector among the livestock sectors in 2005. However, due to relatively high production costs (i.e. costs of corns) and quality problems, the development of this chain is facing challenges (Hu and Liu, 2007).

1.2 Problem statement and research questions

First, inter-organizational communication is a broad concept covering wide range of aspects, such as communication norm and willingness (Eisenberg and Witten, 1987; Heide and John, 1992; Fawcett *et al.*, 2007), information contents communicated, information media adopted, people involved, communication frequency, information quality, information direction, and information formality, and so on (Storer, 2005). However, previous studies typically considered communication as an aspect of a broader construct, such as supply management (e.g. Chen and Paulraj, 2004). Or, some studies have studied one or limited aspects of communication. For example, some studies and organization took communication as communication willingness only. The Global Logistics Research Team at Michigan State University (1995) defined information sharing as 'the *willingness* to make strategic and tactical data such as … available to firms forming supply chain nodes'. Some studies took communication as the extent to which companies share information (e.g. Lee *et al.*, 2010). Some others mixed communication intention together with communication actions (e.g. Cai *et al.*, 2010; Nyaga *et al.*, 2010). We posit that as inter-organizational communication is a broad concept covering diverse aspects, an indicating factor might have different influences on different aspects of communication; each communication aspect might have different relationships with other aspects; and different aspects of communication might also have different effects on different aspects of company performance. This research therefore proposes an integrative framework, which is among the first attempts to include different aspects of communication, and examine these diverse aspects by the same sample in one context.

Second, limited researches including doctoral dissertations have been conducted *quantitatively* on *supply chain information systems* in the *food* sector, although some case studies have provided valuable knowledge in a general context. Stock *et al.* (1988/1989, 1993, 2001, 2006) reviewed doctoral studies in supply chain management (SCM) and logistics related areas. They (2006) reported that, during 1999-2004, only 7 out of 410 (1.7%) SCM and logistics related dissertations gave full focuses on supply information systems. Storer (2005), based on an intensive literature review, pointed out there is also a lack of detailed studies of perishable goods systems. Food chains have special product characteristics that other industries rarely have, due to greater uncertainty (Trienekens, 1999). For instance, seasonality in material production, requirements for conditioned transportation and storage means, or quality decay, which would make production planning, transportation, and storage more challenging (Grievink *et al.*, 2002).

Third, some literature has studied inter-organizational communication but dominantly in the context of developed countries. However, in this globalized economy age, the other parts of the world are becoming increasingly important purchasing sources and/or consumption markets. It would be meaningful if more studies in the future examine this issue from other parts of the world. China is the largest and fastest growing emerging economy in the world, with a substantially different market setting compared to the West (Luo and Park, 2001). A study on food chain in this dynamic economy would be meaningful to examine again those revealed relationships and to provide valuable insights. In China, although SCM and Management Information Systems have received much attention in recent years, limited works have specifically addressed information exchange between entities in agribusiness supply chain. So far, no other *quantitative* study is found with a focus on inter-organizational information exchange in a food chain in the Mainland China.

In this research, the study domain is the poultry supply chain in the Mainland China. The poultry sector obtains our research attention, because of the following reasons (Hu, 2003; Liu *et al.*, 2005; Gu and Wang, 2007):

- Poultry, as an important meat product, has high economic value.
- The poultry consumption ranks the second among the meat consumption in China. Moreover, the production and consumption amount of poultry is increasing rapidly with the economic growth in China. However, no study has been found to have a focus on examining information communication and chain collaboration in this important chain.
- The Chinese poultry chain, on one hand, is more integrated compared to many other Chinese food chains, such as the vegetable or the fruit chains. On the other hand, it is still with large numbers of small and scattered producers and traders, and therefore is not highly integrated, especially compared to its counterparts in the West. In this way, it provides a new and meaningful context for the research on inter-organizational communication.
- Food quality management and safety control play an important role in the poultry chain. Other innovative issues, such as traceability, are under consideration or are likely to play an important role soon.
- It is with large variance in information tools. During the current developing process of industrial integration in the poultry chain, some large-sized companies have started to adopt modern information tools to communicate with their business partners, such as electronic data interchange and intranet.

Last but not the lease, most prior studies still focused on the perceptions of buying firms only or suppliers only, and did not reflect the perceptions of both sides. Therefore, there are questions concerning whether both customers and suppliers benefit from information sharing and collaboration (Nyaga *et al.*, 2010). Corsten and Kumar (2005) found that even though both parties benefited from the collaboration, there was greater feeling of inequity in the relationship on the part of suppliers. In other words, suppliers may believe that they receive less than they deserve. Besides, customers and suppliers normally have their own interests. Customers might focus more on relationship outcomes while suppliers look to safeguard their transaction specific investments through information sharing and joint relationship effort (Nyaga *et al.*, 2010). Thus, researchers have called to 'compare both sides of the equation' (Nyaga *et al.*, 2010). It would be valuable to address the perceptions of both customers and suppliers with the same sample(s) in one context, and to analyze perception differences between them. The present research is among the first attempts to reflect both sides of the 'coin' of inter-organizational communication, by collecting data on the focal companies' relationships with their most important customer, and with their most important suppliers, respectively.

The main research question of this research is: '*how inter-organizational communication can be improved and be used to provide better company performance*'. To answer this central research question and to achieve the desired research objective, the following specific research questions are formulated:

- Research Question A: *What are the impacts of transaction attributes and governance structure on inter-organizational communication (IOC)?*
- Research Question B: *What are the main aspects of inter-organizational communication, and what are their interrelationships?*
- Research Question C: *What are the relationships between inter-organizational communication and company performance?*

1.3 Outline of the research

This book consists of seven chapters, which can be divided into three parts, including: theory and research methodology, empirical studies, and the final discussion and conclusion. Figure 1.2 illustrates an overview of the outline of the book.

The first part of this book is on theory and research methodology. Chapter 2 reviews relative theories on Transaction Cost Economics, inter-organizational communication (IOC), and Supply Chain Management. The linkage between inter-organizational communication and the above mentioned theories are examined. The indicators for communication, the main aspects of communication, and

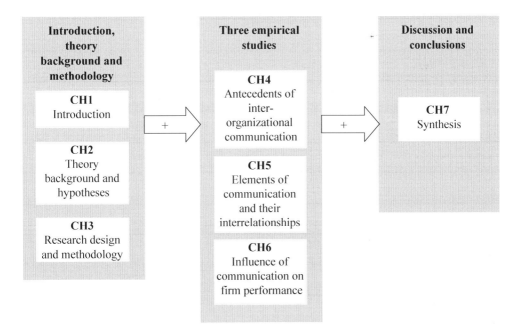

Figure 1.2. The outline of this book.

benefits and values of communication are also discussed. On that basis, related research hypotheses are proposed and research models are developed.

Chapter 3 starts with study population, data collection and company profile. Then, it presents the operationalization of the research constructs. Afterwards, it elaborates construct validity and reliability, and partial least squares modeling, the method used for data analysis.

The second part is composed of three empirical studies. Each study aims to answer one of the three research questions. Chapter 4 first analyzes the validity and reliability of the constructs used in this research. Then, it reports the research results on the influences of transaction attributes and governance structure on communication willingness and behaviors, with intention to reveal indicatory factors that support to improve communication between business partners.

Chapter 5 presents the research results on the interrelationships between communication willingness, communication behavior, communication quality, and perceived communication benefits, with intention to explore the interrelationships of important aspects of communication, and how these aspects interact to provide benefits for companies.

Chapter 6 focuses on the relationships between perceived communication benefits, supply chain compliance, and company performance, with intention to unfold the influence of inter-firm communication on company performance with the mediating role of chain cooperation.

The third part, Chapter 7, provides a synthesis of the findings derived from the three empirical studies. It first summarizes the research results. The answers to the research questions and some pathways to improve information exchange and company performance are addressed. The chapter also highlights the theoretical contributions and managerial implications of this research, as well as the limitations and directions for future research.

This book ends with a full overview of all references used, as well as summaries in English and Chinese.

Chapter 2

Theory background and hypotheses

This chapter discusses theories related to inter-organizational communication (IOC) in supply chains. It starts with a discussion on Transaction Cost Economics (TCE) in Section 2.1, which provides important theoretical insights into inter-organizational relationships and potential antecedents of IOC. Grounded on TCE, we study the potential effects of transaction attributes and governance structure on IOC. Transaction attributes considered are environmental uncertainty and transaction specific investments (TSI), whereas governance structure is modeled by trust and contractual governance. Then, this chapter switches to an introduction on the literature of inter-organizational communication (IOC) in Section 2.2, with the aim of finding the important aspects of IOC and their interrelationship. Thereafter, Section 2.3 sheds light on the theory of Supply Chain Management (SCM) and performance, which helps us understand the potential effects of IOC on supply chain (SC) compliance and performance.

Furthermore, Section 2.4, 2.5, and 2.6 contribute to refining the theoretical content of each concept and the three research models of this study. Specifically, Section 2.4 deals with transaction attributes and governance structure, and ends with a model on the antecedents of IOC (the Communication Antecedents Model). Section 2.5 discusses the main aspects of IOC, and proposes a research model on the interrelationships of the main aspects (the Communication Elements Model). Section 2.6 offers insights into the performance measures employed and how IOC affects SC compliance, and further affects company performance, and sequentially proposes a research model on the performance results of IOC (the Communication-Chain compliance-Performance Model). Figure 2.1 shows the theory framework of this research.

The chapter ends with concluding remarks in Section 2.7, with a research framework for the three main parts of this research (Figure 2.9).

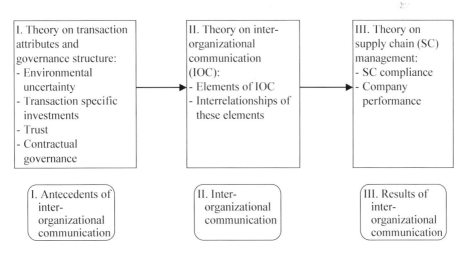

Figure 2.1. Theoretical framework.

2.1 Transaction cost economics

Transaction Cost Economics (TCE) has arguably been the dominant theory for analyzing economic organization between firms (Rindfleisch and Heide, 1997; Masten, 2000; Leiblein, 2003). Over the past decade, TCE has received considerable attention not only in economics, but also in management information systems (Bakos and Kemerer, 1992; Subramani, 2004), as well as in organization theory (e.g. Barney and Hesterly, 1996), business strategy (Hennart, 1988), corporate finance (Smith and Schnucker, 1994), marketing (Anderson, 1985), contract law (Palay, 1994), sociology (e.g. Granoveter, 1985), and political science (e.g. Moe, 1991).

TCE, together with agency theory, belongs to the 'New Institutional Economics' (sometimes referred to as Organizational Economics) paradigm and focuses on 'economic governance'. *Governance* is broadly defined as a 'model of organization' (Williamson, 1991), which is viewed in terms of particular mechanisms supporting an economic transaction where is an exchange of property rights. Meanwhile, Dixit (2009: 5-6) defines '*economic governance*' as 'the structure and functioning of the legal and social institutions that support economic activity and economic transactions by protecting property rights, enforcing contracts, and taking collective action to provide physical and organizational infrastructure... Good economic governance thus underpins the whole Smithian process whereby individuals specialize in different tasks and then transact with one another to achieve the full economic potential of the society'.

TCE asserts that the total cost incurred by a firm can be classified into two components: transaction costs and production costs. *Transaction costs*, namely, coordination costs, are defined as the costs of 'all the information processing necessary to coordinate the work of people and machines that perform the primary processes'. Meanwhile, *production costs* are defined as the costs incurred by 'the physical or other primary processes necessary to create and distribute the goods or services being produced' (Malone *et al.*, 1987). The key premise of TCE is that companies strive to minimize their transaction costs under a certain set of contingencies by choosing the optimal governance mechanism (Williamson, 1985; Barney and Hesterly, 1999). TCE includes *three assumptions* that underlie decisions on a given governance mechanism (Rindfleisch and Heide, 1997; Leiblein, 2003). First, individuals in any economic system have a bounded rationality. While people intend to be rational, in reality, their cognitive capabilities are limited. Second, at least some individuals behave opportunistically in business transactions and seek to serve their own interests with guile, which makes it difficult to know beforehand who is trustworthy and who is not. Third, information is asymmetrically distributed. Thus, people only have access to incomplete, imperfect or unbalanced information; no perfect information exists and exchanges are not costless. Based on these three assumptions, TCE explicitly considers the efficiency implications of adopting alternative modes of governance in transactions.

The logic of TCE is that collaboration in a buyer-supplier relationship strives for the lowest transaction costs (Rindfleisch and Heide, 1997; Bijman, 2002). According to TCE, any transaction has *ex ante* transaction costs and *ex post* transaction costs. *Ex ante transaction costs* are the costs arising before the transaction, such as searching and screening potential exchange agents and bargaining. *Ex post transaction costs* are the costs arising after the transaction such as monitoring compliance with contractual terms and enforcing sanctions in the event of non-compliance.

Meanwhile, TCE has conceptualized three alternative *governance mechanisms*, including spot-markets, vertical integration, and hybrid or intermediate mechanisms. Spot-markets are the most decentralized control structures where supply chain demand is regulated by way of the price mechanism. Vertical integration concerns centralized control structures where a central authority is deemed to possess sufficient information to perform all the coordination of supply and demand requirements (Bakos and Kemerer, 1992). In cases of lower levels of collaboration, the buyer-supplier relationship will be or will approximate the spot-market mode of governance; whereas in the case of a high level of collaboration, the buyer-supplier relationship will resemble the vertical integration model of governance. Between these two extremes, several types of hybrid relationships have been distinguished, which range from collaboration with a short-term focus, long-term focus, to without end cooperation date. Based on these, supply chain researchers further distinguished seven types of chain partnerships, which is elaborated in Section 2.3 and shown in Figure 2.4. According to TCE, if transaction costs are low, economic organizations will favor market governance. However, if transaction costs are high enough to exceed cost advantages of markets, firms will favor contracting or internal organization (Masten, 2000).

In the original framework to study governance mechanisms, Williamson (1985) identified three critical *transaction dimensions*, namely, transaction specific investments, uncertainty (associated with the transaction), and frequency (of the transactions). Of these, the concept of transaction specific investments is the dimension most frequently used to determine the optimal governance mechanism for transactions. *Transaction specific investments* (TSI) refer to human and physical assets that are dedicated to a particular relationship and cannot easily be redeployed. The idiosyncratic nature of these assets gives rise to a safeguarding problem, and consequently a mechanism must be designed to minimize the risk of subsequent opportunistic behavior (Anderson and Gerbing, 1988). TSI are so critical that they transform the nature of the exchange; rendering firms to both valuable and vulnerable positions (Williamson, 1996).

Uncertainty and complexity are the central problems of transactions. TCE explicitly acknowledges and pays particular attention to the role of information in alleviating problems caused by uncertainty (Bakos and Kemerer, 1992). Uncertainty may arise from rapidly changing technology, markets, and consumer preferences. Uncertainty has often been divided into environmental uncertainty and behavioral uncertainty. *Environmental uncertainty* refers to 'unanticipated changes in circumstances surrounding an exchange' (Noordewier *et al.*, 1990: 82). Meanwhile, TCE views *behavioral uncertainty* as arising from the difficulties associated with monitoring the contractual performance of exchange partners (Williamson, 1985). Of all the TCE constructs, environmental uncertainty seems to be the most problematic from a measurement standpoint. Specifically, there appear to be two competing operationalizations of this construct. The most commonly held perspective emphasizes the unpredictable nature of the external environment, whereas the second view examines both unpredictability and complexity. As for behavioral uncertainty, compared to environmental uncertainty and TSI, it involves far fewer operationalizations (Rindfleisch and Heide, 1997).

The *frequency* with which a transaction occurs can be a relevant determinant of which governance structure the cost economizing solution will be. Frequency usually affects governance only in conjunction with the asset specificity involved in the transaction (Boger, 2001a). Existing TCE studies have been largely unsuccessful in confirming the hypothesized effects of frequency on the governance model, therefore, frequency has received limited attention (Rindfleisch and Heide, 1997).

To address safeguarding against problems that result from TSI and to reduce risk and uncertainty, trust and contractual governance are proposed as two important governance concepts in TCE. In recent decades, the economic theory of contracts has developed rapidly. It has received contributions from several areas, of which TCE and agency theory are the most important (Bogetoft and Olesen, 2004). In TCE, a *contract* between a buyer and a supplier means specific transactions, agreements and promises, and the terms of the exchange are defined by price, asset specificity and safeguards, on the assumption that quantity, quality and duration are all specified (Williamson, 1996). TCE is concerned with the costs of making and administering a contract. Transaction costs lead to incomplete contracts that do not specify all possible contingencies. There are four types of direct transaction costs involving a contract (Bogetoft and Olesen, 2004). The first is the difficulty of foreseeing the possible contingencies in a complex world, i.e. the difficulty in setting up a complete set of possible outcomes. The second is the cost of wording a contract. To reach an agreement taking different contingencies into account, the parties have to find a common language describing the different contingencies. The third is the cost of writing a legally binding contract. The above three costs are the principle transaction costs when entering a contract. The fourth type of transaction cost is influence costs, which arise when one party tries to increase his utility by influencing the decisions made by another party. The influence activities may involve holding back information, distorting information, exploiting connections, and withholding specific knowledge (Milgrom and Roberts, 1990, 1992; Hansmann, 1996).

Different from TCE, relational contracting theory (RCT) takes another perspective regarding contract. In RCT, the concept of a contract is expanded to refer to relationships between people who have exchanged, are exchanging, or expect to exchange in the future (MacNeil, 2000). RCT describes a set of relational contracting norms, which are adaptations of the norms common to all contracts (MacNeil, 2000). To distinguish between TCE and RCT approaches to contract, the earlier literature has referred to contracts as hard and soft, explicit and normative, formal and informal, and written and unwritten (Heide, 1994; Lusch and Brown, 1996; Antia and Frazier, 2001).

Trust is viewed as another critical governance mechanism in TCE in establishing a 'hybrid' or 'relational' model of governance structure (Son *et al.*, 2005). According to TCE, trust is a key relational characteristic in building long-term hierarchical relationships between organizations, as it motivates firms to tolerate short-term inequities in the belief that things will 'balance out' in the long term. In other words, trust can lead the parties to believe that short-term inequities would be compensated by mutual benefits in the long term. The main benefit of trust is to provide one party with an optimistic anticipation of the behavior of another party in an exchange relationship. Trust is regarded as relational governance mechanism, safeguarding against opportunism, and an important non-contractual element of the buyer-supplier relationship (Gulati, 1995; Gopal and Koka, 2009).

Gibbons (2010) summarized the accomplishments of TCE in three parts: (1) *methodology* for studying particular governance structures (by microanalysis of transaction detail) and comparing them to others (comparative institutional analysis); (2) *assumptions* about the nature of certain important economic transactions and the devices available for governing them; and (3) applications, mostly to the boundary of the firm, including TCE's theory and evidence on vertical integration, and TCE's theory and evidence on contracts between firms.

TCE has generated considerable interest in the field of management information systems as in other academic disciplines. Two areas of information systems (IS) have been proposed as promising applications of TCE (Bakos and Kemerer, 1992). At the microscopic level, the systems development process is suggested as amenable to analysis through the TCE lens. Ciborra (1985) argued that, existing models of the systems development process were excessively rational in their expectations about how the end users viewed the systems being developed for them. He noted that, the parties to systems development projects have 'mixed interests', and systems development methodologies should explicitly recognize this. Beath (1987) carried this point of view further by studying fourteen actual projects and an in-depth examination of four case studies. She reported clear relationships between project performance and the degree to which the governance structures 'fit' the problem domain.

At the macroscopic level, TCE has been employed to explain and predict changes in industry structure, which were resulted from information technology (IT). Malone *et al.* (1987) highlighted the role of IT in predicting and interpreting a number of probable changes in the structure of markets and in so doing proposed the terms 'electronic markets' and ' electronic hierarchies'. They further argued that IT will decrease coordination costs and will lead to more goods and services being provided through market, rather than hierarchical structures. Clemons and Row (1989) supplemented arguments based on TCE with reasoning from a resource-based view of a company, and concluded that other competitive outcomes are possible as well.

Meanwhile, an emerging stream of research attempts to document the impact of information systems (IS) on industrial structure variables, such as vertical integration and firm size. Brynjolfsson *et al.* (1988) analyzed longitudinal data on IT investments in a number of industries in the U.S.A., and found that increased IT investments led to a move towards market-oriented governance structures, possibly because of reduced transaction costs. And it was further reported that, the decline in firm size was the greatest, after two years since the increased levels of IT was used within an industrial sector (Brynjolfsson *et al.*, 1994). Claro (2004) conducted a case study and survey of the Dutch potted plant and flower industry, and found that information obtained from business networks affected buyer-supplier relationships in terms of transaction specific investments and suppliers' trust, as well as flexibility.

Earlier studies applying TCE has primarily focused on hypothesis creation. In the future, empirical work is needed at both the microscopic (systems development) and the macroscopic (organization of economic activity through markets or hierarchies) level to test and subsequently refine these hypotheses. At the micro level, this will most likely take the form of survey-type instruments to judge the extent to which different governance structures are employed. At the macro level, measures of the proportions of transactions consummated in market versus hierarchical settings are desirable. Another promising application of TCE is the debate about the relative merits of outsourcing IS and services. TCE's clear focus on the distinction between internal and market-based solutions seem to provide a solid theoretical support base for launching investigations into this area of 'current' practical concern (Bakos and Kemerer, 1992).

As some other theories, TCE also has its drawbacks. An extensive overview can be found in the work carried out by Rindfleisch and Heide (1997) and Ghoshal and Moran (1996). The first criticism of TCE is that transactions are considered as a phenomenon isolated from their environment. TCE focuses on a single transaction as the unit of analysis, ignoring other relationships that surround the focal transaction and could be contingent on them (Cook and Emerson, 1978). Second, TCE does not explicitly consider the dynamic evolution of governance mechanisms and transactions (Ring and Van de Ven, 1992). Third, ECE can be challenged based on its view of individuals as being motivated by self-interest with guile (Powell, 1990). It seems that many forms of organizational interactions are based on a gradual development of trust, helping firms to lower the part of transaction costs related to safeguarding against opportunism (Anderson and Narus, 1990). Fourth, a common criticism of TCE is that it is so broad and 'loose' that it explains 'everything'. In effect, it explains nothing because the predictive power of the theory is too weak (Bogetoft and Olesen, 2004). Fifth, TCE generally overlooks the implications of the affective elements and other features of trust (Barney and Hesterly, 1999; Claro, 2004). Being aware of these drawbacks of TCE, we will discuss trust further in Section 2.4.4 for a better understanding of inter-organizational communication.

We have developed a research framework for antecedents of IOC (Figure 2.2) with the aim of revealing important factors that may help to improve IOC. In Section 2.4, we examine these relevant concepts in more detail.

In the next section theory on IOC will be addressed related to the second research question, 'what are the important aspects of IOC and what are their interrelationships? And how can IOC be used to provide benefits for companies?'

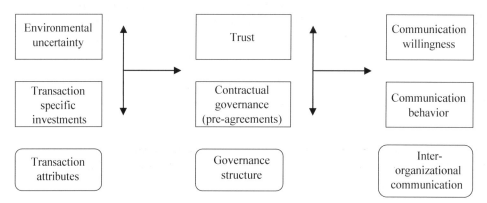

Figure 2.2. Research framework for antecedents of inter-organizational communication (IOC).

2.2 Theory on inter-organizational communication (IOC)

Nowadays it is acknowledged that *inter-organizational communication* (IOC) is an essential enabler to improve the performance and comparative edge of a company and a *supply chain* (SC). This holds true, especially for the food sector, because of agri-product market globalization and given the specific characteristics of perishable foods, such as shelf-life constraints and food safety. These characteristics result in a critical need for fast, real-time, relevant, reliable and adequate communication of information flows in perishable food supply chains.

As pointed out by Cunningham and Tynan (1993), one of the fundamental problems of management information system (MIS) studies is the precise definition of terms employed. Various definitions of inter-organizational communication (IOC) can be found in the existing literature, which were developed for a particular research or for a specific situation. Here we list some of the main definitions of IOC:

- Interfirm information communication refers to information shared between a buyer and key suppliers that is detailed enough, frequent enough (summarized by Carr and Kaynak (2007: 349) based on: Humphreys *et al.* (2004), Carr and Smeltzer (2002) and Krause and Ellram (1997)).
- Information sharing in a supply chain is the regulated flow of information from one unit (e.g. firm, work group, or individual) to the other unit (Kim and Umanath, 2005).
- Inter-organizational information communication systems are the systems that aim to manage relationships with customers and suppliers and to build competitive advantage, while the information is that used for management purposes, and more specifically, is that used to manage third party organizations based on the management science and behavioral science approaches (Storer, 2005: 35).
- Information communication is 'communicating needs, sharing proprietary information, providing helpful information, keeping each other informed of events or changes that may affect them' (Mohr and Sohi, 1995).
- Inter-organizational communication in market channels can serve as the process by which persuasive information is transmitted (Frazier and Summers, 1984), participative decision making is forecasted (Anderson *et al.*, 1987), programs are coordinated (Guiltinan *et al.*, 1980), power is exercised (Gaski, 1984), and commitment and loyalty are encouraged. (Mohr and Nevin, 1990: 36).
- Information exchange is defined as a bilateral expectation that parties will proactively provide information useful to the partner, such as long-term forecasting, structural planning information, future product design, and production planning schedules (Noordewier *et al.,* 1990).
- Inter-organizational information sharing system is a general term referring to systems that cross organizational boundaries, involve resources shared between two or more organizations, and benefit all participants (Barrett and Konsynski, 1982: 94).

Based on existing literature and for the purpose of this present research, *inter-organizational information communication* (IOC) here refers to the information transmission process among supply chain members for management purposes.

A good understanding of the values of IOC promotes SC information integration that fosters competitive SC. Forrester (1958, 1961) introduced the theory of *Industrial Dynamics*, which anchors our current understanding of inter-organizational information coordination. He explained the dynamics of how the delays, amplifications, and oscillations in the flow of demand information adversely affected SC operations, most noticeably inventory levels and production rates. He further stated that, management was on the verge of a breakthrough in understanding how industrial company success depended on the interaction between the flows of information, materials, money, manpower, and capital equipment. The way these five flow systems interlock to amplify one another and cause changes forms a basis for anticipating the effects of decisions, policies, organizational forms, and investment choices. Only through this understanding and the continued development of the 'tools of progress', such as advances in today's information technologies (IT), can new management concepts be implemented. Forester's concepts were largely neglected, as pointed out by Sahin and Robinson (2002), until the co-emergence of e-commerce promoted by advanced IT and Supply Chain Management (SCM) philosophies in the early 1990s.

According to Barrett and Konsynski (1982), most information sharing systems (IS) development efforts had been limited to the replacement of manual IS within a given organization, with the exception of innovations such as decision support systems. Such internal focus was changing with the proliferation of new networking technologies and system development techniques. Initial incentives for inter-organizational information systems (IOIS) development are economic and involve three potential benefits, namely cost reductions, productivity improvements, and product and market strategy. The information resources shared in these systems include hardware, software, transmission facilities, rules and procedures, data and databases, and expertise. Barrett and Konsynski (1982) discussed the concepts underlying the growth of IOIS, presented a classification scheme by which IOIS may be classified and researched, and explained the issues of cost commitment, responsibility, and complexity of the cooperating environment. They foresaw and foretold that the development of IOIS would significantly affect the conduct of business in the future (Storer, 2005).

In an inventory management experimental context, Sterman (1989) showed that the variances of orders amplify as one moves up in the SC in the 'Beer Distribution Game'. Lee and his colleagues further developed the term of *bullwhip effect* (also known as *Forrester effect*) rooted in Forrester's *Industrial Dynamics* (1961), and made use of it to explain the phenomenon of order information distortion and amplification as demand orders move up a SC. Considering a series of companies in a supply chain (SC) that order from their immediate upstream members, the *bullwhip effect* occurs when the demand orders' variability in the SC is amplified as they move up the SC. The bullwhip effect can misguide upstream members in their inventory and production decisions. Four major causes of the bullwhip effect were identified as demand signal processing, rationing game, order batching, and price variations. On the normative side, the bullwhip effect may be mitigated through the combination of planning and sell data, exchange of inventory status information, order coordination and simplified pricing schemes. However, why retailers should share information with manufacturers on sale data and inventory status is an interesting and challenging question. Meanwhile, how to split gains and costs of SCM deserves attention. (Lee *et al.*, 1997a,b). Lee *et al.* (2000) further highlighted the almost total lack of research specifically addressing information communication in SC, while there existed several works on information sharing in the general context (Barratt, 2004: 36). Since then, substantial works have contributed to issues on supply chain information communication systems.

These combined works, especially those conducted by Forrester (1958, 1961) and Lee *et al.* (1997a,b), laid the foundation for understanding industrial dynamics, the impact of information distortion in the SC, and the salient values of IOC for effective and efficient SCM. Other researches have helped fill in some of the gaps by clarifying basic principles and testing the concepts in a variety of problem environments (Storer, 2006). Below we classify them into several groups.

The first group of previous studies examined the norms and willingness of IOC. *Communication norms* are shared expectations for communication behaviors, which specify and guide appropriate conduct of the parties in a communication relationship (Heide and John, 1992). Norms of information sharing were found to be positively associated with communication frequency, bidirectionality, and formality (Mohr and Sohi, 1995). As for *communication willingness*, it refers to a company's openness to communicate relevant information honestly and frequently (Eisenberg and Witten, 1987; Fawcett *et al.*, 2007: 360). Communication willingness was found to impact operational performance and to be critical to the development of a real information sharing capability. However, many companies place most of their emphasis on connectivity, and often overlook willingness. As a result, information sharing between firms seldom delivers on its promise to enable the creation of the cohesive supply chain team (Fawcett *et al.*, 2007).

The second group of researches focused on *communication behavior*, such as: communication media used (Lindgreen *et al.*, 2004), types/contents of information communicated, communication frequency, information intensity, key people and departments involved, information direction, and communication formality. For an extensive review, refer to (Storer *et al.*, 2006). Meanwhile, some studies employed diagrams to map out or to model processes and information flows through the chain (e.g. Trienekens, 1999; Van der Vorst, 2000; Simons *et al.*, 2003; Van Dorp, 2004). Silver *et al.* (1998) distinguished two dimensions of information management: local versus global information, and centralized versus decentralized control[1]. According to Silver *et al.* (1998), the best solutions are obtained by using global information and centralized control, because the decisions are made with visibility of the entire system using information from all locations.

The third group involved *communication quality*, such as information quality, and satisfaction with communication. In the opinion of O'Reilly (1982), and Stohl and Redding (1987), the assessment of information quality is a function of completeness, credibility, accuracy, timeliness, and adequacy of communication flows. Mohr and Sohi (1995) addressed for the first time a channel member's satisfaction with communication, and found empirical evidence that information quality is positively linked to satisfaction with external communication.

The fourth group studied the *benefits/values of IOC*, including cost reductions through increased channel efficiency, product quality improvement, as well as strategic benefits by developing and maintaining market position (Wilson and Vlosky, 1998). It is reported that information sharing improves the performance of both actors and chains (Mahmoudi *et al.*, 2007). Near-complete information sharing that involves sharing more than one type of information results in better (firm level) performance in volatile market conditions (Li *et al.*, 2006). According to Lee and Whang (2000), the key potential benefits of information sharing are: the improved quality of customer service, reduction in payment cycle, and savings in labor costs of manual operations. More benefits in detail include: productivity improvements and product/market strategy (Barrett and Konsynski, 1982); Pareto improvement in chain level performance, the elimination of order verification, reductions in inventory and costs, product quality and on-time delivery; lower demand uncertainty that leads to lower costs, higher order fulfillment rates, shorter order cycle times; agility and flexibility, together with improved stability and performance of the whole SC; and support for procurement. However, we can hardly find a report directly involving financial impact (such as turnover or profitability) except those conducted by Fawcett *et al.* (2007) and Li (2002). We assume strategic values such as a firm's profitability and competitive performance may be indirect results of IOC. Comparatively, direct results might be cost reductions, problem resolution, as well as delivery and quality control.

---

[1] *Local information* implies that each location sees demand only in the form of orders that arrive from the locations it directly supplies. *Global information* implies that the decision-maker has visibility of the demand, costs, and inventory status of all the locations in the system. Meanwhile, *centralized control* implies that attempts are made to jointly optimize the entire system, usually by the decision of one individual or group (pushing stock to locations where it is needed). *Decentralized control*, on the other hand, refers to cases in which each individual unit in the SC makes decisions based on local information (Lee *et al.*, 1993).

The fifth group studied *factors that could affect IOC*. These studies reported associations between IOC and the nature of the inter-organizational relationship or the environment (Storer, 2005). Bandyopadhyay *et al.* (1994) found that the level of relationalism (in term of trust, relationship duration, commitment, benefits, and flexibility) is positively associated with the level of bidirectional communication, communication frequency, formal communication, and use of indirect influence strategies. In addition, specific investments (Bensaou, 1999; Son *et al.*, 2005), control (Mohr *et al.*, 1996), trust (Son *et al.*, 2005), symmetric dependency (Ganesan, 1994; Collins, 2002), shared goals and objectives, strategic importance and relationship complexity (Spekman *et al.*, 1998), commitment (Hardman *et al.*, 2002), the character and experience of individual (van der Vorst, 2000), as well as uncertainty in future transaction relationship (Son *et al.*, 2005), and uncertainty of supply, (changing) demand, process, and planning and control (Van der Vorst, 2000), were found associated with inter-organizational information systems.

To summarize, IOC itself is a broad concept covering a wide range of aspects as shown above. However, previous studies have typically considered communication as an aspect of a broader construct, such as supply management (e.g. Chen and Paulraj, 2004); or have studied one or limited aspects of IOC. How to describe IOC comprehensively? What are the main aspects of IOC and what are their interrelationships? This still remains more or less a 'black box'. Meanwhile, researchers tended to take one of two approaches in conceptualizing and defining IOC: either focusing on the flows of communication between channel members or focusing on evaluative/summary judgment regarding the communication exchange (Mohr and Sohi, 1995). We therefore developed a research framework (Figure 2.3) that constitutes four important parts of IOC, including communication willingness, communication behavior, communication quality, and perceived communication benefits.

Section 2.5 will examine these four parts of IOC in more detail. Prior literature suggested that, IOC is the glue that holds together the entities in a supply chain (Mohr and Nevin, 1990), and is a general cure for supply chain ailment (Sahin and Robinson, 2002). Thus, we now resort to the theory on Supply Chain Management in Section 2.3 with the aim of answering the third research question: 'what is the relationship between IOC and company performance, and how can IOC be used to improve company performance?'.

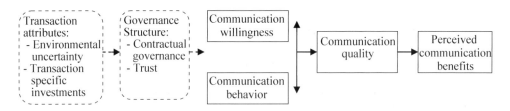

Figure 2.3. Research framework on elements of inter-organizational communication.

2.3 Theory on supply chain management

The term 'supply chain management' (SCM) first appeared in logistics literature in 1982, as an inventory management approach with an emphasis on the supply of raw materials (Oliver and Webber, 1982). In

1990, academics first described SCM from a theoretical standpoint and clarified how it differed from the traditional approaches to managing the flow of materials and the associated flow of information (Ellram and Cooper, 1990). Lee and Billington (1992) stated that supply chain (SC) analysis was much more than just inventory modeling. It can be extended to distribution strategy analysis and to other types of SC problems. Later papers indicated that SCM also includes co-operative efforts between chain members in areas such as: marketing research, promotion, sales, information gathering, research and development, product design, and total system analysis. In 1998, the Council of Logistics Management modified its definition of logistics and indicated that logistics is a subset of supply chain management and the two terms are not synonymous (Lambert *et al.*, 1998). While all business processes need a certain level of upstream and/or downstream (vertical) coordination, the network perspective added that some of these efforts need partnership on the horizontal level as well. Lazzarini *et al.* (2004) described two viewpoints used for analyzing supply across the borders of a firm: the supply chain and the supply network perspective. They tried to integrate these two perspectives and introduce the new term 'netchains' as an abbreviation for the often-used combination of 'chains and networks'. But this term is not widely used so far, and the concept of 'chains and networks' as two perspectives on the same phenomenon is common. Furthermore, Omta *et al.* (2001) set a baseline for the discussion on the contents and scope of chain and network theory, in the opening article of the first issue of Journal on Chain and Network Science.

An extensive review of the definition, literature and research on SCM was provided by Bechtel and Jayaram (1997), and Van der Vorst (2000). In addition, there is a growing number of alternative terms, such as 'demand chain management', 'value chain management', 'value stream management', 'supply base management', 'supply chain pipeline management', 'network sourcing', 'supply strategy', 'supplier integration', 'buyer-supplier partnerships', 'strategic alliances', 'supply chain synchronization', 'network supply chain', etc. (Chen and Paulraj, 2004; Van der Vorst, 2004). It is suggested that particular attention should be paid to differences in the scope of SC analysis in these definitions. Five possible levels of analysis can be distinguished, including (Hoogewegen, 1997):
1. Single organization; for example, a manufacturer.
2. Dyad, referring to the relationship between two organizations, a buyer and a supplier.
3. Entire SC; incorporating the supplier's supplier and the buyer's customer.
4. Industry level (for example, manufacturers).
5. Total network of organizations that participate in a specific part of the economy.

The goal of SCM is to provide high buyer value, achieve significant performance gains, and build competitive chain advantages (Cooper *et al.*, 1997). SCM is rooted in strategic-level decision making. Meanwhile, SCM includes implementation and operational aspects in which day-to-day operations are managed below the senior management level (Ganeshan *et al.*, 1999). Although SCM has received much attention from practitioners and researchers during the last few decades, the term SCM is often misused and no clear definition of SCM exists. Hult *et al.* (2004: 241) defined *strategic supply chains* as: supply chains where the 'members are strategically, operationally, and technologically integrated' and are anticipated for long-term stable relationships with the ability to adapt to the demands of the environment. A relatively official definition of supply chain management was developed in 1994 and modified in 1998 by members of The Global Supply Chain Forum as: *supply chain management* is the integration of key business processes from end users through original suppliers that provides products, services, and information that add value for customers and other stakeholders (Lambert *et al.*, 1998: 1).

Meanwhile, several commonalities in the definitions of SCM are (Cooper *et al.*, 1997; Croom *et al.*, 2000):

1. It evolves through several stages of increasing inter-firm integration and coordination; and in its broadest sense and implementation, it spans the entire chain from primary producer to ultimate end consumer.
2. It potentially involves many independent firms. Thus, managing intra- and inter-firm relationships is of essential importance.
3. It includes the bidirectional flow of products (materials and services) and information, and the associated managerial and operational activities.
4. It seeks to fulfill the goals of providing high buyer value with an appropriate use of resources, and building competitive chain advantages.
5. It takes into account the external environment of a firm.

Nowadays, as stated by Lambert *et al.* (1998), one of the most significant changes in business management is that companies no longer compete as solely autonomous entities, but rather as supply chains. Business management has entered an era of inter-network competition. The ultimate success of a firm depends not only on its own implementation, but also on its ability to integrate its intricate network of business relationships.

As introduced above in Section 2.1, TCE has conceptualized three alternative governance mechanisms, including spot-markets, vertical integration, and hybrid or intermediate mechanisms. Between the two extremes of spot-markets and vertical integration, several types of hybrid relationships have been distinguished, which range from collaboration with a short-term focus, long-term focus, or without end cooperation date. Based on these, supply chain researchers further distinguished the following seven types of supply chain partnerships (Figure 2.4) (Cooper and Ellram, 1993; Slack *et al.*, 1998):

1. Spot market (arm's length contracts), which represent market transactions as positioned by Williamson (1985). The fundamental assumption is that trading partners are interchangeable.
2. Short-term focus. The partnership has a short-term focus. The companies involved recognize each other as partners, and on a limited basis coordinate activities and planning.
3. Long-term focus. The companies involved progress beyond coordination of activities to integration of activities.
4. Coordinated profit sharing, which requires a certain degree of legal formalization, and is often used for licensing and franchising in the service sector (e.g. fast food).
5. Alliance without end of cooperation date. The companies share a significant level of operational integration and view each other as extensions of the own firm.

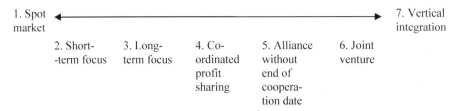

Figure 2.4. Typology of supply chain partnerships (Adapted from Cooper and Ellram (1993) and Slack et al. (1998)).

6. Joint ventures, which are newly created and independent firms and separated from the companies forming the alliance. Power in this partnership is based on equivalence.
7. Vertical integration, or, the merger of parties in (part of) the supply chain. Here, all activities from sourcing raw materials to delivering the products to end consumers and supporting activities are coordinated by one company.

Fawcett *et al.* (2008) grouped the forces, benefits, barriers, and bridges to effective SCM. By making use of a triangulation method consisting of an extensive literature review, cross-channel analysis, and case studies, they found customer satisfaction and service is perceived as more enduring than cost savings; and all managers recognized technology, information, and measurement systems as major barriers to successful supply chain collaboration. Meanwhile, they pointed out that the people issues, such as culture, trust, aversion to change, and willingness to collaborate, are more intractable.

Supply chain collaboration is essential for approaching optimal performance and obtaining competitive advantage. SC collaboration is the collaboration of two or more autonomous companies that form long-term relationships and work closely to plan and execute SC operations toward common goals, thereby achieving more benefits than acting independently (Simatupang and Sridharan, 2005; Sheu *et al.*, 2006). It is a partnership where the parties work together, share information, resources and risk, and make joint decisions to accomplish mutual beneficial outcomes (Bowersox *et al.*, 2003). Two collaborative efforts are especially important for perishable food sector: SC compliance with logistics requirements and with quality requirements.

The logistics compliance and quality compliance is the extent to which companies comply with their business partners' requirements regarding logistics activities and quality control. The logistics compliance and quality compliance tend to differ widely amongst different outlets, producing various types of transaction costs and offering different incentives for suppliers and customers to improve their production systems and marketing regimes (Ruben *et al.*, 2007) Suppliers can be successful only when they are able to deliver right products to right markets at right time. Customers, on the other hand, should also be able to purchase the right products from the right market at right time in order to achieve a good market performance.

SCM theory has its limitations. Researchers criticized the fact that most literature about SCM is primarily empirical, and lacks a clear definition and a robust conceptual framework, due to its multidisciplinary origin and evolution. Sachan and Datta (2005) examined the state of logistics and SCM research from the standpoint of existing methodologies. Their major findings regarding the research gaps and direction of future research are: (1) there are very few interdisciplinary studies. The development of a new discipline is based on the usage of concepts, definitions, theories, rules and principles from other disciplines. For example, Stock (1997) recommended 53 theories of other disciplines like anthropology, computing, economics, psychology, which can be used in logistics research. However, the theories and methods of other disciplines are applied in very few papers in SCM (e.g. Pfohl and Buse, 2000; Lemke *et al.*, 2003). (2) Innovative application of secondary data is few. Secondary data were simply taken from government reports. (3) The research at the inter-organizational level is scanty, though the objective of the SCM is to integrate all the firms in the value chain and treat them as a single entity. (4) Most of the authors in published papers are from North America (mainly USA) and Europe, and the context used by them are also from these regions. It would be valuable if more studies in the future look at supply chain issues from other parts of the world, especially the developing and transitional countries, which are becoming either the sourcing centers or markets of the global economy. In this present research, by combining SCM theory with theories on inter-organizational communication (IOC), and Transaction Cost Economics, we try to extend the research on 'how IOC can be used to improve company performance' by taking a perspective of Supply Chain Management.

Additionally, an important debate regarding SCM is *performance measurement*. Measuring supply chain performance can facilitate a better understanding of a chain, positively influence actors' behavior, and improve its overall performance (Chen and Paulraj, 2004: 145). According to Neely *et al.* (1995: 81),

1. *Performance measurement* is defined as the process of quantifying the efficiency and effectiveness of action.
2. A *performance measure* is a metric used to quantify the efficiency and/or effectiveness of an action.
3. A *performance measurement system* is the set of metrics used to quantify both the efficiency and effectiveness of actions.

Here, *effectiveness* refers to the extent to which a customer's requirements are met, and *efficiency* measures how economically a company's resources are utilized when providing a pre-specified level of customer satisfaction (Shepherd and Günter, 2005).

A number of approaches to performance measurement were identified, including: the balanced scorecard, the performance measurement matrix, performance measurement questionnaires, criteria for measurement system design, and computer aided manufacturing approaches (Neely *et al.*, 1995). Extensive overviews of performance measurement were provided by Neely *et al.* (1995) and Aramyan (2007).

Three main streams can be found in the literature of performance: financial, organizational, and strategic. In the financial stream, accounting-based (financial) indicators, such as efficiency, sales growth rate, and profitability, are popular dimensions (Murphy *et al.*, 1996; Taweesak, 2002). In the organizational stream, three fundamental approaches, namely, goal-based approach, system approach, and multiple constituency approach, are used to measure organizational performance. The strategic stream integrates the above two approaches, and tries to measure performance by multiple constructs, such as financial, operational, and multiple constituencies (Venkatraman and Ramanujam, 1986). Additionally, both objective and subjective measures are commonly used among researchers. An *objective performance measure* (e.g. profitability) can be collected without directly asking informants, while *subjective measures* are collected by asking managers to give their evaluation of certain criteria, like overall performance (Venkatraman and Ramanujam, 1986). Both types of measures have their advantages and disadvantages (Scholten, 2006).

While research on performance measurement at the organization level has proven arduous, it is even more difficult to measure the performance at the supply chain level. Each entity is likely to adopt idiosyncratic performance criteria, which might even be conflicting. Moreover, performance measures change over time as the buyer-supplier relationship evolves (Claro, 2004). Shepherd and Günter (2005) contributed an excellent overview of *performance measurement of supply chains*. They provided taxonomy of measures of supply chain performance, delineated according to the processes identified in the Supply Chain Operations Reference (SCOR) model[2]: plan, source, make, deliver or return

---

[2] The SCOR model was developed by the Supply Chain Council in 1997, and has been described as a 'systematic approach for identifying, evaluating and monitoring supply chain performance' (Stephens, 2001).

(customer satisfaction); whether they measure cost, time, quality, flexibility or innovativeness; and, whether they are quantitative or qualitative. A guiding principle here is that, supply chain performance must be measured at multiple levels and a balanced approach is crucial. Single indicator measurement (e.g. cost or time) is not adequate for measuring (supply chain) performance. So far, there is widespread recognition of the importance of adopting a systematic and balanced approach to measure supply chain performance (Shepherd and Günter, 2005). However, identifying key drivers or key performance indicators (KPIs) for those key performance areas remains a big challenge for each supply chain.

Based on the above, this research uses multiple indicators to measure company performance, including financial (e.g. profitability) and non-financial indicators, subjective indicators (e.g. satisfaction), operational indicators (efficiency) and strategic indicators (e.g. sale growth, and market share) (see Attachment A for the questionnaire). Furthermore, by collecting data from both customers and suppliers at each stage of the supply chain, we are able to measure and describe the performance for the entire supply chain and network of this research.

We therefore propose a research framework (Figure 2.5), with the aim of revealing the relationship between perceived (realized) communication benefits, SC collaboration, and company performance. Section 2.6 examines these three aspects in more detail, and further proposes our hypotheses and a research model on results of IOC (the Communication-Chain compliance-Performance Model).

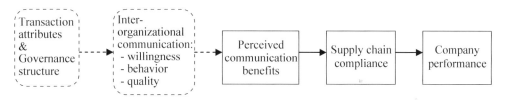

Figure 2.5. Research framework on performance results of inter-organizational communication.

2.4 Hypotheses on antecedents of inter-organizational communication

Section 2.2 introduced two transaction attributes (uncertainty and transaction specific investments) and two governance structure (trust and contractual governance). This section introduces the generalization of hypotheses regarding these aspects.

2.4.1 Uncertainty

Along with asset specificity, *uncertainty* is regarded as a critical dimension for characterizing the governance of transactions for an exchange party (Williamson, 1979, 1985). Several types of uncertainty have been used in previous empirical studies using the TCE framework (Rindfleisch and Heide, 1997). In addition, uncertainty has been a central concept in organization theory (Milliken, 1987), and was defined as a main problem facing top-level organizational administrators (Thompson, 1967: 159). Uncertainty can originate either from the broad environment surrounding an economic exchange between parties (i.e. market uncertainty), or from transaction partners within exchange relationships because of these partners' opportunistic behavior (i.e. supplier or buyer behavioral uncertainty).

While Transaction Cost Economics (TCE) assists us in identifying the primary sources of uncertainty (broad transaction environment vs. transaction partners), it appears that no universal definition exists for the uncertainty construct itself in the existing literature (Son *et al.*, 2006). In existing studies, uncertainty is often defined as a probability of loss from a transaction (Bauer, 1960; Peter and Ryan, 1976; Taylor, 1974). While in other streams of research, it is also viewed as a lack of information needed to make a decision about a future event or transaction (Brindley and Ritchie, 2004; Downey and Slocum, 1975; Rowe, 1977), or as the difference between the information needed to make a decision and the information at hand (Galbraith, 1977; Lamberti and Wallace, 1990).

In this study, there is a certain focus on environmental uncertainty. *Environmental uncertainty* refers to unanticipated/unpredictable changes in circumstances surrounding an exchange, which influence coordination costs (Noordewier *et al.*, 1990) and negotiation costs (Hobbs, 1997). Coronado (2010: 42) reported that environmental uncertainty has been measured in terms of demand uncertainty (Anderson, 1985), volume uncertainty (Noordewier *et al.*, 1990) (Davis, 1993, and Raynaude *et al.*, 2005), and price uncertainty (Fafchamps *et al.*, 2008; Kyeyamwa *et al.*, 2008).

Williamson (1991) has argued that in the case of environmental uncertainty (and absent asset specificity), contractual governance is preferred because of its low cost and strong performance incentives. When a business environment is highly uncertain, more explicit clauses with contract arrangements facilitate adjustments as events unfold, and prevent constant renegotiations and opportunism (Masten, 1993). Empirically, Barthelemy and Quelin (2006) have found that the greater the uncertainty about future needs, the more explicit the contract regarding contingencies, which fosters adoption of the exchanges, given that level of uncertainty. Arana (2010) recently found that as environmental uncertainty increases, contractual governance is preferred over relational governance (information exchange, commitment, and expectation of continuity). Accordingly, we formulate the following hypothesis:

> H_{iA}: *The level of environmental uncertainty is positively associated with the level of contractual governance.*

2.4.2 Transaction specific investments

'Transaction specific investments' is an important and distinctive construct in Transaction Cost Economics (Williamson, 1996). *Transaction specific investments* (TSI) refer to the degrees to which an asset cannot be redeployed to alternative uses and by alternative users without sacrifice of productive value (Williamson, 1991). Investments with a high specificity represent *sunk costs* that have significantly lower value or even no value outside a particular exchange relationship. In buyer-supplier relationships, TSI are usually represented as customization (tailoring) of products, services or production processes by the supplier on behalf of the buyer (Buvik and Reve, 2001). In many studies, TSI is recognized as the most important dimension that determines the form of governance of a transaction (Rindfleisch and Heide, 1997; Leiblein, 2003; David and Han, 2004). Williamson (1989) has distinguished five types of TSI: site, human, physical TSI, dedicated TSI and brand name.

Prior studies have primarily centered on the human and physical dimensions of TSI (Claro, 2003; Grover and Malhotra, 2003). Transactions with business partners are necessarily dependent on the use of physical materials and human resources. So it is essential that these physical materials and human resources meet certain specifications of business partners. For example, firms might have to invest in specific physical assets (such as cooling, packaging or communication equipment) to comply with buyer requirements. Or, they might also have to invest in specific human assets to communicate well with their buyer, and thus ensure the persistence, efficiency and quality of the transactions.

Although TSI creates dependency and the risk of opportunism, there are certainly advantages in investing in idiosyncratic assets, especially in business relationships that encompass recurrent transactions. First, TSI is an important mechanism for establishing stable buyer-supplier relationships. The deliberate creation of specific investments for the purpose of making it difficult for a partner to end the relationship will also provide sufficient reason for the buyer and the supplier to continue to work closely together and communicate with each other, especially when firms are highly dependent on each other (Williamson 1985). Second, TSI sends a powerful signal to the trading partner and is more than a hollow promise. Observing the other party's investments causes the trading partner to be more confident about the other party's compliance, because the other party will suffer economic consequences if the relationship ends (Heide and John, 1988; Anderson and Weitz, 1992). As a result, TSI made by a firm tends to promote a long-term and stable relationship with its trading partner by encouraging the partner to increase the level of cooperation.

According to Transaction Cost Economics (TCE) logic, 'failures of alignment' occur when one part of the buyer-supplier relationships chooses a governance structure that is inappropriate for a given level of asset specialization (Dyer, 1996). It is not an easy task to select an appropriate alignment in the presence of the complicated and turbulent transaction environment. However, despite all pitfalls and constraints, many efforts have been made to empirically investigate the influences of the transaction attributes on governance structure since the early 1980s (Han *et al.*, 2009). Among these efforts, trust has been widely accepted as a relational and informal governance institution (e.g. Joskow, 1987; Poppo and Zenger, 2002; Poppo *et al.*, 2008), whereas contract governance has been examined as a formal governance structure.

Previous studies provided certain (conflicting) evidences of the relationship between TSI and the use of trust as a relational and informal governance structure. Empirically, Katsikeas *et al.* (2009) recently reported that, exporters' transaction specific assets enhanced importers' trust, while mitigating exporters' opportunism. In the Chinese context, Han (2009) reported mixed findings from a survey of pork processors. The level of asset specificity is found to be positively linked to long-term cooperation and trust in processors' customers, but not to processors' suppliers. This might imply that pork processors pay more attention to long-term cooperation and trust in customers to safeguard their specific investment. It is noteworthy that, though Suh and Kwon (2006) asserted that a firm's trust in their supply chain partner is strongly associated with both sides' specific asset investments, they found conflicting relationships between trust and TSI. Their study showed that focal firms' asset specificity was negatively related to their trust in the partners, whereas partners' asset specificity was positively linked to focal firms' trust in partners. To examine the relationship between TSI and trust again, we therefore propose:

H_{iB1}: *The level of transaction specific investments (TSI) is positively associated with the level of trust in the partners.*

Prior studies also examined the relationship between TSI and the use of contractual governance as a formal governance structure. Boger (2001b) summarized the major results of empirical studies on transaction costs and contractual governance in the agri-food sector. Bogetoft and Olesen (2004) pointed out that TSI, together with uncertainty and asymmetric information, are those variables necessitating contractual safeguard, according to TCE and agency theory. The recent relevant studies in the Chinese context include Lu *et al.* (2007), Zhou *et al.* (2008), and Han *et al.* (2009). Lu (2007) reported that vegetable processing firms were more likely to use contracts to conduct transactions with the downstream customers while the degree of TSI was high. However, he also reported a conflicting finding that TSI was negatively associated with contractual governance when the vegetable processing firms conducted business with suppliers (farmers). Meanwhile, it is interesting that, Lu (2007) did not find empirical evidence on the significant association between the level of TSI and the application of contractual governance by the vegetable farmers that transacted with downstream processors; Zhou *et al.* (2008) failed to find such evidence on the relationship between TSI and contractual governance in commercial machinery, computer equipment, and electronic component manufacturing. Comparatively, Han (2009) found strong empirical evidence and reported that asset specificity was positively associated with contractual governance in transactions between pork processors and suppliers, and between pork processors and customers.

H_{iB2}: *The level of transaction specific investments (TSI) is positively associated with the level of contractual governance.*

2.4.3 Trust

Trust is an essential social element of buyer-supplier relationships (Anderson and Narus, 1990). The importance of trust for chain collaboration is widely accepted (Harland, 1999), and it has been regarded as a prerequisite for collaboration (Morgan and Hunt, 1994; Alvarado and Kotzab, 2001; Kottila and Rönni, 2008). Omta *et al.* (2001) stated that in network theory, forms of collaboration are not just based on economic motivations; power and trust are key concepts in this approach. Some trade partnerships are based on trust and loyalty, while others are based on opportunism. Trust helps to reduce complexity in transaction making (Powell, 1990), enables partners to manage risk and opportunism in transactions (Nooteboom *et al.*, 1997), and reflects the extent to which negotiations are fair and commitments are sustained (Anderson and Narus, 1990). The absence of trust is a reason for the failure of supply network projects (Camps *et al.*, 2004). In New Institutional Economics, trust becomes operational via transaction costs, and searching and monitoring in complex transactions is less necessary with trusted business partners (Uzzi, 1997).

Various definitions of trust have been proposed by researchers with different theoretical perspectives, research interests, and levels of analysis (Bigley and Pearce, 1998). At the individual level, *trust* was originally defined as an individual's optimistic expectations of others (Deutsch, 1958). In inter-organizational relationships, *trust* was defined as 'the willingness of a party to be vulnerable to the actions of another party based on an expectation that the other will perform a particular action important to the trustor, irrespective of the ability to monitor or control that other party' (Mayer *et al.*, 1995). Despite the various definitions of trust, vulnerability is always a consideration: by engaging in trusting actions, the trustors expose themselves to risky situations in which they have no control over possible negative consequences (Yang and Jarvenpaa, 2005).

It is assumed that previous and existing interactions between the two related parties are the main basis for trust development (experience-based trust). Through interactions, the two parties can accumulate rich information (or knowledge) about each other by observing their activities. The more shared experience with and the more information about trading partners, the greater the trust between them (Yang and Jarvenpaa, 2005).

Trust has been identified as an important factor influencing the adoption and use of inter-organizational information systems (IOIS) (Hart and Saunders, 1997, 1998; Gang *et al.*, 2006). Trust and cooperation are also regarded as critical ingredients in a supply chain (SC) partnership (Lee and Whang, 2000). Hardman *et al.* (2002) surveyed a South African apple chain and found that, higher levels of trust led to improved communication, and then to greater cooperation on delivery scheduling and quality control. According to Klein (2007), trading partners' level of trust in the client positively influences their information exchange behavior and, in turn, information communication positively affects client customizations (Klein, 2007). Furthermore, both information communication and information quality are influenced positively by trust in SC partners (and by shared vision between SC partners), but negatively by supplier uncertainty (Li and Lin, 2006). Kottila and Rönni (2008) reported that, their case studies of organic food chains supported the previous research that trust, while being a prerequisite for collaboration (Alvarado and Kotzab, 2001; Morgan and Hunt, 1994), also increases communication quality (Weitz and Sjap, 1995). Son *et al.* (2005) proposed and reported only an *indirect* effect of trust on Electronic Data Interchange (EDI) usage. However, it was reported that, high frequency of communication is not an indication of trust and collaboration, and is less important than communication quality (Kottila and Rönni, 2008). In any case, completely open trust is often unfeasible in real-life business. In real life, 'an alternative position, between trusting and mistrusting tends to yield more favorable outcomes' (Butler, 1999). Based on the existing arguments, we formulate the following hypothesis, and check inter-organizational communication in terms of two different constructs, i.e. willingness and behavior:

> H_{iC}: *The level of trust is positively associated with the level of inter-organizational communication (IOC), in term of communication willingness and behavior.*

2.4.4 Contractual governance

According to TCE and agency theory, TSI, uncertainty, and asymmetric information are all variables that necessitate contractual safeguard (Bogetoft and Olesen, 2004). First, *TSI* in physical or human assets transforms an exchange from a world of classical contracting in which the 'identity of parties is irrelevant' into a world of neoclassical contracting in which the identity of exchange partners is of critical importance (Williamson, 1991). Severing the relationship leads to the loss of value of these specialized investments. To safeguard against such hold-up behavior, organizations adopt neoclassical contracts, with provisions to promote the longevity of exchanges by specifying not only required actions and conditions of contractual breach, but also a framework for resolving unforeseen disputes. Second, *uncertainty* is another exchange hazard in that it requires the parties to adapt to problems arising from unforeseeable changes. Contracts, however, give access to such capabilities through the specification of clauses and procedures facilitating negotiations that invariably arise from unexpected change. Third, agency theory scholars focus on *asymmetric information*, and they distinguish between information asymmetry before contracting (adverse selection) and after contracting (moral hazard).

According to agency theory, contracts are explicitly drafted with provisions to safeguard against uncertainty and asymmetric information, and to promote the longevity of exchanges between two business parties (Bogetoft and Olesen, 2004). Zhou and Poppo (2010) pointed out that one function of contracts is coordination, by working as a 'technical aid' to manage the exchange relationship (Woolthuis *et al.*, 2005; Carson *et al.*, 2006). For example, a contract may specify shared goals, delivery information related to system interactions (Mayer and Argyres, 2004), specific coordination mechanisms such as face-to-face meetings, project groups, or steering committees (Hoetker and Mellewigt, 2009), as well as processes for resolving disputes, and adapting exchanges to unforeseen contingencies (Poppo and Zenger, 2002). These coordination devices foster more frequent communication and a greater flow of information (Zhou and Poppo, 2010). However, we fail to find direct empirical evidence in prior studies on the relationship between contractual governance and information exchange. Thus, we propose:

H_{iD}: *The level of contractual governance is positively associated with the level of inter-organizational communication, in term of communication willingness and behavior.*

Based on the discussion in this section, the Communication Antecedents Model (Figure 2.6) is proposed to show the hypothesized relationships between Environment uncertainty, TSI, trust, and contractual governance, and IOC.

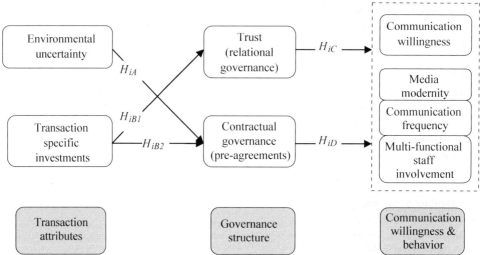

Figure 2.6. Research model on antecedents of inter-organizational communication (the Communication Antecedents Model).

2.5 Hypotheses on inter-organizational communication

From the literature, as identified in section 2.2, we learnt that inter-organizational communication (IOC) is a broad issue covering diverse aspects. Mohr *et al.* (1990, 1996) approached communication through four facets, namely frequency, direction, modality/formality, and content. Clare *et al.* (2002) suggested that information may be measured in terms of information sharing (depth and intensity) and information quality (timeliness, accuracy, adequacy, conciseness and credibility). Claro (2004) described supports of information in terms of defining prices and quality, facilitating logistics operations and production processes, and foreseeing future actions. Based on an intensive literature review on inter-organizational information systems, Storer (2005) summarized that communication between buyers and suppliers can be described in terms of elements including: information contents (the types of information communicated), communication media used, communication frequency, communication formality (formal and informal communication), information quality, information direction (e.g. forward or backward information through supply chains), people and departments involved. In addition, other main elements of IOC found in previous literature are: communication norms (Heide and John, 1992), communication willingness (Fawcett *et al.*, 2007), and (potential, realized, and perceived) benefits/values of IOC (Storer, 2005). A better understanding of IOC can be approached by examining these elements comprehensively. The following sections introduce these elements in more detail.

First, a company's *communication willingness* refers to its positive attitude and openness to communicate relevant information honestly and frequently (Fawcett *et al.*, 2007: 360). According to organizational theory, company culture influences how willing its staff are to share information (Constant *et al.*, 1994; McKinnon *et al.*, 2003; Al-Tameem, 2004). This cultural influence holds true for communication across organizations in the SC as well as across internal functions such as new product development, marketing, and engineering.

Second, some previous literature discussed *communication behavior*. *Communication media* employed by buyers and suppliers, in order of decreasing richness, include: face-to-face communication, videoconference, phone calls, instant messaging, faxes, e-mail, Electronic Data Interchange (EDI), letters/memos/newsletters, and numeric (Storer, 2005; Ambrose *et al.*, 2008). According to Media Richness Theory, communication media have varying capacities for resolving ambiguity, negotiating varying interpretations, and facilitating understanding.

The *types/contents* of information communicated among SC partners include (Storer, 2005): general understanding of the market, the chain, the product and norms for information sharing (Anderson *et al.*, 1987; Jonsson and Zineldin, 2003), problem resolution (Hardman *et al.*, 2002), product and performance feedback generally (Bowersox and Closs, 1996; Huan *et al.*, 2004), product quality and freshness and traceability (Bowersox and Closs, 1996; Van Dorp, 2004), on-time delivery, completeness of orders, flexibility to change orders (Bowersox and Closs, 1996; Huan *et al.*, 2004), prices, costs, and profitability (Issar *et al.*, 2004; Lindgreen *et al.*, 2004), supply and demand forecasts (Trienekens, 1999; Lefebvre *et al.*, 2003), promotions (Trienekens, 1999; Van der Vorst, 2000), new product development (Bensaou, 1995; Claro, 2004), and opportunities and threats (Trienekens, 1999).

Communication frequency reflects how often business partners have contact with each other (Brown, 1981; Mohr and Nevin, 1990). *Frequency* was measured in terms of frequency of using communication media, meeting frequency, frequency of positive feedback, frequency of visits, and frequency of interactions. (Anderson *et al.*, 1987; Jonsson and Zineldin, 2003). Meanwhile, channel information *intensity* refers to the amount of resource flows and the frequency of information flows.

People involved in IOC may be managers from different functions (Vlosky *et al.*, 1994; Lindgreen *et al.*, 2005) and at different hierarchical levels (transactional, operational, policy and strategic) (Siemieniuch *et al.*, 1999). The people factor may be the most important risk factor for the success of IOC. When the *involvement of relevant people* in information sharing is poor, they may communicate less frequently with SC members, and the information quality may be poor too (Vries, 2009).

Formality is mentioned in the literature in terms of formal communication channels, written relationship terms, expectations communicated in detailed and explicit discussion of relationship terms, formal communication of expectations, formal solicitation of feedback and/or conducting surveys (Anderson *et al.*, 1987; Storer, 2005). However, we noticed that informal communication is dominant in the Chinese poultry chain of the present research.

Third, some prior studies focused on *communication quality*. *Information quality* is often assessed in terms of reliability, timeliness, speed, accuracy, adequacy, completeness, relevancy, depth and range of content, ease of access, presentation, inter-activity, and overall satisfaction (Bensaou, 1995). Meanwhile, we noticed that, companies should *be well aware of the (changing) requirements and expectations of their business partners.* On the one hand, they should be aware of their customers' demands, requirements and expectations, so as to service their customers' needs better (market-oriented theory) and avoid potential risks. On the other hand, they should also present their own business and requirements to their suppliers and help them understand properly in order to get a better service from their suppliers (Wilson and Vlosky, 1998). To distinguish these two types of communication quality, we formulated two constructs to test in the model, including (regular) 'information quality' and 'knowledge on business partners' (changing) requirements and expectations'.

Fourth, *potential benefits* of effective and efficient IOC are immense, including improved efficiency, cost reduction, improved product quality, improved competitive edge and firm performance (Wilson and Vlosky, 1998; Amanor-Boadu *et al.*, 2002). Previous researches examined more on firm performance such as market share and profitability. We assume these are indirect and further, rather than direct benefits of IOC. In this research, we try to examine direct benefits of IOC in Chapter 5, with the aim of revealing how IOC leads to direct supports for focal firms; and in chapter 6 we look at both the direct and indirect benefits of IOC, with the aim of revealing how perceived communication benefits lead to better company performance ultimately.

We therefore developed 'the Communication Elements Model', comprising important aspects of IOC, including communication willingness, media modernity, knowledge on each other's requirements and expectations, information quality, perceived communication benefits for firms in relationships with suppliers, and perceived communication benefits for firms in relationships with customers. Some elements are not considered here, because they are less relevant in this research. For example, communication formality is not included in the model, because informal communication is prevalent in the Chinese poultry supply chain. The following sections introduce these constructs, our hypothesis, and the Communication Elements Model proposed in this research.

2.5.1 Communication willingness and communication quality

Different companies often have different attitudes towards information communication with their supply chain (SC) partners. Some companies are unwilling to share information, although they sometimes share under pressures from business partners. On the one hand, they are afraid that information provided to their customers or suppliers may be abused and place their organizations at a competitive disadvantage. On the other hand, some doubt the value of IOC compared to the financial, physical and human costs.

Differently, some companies define and manage IOC as a technology issue. They invest heavily in information technology (IT), believing that this will help connect people and companies, and therefore lead to improved information sharing and SC cooperation. Yet, it is reported that the sought after information sharing quality and higher levels of cross-enterprise collaboration do not always materialize in many companies that invest heavily in IT (Fawcett *et al.*, 2007).

A few firms, however, seem to treat IOC quite differently. They act as though interfirm communication is a behavior embedded in organizational cultures. In such cases, sensitive information involving cost, technology plans and production plans are shared. This open information communication augments their investments in technology to create better relationships and raise the level of SC cooperation (Fawcett *et al.*, 2007).

Mohr and Sohi (1995) for the first time studied and reported the positive relationship between norms of information exchange and specific communication flows (in term of frequency, bidirectionality and formality). It appears that communication norms encourage members' willingness to initiate and establish routines and procedures for communication. Fawcett *et al.* (2007) examined empirically how ICT is used to enhance SC performance, and they found that communication willingness affected operational performance and was critical to the development of a real information sharing capability.

We assume that willingness ultimately affects the extent and quality of IOC that takes place. Unwillingness to share relevant information among organizations can negate huge investments in technology, diminish potential values, negatively affect SC cooperation, and further decrease organizations' competitive edge (Lee *et al.*, 2000; Mendelson, 2000; Fawcett *et al.*, 2007). Thus, to examine the role of communication willingness in improving communication quality and realizing potential communication benefits, we propose the following hypothesis:

> $H_{ii.A}$: *The level of communication willingness is positively associated with the level of communication quality.*

2.5.2 Communication behavior and communication quality

Based on an extensive literature review, Storer (2005) reported the existence of some quantitative proofs about potential interactions between other aspects of IOC. Communication quality was found to be positively associated with communication frequency, but not with bi-directionality or formality; satisfaction with communication was found to be positively associated with information quality, bidirectionality, and communication frequency (Mohr and Sohi, 1995). Channel information intensity was found to be correlated with EDI use, formalization, channel cooperation and performance, but not with information quality, conflict, or satisfaction. Formality was found to be negatively correlated with distortion and withholding (Mohr and Sohi, 1995). It was reported that, a wide range of organizational departments were involved in communications with customers and suppliers in food sectors, and staff involvement is positively associated with IOC communication. Channel information quality was also found to be correlated with formalization, channel cooperation, performance, and satisfaction but not with EDI use, channel information intensity or conflict. Satisfaction with communication was positively associated with frequency, bi-directionality, and communication quality (Storer, 2006). Thus, to scrutinize the role of communication behavior in improving communication quality and realizing potential supports of IOC, we propose:

H_{iiB}. *The level of communication behavior (regarding modern media, communication frequency, and multi-functional staff involvement) is positively associated with the level of communication quality.*

2.5.3 Communication quality and perceived communication benefits

Information quality is high when information is relevant, timely, precise, reliable, adequate, and complete (O'Reilly, 1982; Stohl and Redding, 1987; Mohr and Sohi, 1995). Previous research has found that information quality is strongly associated with satisfaction in communication (Mohr and Sohi, 1995). Information about the capacities, history, and development trends, of business partners, of competitors, and of the own organization must be available at the right time, at the right place, and in the right form. A company should not only be aware of the (changing) demands, requirements, and expectations of its business partners, but also should help business partners to obtain its own relevant knowledge. Understanding customer requirements is the basis of a customer orientation that has been shown to improve performance (Jaworski and Kohli 1993; Narver and Slater 1990). Meanwhile, the more in certain range you let partners understand about the business of your own company, the better they are able to service your needs (Wilson and Vlosky, 1998). It has also been proved by a great deal of commercial fraud that a closer look at partners' affairs could prevent potential risks and huge losses (Case, 2007). However, it was found that agribusiness organizations did not receive timely indicators of changing customer requirements (Storer *et al.*, 2006). Thus, to check the role of communication quality in realizing potential communication benefits, we propose:

$H_{ii}c$. *The level of communication quality is positively associated with the level of perceived communication benefits.*

Based on the discussion above, a research model on important aspects of IOC and their interrelationships (the Communication Elements Model) is proposed here (Figure 2.7). With the Communication Elements Model, we intend to examine two issues, namely: (1) what are the relationships between communication willingness and behavior and communication quality; (2) what are the relationships between communication quality and perceived communication benefits. This Communication Elements Model can be used to draw managerial implications, and to reflect the diversity of IOC in a SC (network) setting as well.

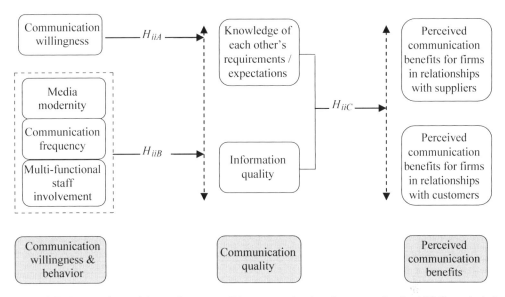

Figure 2.7. Research model on elements of inter-organizational communication (IOC) and their interrelationships (the Communication Elements Model).

2.6 Hypotheses on inter-organizational communication, supply chain collaboration, and performance

2.6.1 Inter-organizational communication and supply chain collaboration

The theory of Supply Chain Management (SCM) asserts that, the way companies pursue their objectives is to seek cooperation through supply chains (SC), since chains can raise performance levels above those attainable in spot-market operations. Meanwhile, earlier studies reported that, inter-organizational communication (IOC) is imperative glue that holds supply chain partners together (Mohr and Nevin, 1990: 36). IOC is a critical factor in promoting SC compliance among firms, and is also a generic cure for SC ailments (Forrester, 1958; Lee *et al.*, 1997b; Sahin and Robinson, 2002). IOC can help reduce conflicts and operating costs, improve efficiency and productivity, lead to higher revenues, strengthen inter-firm collaboration (Cao, 2007), and induce joint knowledge creation between partners (Tyndall *et al.*, 1998; Lee, 2000).

A survey among 127 logistics executives in varying-sized USA companies revealed that, integrated logistics management was positively associated with better performance, such as customer service, productivity, costs, strategic focus, cycle time, and quality, and competitive position. Furthermore, the survey showed that the most important ingredients for successful implementation of integrated logistics were: top management support, corporate-wide commitment, intra-organizational communication/ training, availability of good information, and system flexibility (Daugherty *et al.*, 1996).

SC collaboration is essential for approaching optimal performance and obtaining competitive advantage. In SCM, SC compliance with logistics requirements and with quality requirements are two important aspects. Thus, we propose the following hypotheses:

> H_{iiiA}: *The level of perceived communication benefits is positively associated with the level of supply chain compliance.*

2.6.2 Supply chain compliance and performance

Previous studies have revealed that customers and suppliers that comply with business partners' requirements, for example, in the area of logistics and quality, are likely to perform better. However, some of the findings are different or even conflicting in recent studies in the Chinese context. Lu (2007) studied Chinese vegetable chains, and found that vegetable companies' compliance with buyers' delivery requirements had positive effects on quality and price satisfaction, on profitability, but not on efficiency, whereas companies' compliance with quality requirements had no significant effect on any of these aspects of performance. Adversely, Han (2009) found that the association between integrated logistics management and performance was not supported in the Chinese pork chain, but the relationship between quality management practices and performance was supported.

We suppose these conflicting results might come from sector effect. To scrutinize the relationship between supply chain management and performance further, this present research examines the Chinese poultry chain, and distinguishes not only different aspects of IOC, but also different aspects of performance, including efficiency, customer satisfaction, and profitability and competitive edge. Thus, we propose:

> H_{iiiB}: *The level of supply chain compliance is positively associated with the level of company performance.*

Based on the considerations, we designed the third research model, the Communication-Chain compliance-Performance Model (Figure 2.8).

The above hypotheses of the three models are summarized in Table 2.1 and are quantitatively tested by partial least squares (PLS) modeling in Chapter 4, 5, and 6, respectively. These three research models are applied to both the supplier and the customer sides of the focal companies. And the hypotheses are formulated for both the company-supplier and the company-customer models.

2.7 Concluding remarks

This chapter elaborated three theories that are of importance for studying inter-organizational communication (IOC) in supply chains. Transaction Cost Economics sheds light on potential antecedents of IOC; the literature on inter-organizational communication offers insights into the important aspects of IOC and their interrelationships; whereas the theory on supply chain management provides a means of researching the potential performance improvement that could be contributed by IOC. Meanwhile, they overlap to some extent and provide rather complementary explanations. Thus, the combination of these theories provides a rich theoretical understanding of the issues being studied.

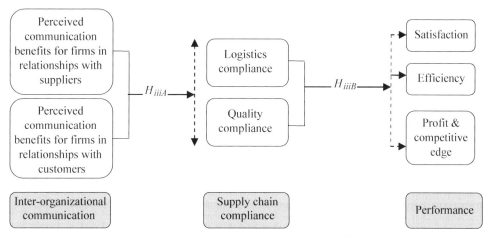

Figure 2.8. Research model on inter-organizational communication (IOC), supply chain compliance, and performance (the Communication-Chain compliance-Performance Model).

Table 2.1. The hypotheses for the three models on antecedents, inter-organizational communication (IOC), and performance.

I. Hypotheses on antecedents of inter-organizational communication (IOC) in the Communication Antecedents Model

H_{iA} The level of environmental uncertainty is positively associated with the level of contractual governance.

H_{iB} The level of transaction specific investments (TSI) is positively associated with the level of trust (H_{iB1}) and of contractual governance (H_{iB2}).

H_{iC} The level of trust is positively associated with the level of inter-organizational communication (IOC) (in terms of communication willingness and behavior).

H_{iD} The level of contractual governance is positively associated with the level of inter-organizational communication (in terms of communication willingness and behavior).

II. Hypotheses on important aspects of IOC and their interrelationships in the Communication Elements Model

H_{iiA} The level of communication willingness is positively associated with the level of communication quality.

H_{iiB} The level of communication behavior (in terms of media modernity, communication frequency and multi-functional staff involvement) is positively associated with the level of communication quality.

H_{iiC} The level of communication quality is positively associated with the level of perceived communication benefits.

III. Hypotheses on performance results of IOC in the Communication-Chain compliance-Performance Model

H_{iiiA} The level of perceived communication benefits is positively associated with the level of supply chain compliance.

H_{iiiB} The level of supply chain compliance is positively associated with the level of performance.

Grounded on these theories, this present research formulated three research models and then proposed hypotheses (Table 2.1). These models are: (1) The Communication Antecedents Model on potential antecedents of IOC; (2) The Communication Elements Model on important aspects of IOC and their interrelationships; and (3) The Communication-Chain compliance-Performance Model on performance results of IOC. In Section 2.4., Section 2.5, and Section 2.6, we enhanced our understanding of these relevant concepts gleaned from the theories, and the interrelationships between these concepts. Figure 2.9 summarizes the research framework of this research.

It is noteworthy that, the development of a relationship is non-linear and is not always a sequential process (Claro 2004). It is important to stress that some variables might mutually affect each other. For example, perceived communication benefits and performance might positively affect communication willingness and transaction specific investments. And good communication quality might improve trust.

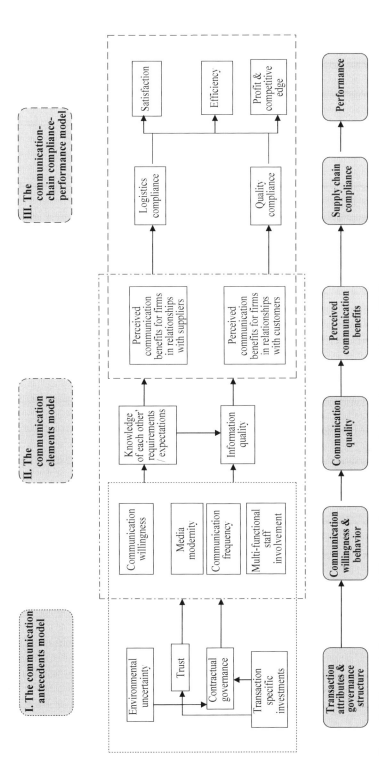

Figure 2.9. Research framework of this research on inter-organizational communication (IOC).
Notes: ▢ : research model I; ⌐ ¬ : research model II; ⌐‾¬ : research model III on inter-organizational communication (IOC).

Chapter 3

Research design and methodology

This chapter introduces the methods employed in this research project. Section 3.1 describes the study population and data collection. Section 3.2 presents the operationalization of the constructs employed. Section 3.3 first introduces definitions of formative constructs and reflective constructs, as well as the four primary decision rules implemented to specify constructs. Then, it explains how constructs have been specified in this research, and how we have assessed construct validity and reliability. Section 3.4 presents partial least squares (PLS) modeling technique employed for data analysis, and control variables examined.

3.1 Study population, data collection, and company profile

3.1.1 Study population and data collection

The study domain is the poultry supply chain in the Mainland China. Given the vast geographic size of China, this research focuses mainly on *three regions* (Figure 3.1): (1) Beijing city (the capital) and Hebei province, which are located in Northern China; (2) Shandong province, an eastern coastal province; and (3) Guizhou province, a province located in South-west China. All of the three regions have long history of producing and consuming poultry. Comparatively, Beijing, Hebei, and Shandong represent

Figure 3.1. The locations of the survey (Beijing & Hebei, Shangdong, and Guizhou).

the more developed regions in China, whereas Guizhou is a less developed province. In addition, in order to study the potential impacts of different locations on inter-organizational communication and company performance, this research also examines administrative level of a location as a control variable in Chapter 4, 5 and 6.

To gather empirical data on the constructs in this research, the steps below were followed. First, based on the configuration of the poultry chain in China we identified six types of participants including commercial poultry farms, processors including slaughterhouses, intermediaries, traders, supermarkets, and restaurants. Individual poultry farmers are not included in this research, considering that they are small and scattered, and they are normally with a focus on primary agriculture activities instead of commercial activities like other entities in this research. In addition, individual farmers conduct information exchange more like individuals than organizations; whereas this research focuses on the communication between organizations. Second, based on a comprehensive study of previous literature, a preliminary questionnaire was designed for pilot interviews. The researcher interviewed about twenty relevant experts, officials, and practitioners in the poultry chain. They helped to construct the questionnaire, while providing valuable information on the Chinese poultry sector and on the distribution status of poultry firms in the sampling areas. The insights obtained from the interviews, together with those from the literature, jointly contributed to a structured questionnaire. With this questionnaire, we performed a pre-test with 2-5 selected companies from each stage of the poultry chain. Based on the pre-test, the questionnaire was further revised and resulted in the final structured questionnaire (see Appendix 3.1) for the survey. For both the pre-test and the survey, the questionnaires were first developed in English, then translated into Chinese with the assistance of an independent translator, and finally translated back into English with another translator to ensure conceptual equivalence (Hoskisson *et al.*, 2000). The triangular approach of expert interviews, pre-test, and survey have contributed jointly to the establishment of factors on inter-organizational communication, its antecedents, and performance results in the chain (Yin, 2003).

The survey was conducted between October 2008 and June 2009. The respondent companies were selected based on multistage cluster sampling from the three regions. Due to the lack of integrated statistical data, we could not find an overall list of companies in the poultry chain. However, three main criteria were used to select candidate companies, including company type (supermarket, restaurant, trader, processor, intermediary, and commercial farm), company size (mini, small, middle, large, and super & international) (see Appendix 3.2), and administrative level of location ((national and provincial) capital city, other city, and county). Table 3.1 shows the locations, administrative levels of locations, and firm size of the respondent companies. The sources and other principles employed to select respondent companies are as follows:

1. To select supermarkets, two main sources were used: supermarket associations, and the Yellow Pages of the three regions. For a supermarket or a restaurant with more than one store, the survey was conducted only with its head store or one of its major stores. Most supermarkets have individual consumers as their major customers, thus, we only asked them to fill in the part of the questionnaire concerning their most important suppliers. But for a few membership warehouses with organizations as their main customers, the researcher also asked them for information about their most important customers.

2. With regard to restaurants, though the whole population of restaurants is pretty huge, only those restaurants providing purely poultry products, or providing poultry as one of their main products, were targeted in this research. In any case, restaurants located in small towns mainly purchase

from wet markets. Their purchasing behavior is similar to that of individual citizens. However, the objective of this research is to examine inter-organizational communication, thus, we looked for those restaurants purchasing poultry products from organizations instead of individuals.

3. To select organizations such as restaurants and traders, as well as some processors, the main sources are company information obtained from informants in Administration Offices for Industry and Commerce.

4. In addition, intermediaries, commercial farms, and some processors were selected based on information from informants in Centers for Animal Disease Control and Prevention.

5. For companies involved in multiple businesses, we asked them to answer the questionnaire with a focus on their most important suppliers and customers.

We did not try to conduct the survey by sending post mail directly, because, based on the researcher's earlier research experiences in China, it is almost impossible to get questionnaires back from a postal

Table 3.1. Location, administrative level of a location, and firm size of the total sample: frequency (and percentage).

	Supermarkets	Restaurants	Traders	Processors	Intermediaries	Farms	Others[1]	All firms
Location								
Beijing & Hebei	9	28	15	14	11	12	2	91 (53%)
Shandong	5	2	2	4	3	3	-	19 (11%)
Guizhou	11	12	7	7	8	16	1	57 (33%)
Total	25	42	24	25	22	31	3	172 (100%)
Administrative level of the location								
(Provincial) capital city	6	35	21	11	10	11	3	97 (56%)
Other city	8	1	2	4	4	4	-	23 (13%)
County or town	11	6	1	10	8	16	-	52 (30%)
Total	25	42	24	25	22	31	3	172 (100%)
Firm size[2]								
Mini	2	28	24	10	21	23	2	110 (64%)
Small	8	10	-	5	1	7	1	31 (18%)
Medium	8	2	-	5	-	1	-	17 (10%)
Large	3	2	-	2	-	-	-	7 (4%)
Super & international	4	-	-	3	-	-	-	7 (4%)
Total	25 (15%)	42 (24%)	24 (14%)	25 (15%)	22 (13%)	31 (18%)	3 (2%)	172 (100%)

[1] 'Others' refers to organizations of which the main activities include both scientific research and business transactions.

[2] For firm size, refer to Appendix 3.2.

survey. However, the data collection procedures were greatly facilitated by the researcher's previous working experience and personal *guanxi*[3] network. The targeted firms were contacted mainly through informants in organizations such as Supermarket Associations, Restaurant Associations, Administration Offices for Industry and Commerce, and Centers for Animal Disease Control and Prevention. These organizations, on the one hand, provide administrative or support services, so have close business contacts with the targeted companies. Thus, most of the targeted companies agreed to take part in the survey. If a company hesitated or refused to participate, we tried to find other contacts to communicate with them until they agreed. These measures jointly contributed to a high response rate of over 90%.

To minimize response bias, we have targeted top managers as the *respondents* within each focal firm. They are general or deputy-general managers, company owners, or office managers who have full knowledge of the purchasing and/or marketing activities. The questionnaires, together with the instruction letters, were sent to them after they had agreed to take part in the survey. We asked respondents to select their most important suppliers and customers, and answer the questions related to their most important suppliers and customers. Moreover, if respondents were not sure about certain question(s), we encouraged them to ask their colleagues. To make the survey more appealing and of high quality, certain recommendations of Dillman (1978, 2000) were applied. First, the instruction letter introduced the objectives of the research, the requirements of the questionnaires, and the possible advantages of the outcomes of the research for the respondents. Second, the letter also explained that all information provided by the respondents would be kept confidential. Third, name, phone number, and e-mail address of the researcher were included for possible enquiries. Fourth, to encourage the respondents to answer the questionnaires in full, and to add their names, addresses and email addresses for future contact, we promised to provide a summary of the most important findings of the survey, together with a gift for each comprehensively and conscientiously filled-in questionnaire.

The questionnaires were sent out by various measures according to the requirements of the respondents. They were mostly sent out by *e-mail* to the supermarkets, and by *fax or e-mail* to the processors, intermediaries and farms. As for most of the restaurants and traders, *printed questionnaires* were taken to them by the researcher or informants. Each returned questionnaire was checked timely and carefully. When a questionnaire was found incomplete or confusing, the researcher called or visited the respondents to confirm their answer, in this way to make sure that the respondents understood the questions correctly and provided answers precisely.

Normally, an entity in a supply chain is not only a customer for its suppliers, but also a supplier for its customers. Each respondent company (focal company) was asked to answer the questionnaire according to their business relationship with its most important supplier, and with its most important customer, respectively. By collecting data about both sides (see Figure 3.2), we expect to better depict the differences between the purchasing and marketing perspectives, whereas most previous studies collected data from only supplier or customer side.

Finally, 165 questionnaires were obtained for the company-supplier sample, with answers from respondent firms on the relationships with their most important suppliers; whereas 96 questionnaires

---

[3] Personal relationships are called as *Guanxi* in China. Guanxi functions as information governance, which prevail in social life and business society in China. People rely on *guanxi* to seek valuable information, receive assistance and facilitate business transactions.

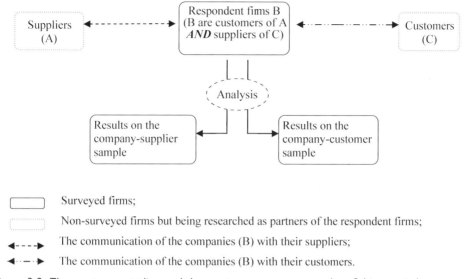

Surveyed firms;

Non-surveyed firms but being researched as partners of the respondent firms;

The communication of the companies (B) with their suppliers;

The communication of the companies (B) with their customers.

Figure 3.2. The company-supplier, and the company-customer samples of this research.

were obtained for the company-customers sample, with answers from focal firms on the relationships with their most important customers. The following section outlines the characteristics of the respondent companies.

3.1.2 Company profile

The sample in this research consists of 172 respondent companies, including 25 supermarkets, 42 restaurants, 24 traders, 25 processors, 22 intermediaries, 31 commercial farms, and 3 other firms (Table 3.2). Two (membership) supermarkets, having organizations as their most important customers, have contributed not only to the customer sample, but also the supplier sample. Other supermarkets and restaurants have individual consumers as their most important customer, thus have contributed only to the customer sample. In addition, there are 21 traders, 20 processors, 20 intermediaries, 24 farms and 2 other companies that have contributed to both the customer and the supplier samples. 'Others' in the table below refers to those organizations whose major activities include both scientific research and business transactions.

Table 3.3 displays the profile of the respondent companies. It is shown that, the firm age of farms and restaurants are significantly different from that of processors. The average firm age was 8.77 years. The oldest organization, an institute with both breeding and selling chicken as main activities, was set up 52 years ago. The youngest organizations, including two restaurants and one farm, were set up just one year ago. The average ages of farms and restaurants are significantly younger than those of processors and other groups of companies.

As for the profiles of the respondents, the results show that 87.8% of the respondents of the survey were senior employees or key employees (there is often no specific senior employee in a small company except

Table 3.2. Company type and numbers of the company-supplier and the company-customer samples.

	Supermarkets	Restaurants	Traders	Processors	Intermediaries	Farms	Others	All firms
The company-supplier sample	25	42	23	24	22	27	2	165
	(=2[a]+23)		(=21[a]+2)	(=20[a]+4)	(=20 [a]+2)	(=24[a]+3)	(=2[a]+0)	(=89[a]+74)
The company-customer sample	2	-	22	21	20	28	3	96
	(=2[a]+0)		(=21[a]+1)	(=20[a]+1)	(=20[a]+0)	(=24[a]+4)	(=2[a]+1)	(=89[a]+7)
Total	25	42	24	25	22	31	3	172

[a] The number of the focal firms that contribute to both samples.

Table 3.3. Profile of the total sample on firm age, respondent position, and poultry types: number (and percentage).

	Supermarkets	Restaurants	Traders	Processors	Intermediaries	Farms	Others	All Firms
Firm age in years[1]:	8.04	6.95	7.17	10.32	9.64	6.84	28.67	8.77
mean and (S.D.)	(5.02)	(5.29)	(4.43)	(6.47)	(5.43)	(5.21)	(20.60)	(7.52)
Respondent position								
– senior or key employee	24	38	20	20	18	28	3	151 (88%)
– others	1	4	4	5	4	3	-	21 (12%)
Poultry type								
– chicks only	-	4	12	12	12	16	2	58 (34%)
– ducks only	-	-	1	5	1	4	1	12 (7%)
– other poultry only	-	1	-	-	-	2	-	3 (2%)
– at least two types of poultry	25	37	11	8	9	9	-	99 (58%)
Total	25	42	24	25	22	31	3	172
	(15%)	(25%)	(14%)	(15%)	(13%)	(18%)	(2%)	(100%)

[1] Independent-samples T test was applied to compare firm age for each pair of types of companies.

the owner). This indicates a high quality of respondents, who should have a clear understanding of what practices their organizations employ, with regard to their most important customers and suppliers.

With regard to poultry types, most respondent companies (57.6%) were involved in at least two types of poultry, while the second largest group of firms (33.7%) were involved in chick products only.

Table 3.4 displays the quality standards employed by respondent companies. Quality standard here is an ordinal construct to measure the highest quality standard applied in an organization. It ranges between 1 and 5, where 1 is 'unknown or no specific standard', 2 is 'QS certificate or similar level of quality standards', 3 is 'standards slightly higher than QS', 4 is 'ISO9000 or Green A or a similar level of standard or international supermarkets', and 5 is 'ISO22000 or Green AA or a similar level of standard'. Among these standards, 'QS' (quality standard) is the basic national standard in China for food products. Green A is a Chinese food standard for non-pollution food, while Green AA is a Chinese food standard for organic food.

Most surveyed companies (58.1%), mainly companies in trade area, such as restaurants, traders, and supermarkets, have applied 'QS' or a similar standard as their highest standard. Quality standard 4 (ISO9000 or HACCP or Green A or a similar level of standard) was applied by 18.6% of the respondent firms, mainly by intermediaries, farms, and processors. Whilst quality standard 5 (ISO 22000 or Green AA or a similar level of standard) was applied by 9.3% of the respondent firms, mainly by processors and intermediaries. The lower quality standards applied in trading companies compared to production companies might imply that there is a higher potential risk of food quality and safety problems in trading companies than in production companies.

Table 3.4. Profile of the total sample on quality standard: number and (percentage).

	Supermarkets	Restaurants	Traders	Processors	Intermediaries	Farms	Others	All Firms
Quality Standard[1]: mean and (S.D.)	2.44	2.05	1.92	3.64	3.59	3.13	4.00	2.74
	(0.77)	(0.22)	(0.28)	(1.35)	(1.10)	(0.96)	(1.00)	(1.08)
unknown or no standard	-	-	2	1	-	1	-	4 (2%)
basic QS standard	18	40	22	7	6	7	-	100 (58%)
standards slightly higher than QS	3	2	-	1	1	12	1	20 (12%)
standards similar to ISO9000 or Green A	4	-	-	7	11	9	1	32 (19%)
standards similar to ISO22000 or Green AA	-	-	-	9	4	2	1	16 (9%)

[1] Independent-samples T test was applied to compare means for each pair of types of companies.

3.2 Constructs operationalization

3.2.1 Antecedents of inter-organizational communication

This research aims to examine two types of potential antecedents of inter-organizational communication (IOC), namely transaction attributes and governance structure. Based on previous studies introduced in Section 2.1 and 2.4, transaction attributes are operationalized with two constructs, namely, 'environment uncertainty' and 'transaction specific investments' (TSI), whereas governance structure is operationalized with two other constructs, namely, 'trust' and 'contractual governance'. All items of these constructs were measured using a 5-point Likert scale ranging from '1 = totally disagree' to '5 = totally agree'. This section introduces the operationalization of these constructs, which is summarized in Table 3.5. For all constructs, Cronbach's alpha for exploratory factor analysis is above the cutoff of 0.60, which supports the internal consistency of these constructs (Straub *et al.*, 2004).

Table 3.5 Operationalization of constructs of transaction attributes and governance structures (see Appendix 3.1 for detailed measures).

Constructs	Operational definition	Source(s)	Measures	Cronbach's α[1]
Transaction attributes				
Environmental uncertainty (EUn)	EUn refers to unanticipated changes in circumstances surrounding a transaction.	Noordewier *et al.* (1990), Han (2009), Arana (2010)	EUn 1-3	CS[2]: 0.74 CC[3]: 0.69
Transaction specific investments (TSI)	TSI refer to an organization's investments made specifically for a transaction with a specific business partner.	Heide and John (1988), Lu (2007)	TSI 1-3	CS: 0.82 CC: 0.67
Governance structures				
Trust	The belief that the business counterparts are honest and sincere.	Anderson and Narus (1990); Zaheer *et al.* (1998); Claro (2004)	Trust 1-3	CS: 0.90 CC: 0.87
Contractual governance (CG)	Transactions are conducted under certain pre-agreed transaction conditions, including price, quality, volume, and delivery.	Bogetoft and Olesen (2004); Lu (2007)	CG 1-4	CS: 0.83 CC: 0.79

[1] Cronbach's α based on standardized items for exploratory factor analysis were obtained by SPSS 17.0.
[2] CS – the company-supplier sample.
[3] CC – the company-customer sample.

Environmental uncertainty refers to unanticipated changes in circumstances surrounding a transaction. Price and volume uncertainties are key aspects of this construct (Noordewier *et al.*, 1990). In addition, this research also considers quality uncertainty, which is critical for meat products. Based on Han (2009) and Arana (2010), three items have been formulated in this research to measure environment uncertainty: market complexity, price volatility, and quality variation. These items are:
- EUn1: Currently, the market of poultry products is complex.
- EUn2: Currently, the price of poultry products is volatile.
- EUn3: Currently, the quality of poultry products is variable.

Transaction specific investments (TSI) refer to an organization's investments made specifically for a transaction with a specific business partner. Two main dimensions of specific investments can be found in the literature, namely, physical investments, and human and knowledge investments. Based on Heide and John (1988), and Lu (2007), three items have been formulated in this research to measure specific investments. They are:
- TSI1: We have made large investments in poultry sales to our most important customer / in poultry procurement from our most important supplier, in the last three years.
- TSI2: We have made large investments in controlling poultry quality of ours / of our most important supplier, in the last three years.
- TSI3: If switching to other customers / suppliers, we would waste a lot of knowledge, regarding the operation methods of our most important customer /supplier (Dropped for the company-supplier sample).

Trust refers to the belief that the business counterparts are honest and sincere and will in no circumstances deliberately do anything to damage the relationship (Anderson and Narus, 1990). Trust has been looked at as a type of relational governance (Zaheer and Venkatraman, 1995). Two dimensions of trust can be found in the literature, namely, interpersonal trust and inter-organizational trust (Zaheer *et al.*, 1998). In this research, three related items were adapted from Claro (2004) and Zaheer *et al.* (1998) to measure both inter-organizational and interpersonal trust jointly. These items are:
Based on experience in the last 12 months, we believe that:
- Trust1: Our most important customer / supplier is credible.
- Trust2: Our most important customer / supplier will keep its promises made to us.
- Trust3: The staff of our most important customer / supplier is credible.

Contractual governance, as a preferred means of coordination when there are higher risks and uncertainties, is designed to minimize transaction costs (Williamson, 1979). Quality, quantity, price, rights and obligations are the main specified items in a contractual agreement. The more items are agreed before actual transactions, the less risk and opportunism there is for ongoing transactions (Bogetoft and Olesen, 2004). This research, following Lu (2007), defines contractual governance between focal firms and their most important business partners with regard to price, quality, transaction volume, and delivery. The items of contractual governance (CG) are:
- CG1: Price is pre-agreed with our most important customer / supplier.
- CG2: Quality is pre-agreed with our most important customer / supplier.
- CG3: Transaction volumes are pre-agreed with our most important customer / supplier.
- CG4: Delivery time and place are pre-agreed with our most important customer / supplier.

3.2.2 Elements of inter-organizational communication

Grounded on previous studies introduced in Section 2.2, 2.4, and 2.5, this research first proposed two distinct dimensions of inter-organizational communication (IOC), communication willingness and communication behavior. Here, communication behavior is operationalized with three constructs, including 'media modernity', 'communication frequency', and 'multi-functional staff involvement'. Thereafter, communication quality is operationalized with two constructs, 'knowledge on each other's requirements and expectations' and 'information quality'. And 'perceived communication benefits' is operationalized with two other constructs, 'perceived communication benefits for firms in relationships with suppliers', and 'perceived communication benefits for firms in relationships with customers'. For all of the above constructs except 'media modernity', a five-pointed Likert scale is used ranging between '1 = totally disagree' and '5 = totally agree'. As for 'media modernity', it is a one item question, measured by '1 = face-to-face or phone', '2 = e-mail', and '3 = EDI or intranet'. This section introduces the operationalization of these constructs, which is summarized in Table 3.6. For all of these constructs, Cronbach's alpha for exploratory factor analysis is above the cutoff of 0.60, which proves the internal consistency of these constructs (Straub *et al.*, 2004).

Communication willingness refers to the positive and open attitude of an organization to communicate relevant information honestly and timely with its business partners (Fawcett *et al.*, 2007). According to Organizational Theory, company culture influences how willing its staff are to share information (Constant *et al.*, 1994; McKinnon *et al.*, 2003; Al-Tameem, 2004). This cultural influence holds true for communication across organizations in the supply chain, as well as across internal functions such as new product development, marketing and engineering. This construct was initiatively measured by three items based on Mohr and Sohi (1995) and Fawcett *et al.* (2007). These items are:
- Willing1: We are willing to provide proprietary information to our most important customer / supplier if the information is helpful to it.
- Willing2: We (Our most important customer/supplier) are expected to provide our most important customer/supplier (us) with proprietary information that may be of help.
- Willing3: We have formal and official channels through which to communicate with our most important customer / supplier (Dropped for both samples).

Media modernity refers to the level of modernity of tools that are employed to communicate information with business partners. Based on Mohr and Sohi (1995), and Storer (2006), this research examines three types of media, which in order of increasing modernity levels, are: face-to-face/phone, e-mail, intranet/EDI (electronic data interchange). The question for this one-item construct is:
Media: *In the last 12 months, the most modern media used to communicate with our most important customer/supplier was:*
1. Face-to-face discussion and/or phone (traditional media).
2. E-mail (moderately advanced media).
3. Intranet/electronic data interchange (modern media).

Communication frequency refers to how often a company exchanges information with business partners. So, 'how often' and 'what information' are two key issues of this construct. In response, four items have been designed in this study for this construct based on (Storer, 2006). These items are:

Table 3.6. Operationalization of constructs of inter-organization communication (IOC) (see Appendix 3.1 for detailed measures).

Constructs[4]	Operational definition	Sources	Measures	Cronbach's α[1]
Communication willingness				
Communication willingness (Willing)	The openness to communicate relevant information honestly and timely.	Mohr and Sohi (1995); Fawcett et al. (2007)	Willing 1-2	CS[2]: 0.74 CC[3]: 0.77
Communication behavior				
Media modernity (Media)	The level of modernity of tools used to communicate with business partners, including: face-to-face/phone, e-mail, intranet/EDI.	Daft and Lengel (1984); Mohr and Sohi (1995); Storer (2006); Ambrose et al. (2008)	Media 1	-
Communication frequency (Freq)	How often a company exchanges information on problem resolution, quality control, delivery, and price, with business partners.	Brown (1981); Mohr and Nevin (1995); Storer (2006).	Freq 1-4	CS: 0.60 CC: 0.79
Multi-functional staff involvement (Staff)	The extent to which staff, involved in communication with business partners, are from different functions and multi-hierarchical levels.	Lindgreen et al. (2004); Vlosky (1994); Siemieniuch (1999)	Staff 1-2	CS: 0.69 CC: 0.79
Communication quality				
Knowledge on each other's requirements and expectations (Know)*	The extent to which a company is aware of the expectations and requirements of its business partners.	Wilson and Vlosky (1998)	Kownledge 1-2	CS: 0.83 CCS: 0.81
Information quality (InfoQuali)	Assessed in term of reliability, timeliness, adequacy, accuracy and credibility.	O'Reilly (1982); Stohl and Redding (1987); Mohr and Sohi (1995)	InfoQuali 1-3	CS: 0.82 CC: 0.84
Perceived communication benefits				
Perceived communication benefits for firms in relationships with suppliers (BenefitA)*	The extent to which a customer benefits directly from information obtained from its suppliers.	Claro (2004)	BenefitA 1-4	CS: 0.74 CC: 0.82
Perceived communication benefits for firms in relationships with customers (BenefitB)*	The extent to which a supplier benefits directly from information obtained from its customers.	Claro (2004)	BenefitB 1-4	CS: 0.78 CC: 0.65

[1] Cronbach's α based on standardized items for exploratory factor analysis were obtained by SPSS 17.0.
[2] CS – the company-supplier sample.
[3] CC – the company-customer sample.
[4] * Constructs proposed and empirically examined for the first time in this research.

In the last 12 months, the frequency with which we communicated on the following information with our most important customer/supplier was:
- Freq1: Problem resolution.
- Freq2: Product quality control.
- Freq3: Timely and precise delivery.
- Freq4: Product price decision.

Multi-functional staff involvement refers to the extent to which staff, involved in communicating with business partners, are from different functions and levels of the organization. Based on Fawcett *et al.* (2007), two items are used for this construct, including:
- Staff1: We use cross-functional teams to communicate with our most important customer/supplier.
- Staff2: Senior level managers, of ours and our most important customer/supplier, interact frequently.

Information quality refers to the extent to which information communicated with business partners is timely, adequate, accurate and credible. The items of this construct are adapted from Mohr and Sohi (1995), and Storer (2006). These items are:
Information communicated between us and our most important customer/supplier is:
- InfoQuali1: Timely.
- InfoQuali2: Adequate.
- InfoQuali3: Accurate and credible.

Knowledge on each other's requirements and expectations refers to the extent to which an organization is aware of the (changing) expectations and requirements of its business partners. Expectation and requirements here include certain issues that are broader and deeper than regular information. Based on the literature, this construct is proposed and empirically examined for the first time in this research with two items:
- Know1: We are well aware of the expectations and requirements of our most important customer/supplier.
- Know2: Our most important customer/supplier is well aware of our expectations and requirements.

Perceived communication benefits for firms in relationships with suppliers (BenefitA) refers to the extent to which a company benefits directly from information obtained from its suppliers. Based on Claro (2004), this construct is proposed and empirically examined with four items in this research, to measure the benefits that customers obtained from the communication with its suppliers. These items are:
We (our customer) get(s) information from our most important supplier (us), which supports us (it) directly in:
- BenefitA1: Problem resolution.
- BenefitA2: Product quality control.
- BenefitA3: Timely and precise delivery.
- BenefitA4: Product price decision.

Perceived communication benefits for companies in relationships with customers (BenefitB) refers to the extent to which a company benefits directly from information obtained from its customers. Based on Claro (2004), this construct is also proposed and empirically examined with four items in this research, to measure the benefits that are obtained by suppliers from the communication with their customers. These items are:

We (our supplier) get(s) information from our most important customer (us), which supports us (it) directly in:
- BenefitB1: Problem resolution.
- BenefitB2: Product quality control.
- BenefitB3: Timely and precise delivery.
- BenefitB4: Product price.

As introduced in Section 2.2 and 2.5, previous literature often examined performance such as market share and profitability as results of information exchange. However, we assume that these are indirect benefits rather than direct benefits of inter-organizational communication. Meanwhile, customers and suppliers might obtain different kinds and levels of benefits from inter-organizational communication in supply chains. Thus, by employing the two distinct constructs of 'perceived communication benefits for firms in relationships with suppliers' and 'perceived communication benefits for firms in relationships with customers', this research intends to examine the perceived direct benefits of inter-organizational communication, and tries to distinguish the benefits of information for customers and for suppliers.

3.2.3 Results of inter-organizational communication

Based on the literature introduced in Section 2.3 and 2.6, supply chain (SC) compliance is operationalized with two constructs, 'logistics compliance' and 'quality compliance'. Meanwhile, company performance is operationalized with three constructs, including 'satisfaction', 'efficiency', and 'profit & competitive edge'. These items of 'logistics compliance' and 'quality compliance' are measured by 5-point Likert scale, ranging between '1 = totally disagree' and '5 = totally agree'. Meanwhile, the items of the three constructs on performance are measured by 7-point Likert scale[4] ranging between '1 = totally disagree' and '7 = totally agree'. For detailed measures, see the questionnaire in Appendix 3.1. This section introduces the operationalization of these constructs, which is summarized in Table 3.7. For all of these constructs, Cronbach's alpha for exploratory factor analysis is again above the cutoff of 0.60, which supports the internal consistency of these constructs (Straub *et al.*, 2004).

Logistics compliance in this research refers to the extent to which suppliers comply with their customers' requirements for logistics activities, such as delivery and packaging. Delivery and packaging are two critical issues, which may affect the quality of perishable food. Thus, this research measures logistics compliance (LC) by two items related to delivery and packaging respectively, which were adapted from Lu (2007). These items are:
- LC1: Our most important supplier (We) delivers products timely and precisely to us (to our most important customer).
- LC2: Our most important supplier (We) packages products according to the requirements of us (our most important customer).

---

[4] During the pre-test of the survey, 7-point Likert scale was used for all items. However, respondents complained that it confused them, and strongly suggested to use 5-point Likert scale. Thus, 5-point Likert scale was employed for most items in the survey. However, to measure the performance more precisely, 7-point Likert scale was kept for those items.

Table 3.7. Operationalization of constructs of supply chain compliance and performance (see Appendix 3.1 for detailed measures).

Constructs	Operational definition	Source(s)	Measures	Cronbach's α[1]
Supply chain compliance				
Logistics compliance (LC)	The extent to which suppliers comply with their customers' requirements for logistics activities, such as delivery and packaging.	Lu (2007)	LC 1-2	CS[2]: 0.74 CC[3]: 0.75
Quality compliance (QC)	The extent to which suppliers comply with their customers' requirements for quality.	Lu (2007)	QC 1-3	CS: 0.75 CC: 0.76
Company performance				
Satisfaction (Satis)	The extent to which customers are satisfied with their suppliers, concerning quality and price.	Bensaou and Venkatraman (1995); Claro 2004; Lu 2007	Satis 1-2	CS: 0.78 CC: 0.74
Efficiency (Effi)	Efficiency relates to financial costs and time costs incurred in a transaction, which reflects the operational performance.	Fawcett *et al.* (2007); Lu (2007)	Effi 1-2	CS: 0.84 CC: 0.77
Profitability & competitive edge (P&C)	The extent to which profit, sales, market coverage, and competitive edge of a focal firm grow faster or slower, compared to its main competitors in the last twelve months.	Nrasimahan and Kim (2002); Fawcett *et al.* (2007); Han (2009)	P&C 1-4	CS: 0.85 CC: 0.82

[1] Cronbach's α based on standardized items for exploratory factor analysis obtained by SPSS 17.0.
[2] CS – the company-supplier sample.
[3] CC – the company-customer sample.

Quality compliance refers to the extent to which suppliers comply with their customers' requirements for quality. This is a three-item construct adapted from Lu (2007). The three items are:
- QC1: Our most important supplier (We) will help us (our most important customer) if we (they) are faced with quality problems.
- QC2: Our most important supplier (We) provides products that meet the quality requirements of us (our most important customer).
- QC3: Our most important supplier (We) provides products of better quality than its (our) main competitors.

This research distinguished three indicators of performance: satisfaction, efficiency, and profitability and competitive edge.

Satisfaction refers to the rating of a company's satisfaction with its selected partner(s). Satisfaction is a subjective dimension, which is supported by the notion that a company's performance is determined partly by how well the business relationship meets expectations (Bensaou, 1995; Claro, 2004). During the pre-test, we noticed that price and quality are the two aspects that obtained the highest attention from poultry companies. Thus, this study measures satisfaction by only two items related to price and quality, respectively, based on Bensaou and Venkatraman (1995), and Lu (2007). The items for satisfaction in this research are:

- Satis1: We (Our most important customer) are (is) satisfied with the product quality of our most important supplier (us).
- Satis2: We (Our most important customer) are (is) happy with the price paid to our most important supplier (us).

Efficiency relates to financial and time costs involved in a transaction, which reflects the operational performance. Transaction costs incurred dramatically reduce the efficiency of an organization. Transaction costs are high in the agri-food sector in China due to a less well-developed infrastructure and market information asymmetry. Companies have to spend a lot of time and efforts in searching for market information, finding transaction partners, and delivering products to markets (Lu, 2007). To measure efficiency, two items were adapted from Fawcett *et al.* (2007) and Lu (2007). These items are:

- Effi1: It costs us less money when we purchase (sell) poultry from our most important supplier (to our most important customer).
- Effi2: It takes us less time to complete an order with our most important supplier (customer) than with others.

Profitability & competitive edge refers to the extent to which the profit, the sales, market coverage, and competitive edge of a focal firm grow faster or slower, compared to its main competitors in the last twelve months. This allows comparisons to be made between companies of different size (Lusch and Brown, 1996). Profitability was initially formulated based on Kaynak (2002), Narasimhan and Kim (2002), and Han (2009), whereas competitive performance was initially formulated based on Narasimhan and Kim (2001), and Straub *et al.* (2007). These items have been employed to jointly measure the construct of 'profitability & competitive performance'. They are:
Compared to our main competitors in the last 12 months, we have achieved a better performance with poultry products in terms of:

- P&C1: Profitability.
- P&C2: Sales growth rate.
- P&C3: Market share (Dropped for both samples).
- P&C4: Overall competitive edge.

3.3 Construct validity and reliability

3.3.1 Formative constructs and reflective constructs

Before distinguishing the properties of formative and reflective constructs, it is important to define the various terms used throughout this research. *Measures*, also known as *items* or *indicators*, are observable and quantifiable scores obtained through observation, self-report, interview, or other empirical means (Edwards and Bagozzi, 2000). Measures are used to examine constructs. A *construct*, namely, a *latent variable*, is a variable that is not observable or measured directly, but is measured indirectly through observable variables that reflect or form the construct (Straub *et al.*, 2004). Constructs are abstractions that describe a phenomenon of theoretical interest (Edwards and Bagozzi, 2000). Constructs may be used to describe a phenomenon that is observable (e.g. communication media) or unobservable (e.g. communication willingness).

A *formative construct*, also known as a *composite variable*, is a construct that is formed and determined by its observed indicators. These observed indicators are called *causal indicators* or *formative indicators* (1964). These observed indicators represent different dimensions of, and determine, the formative constructs. Changes in a formative indicator should cause changes in the formative construct, but not vice versa. Dropping a formative indicator may alter the conceptual domain of the formative construct (Bollen and Lennox, 1991; Diamantopoulos and Winklhofer, 2001). Conversely, a *reflective construct* is the common cause of its indicators, namely, *reflective indicators* or *effect indicators* (Bollen and Lennox, 1991; Edwards and Bagozzi, 2000). Reflective indicators 'reflect' the reflective construct and, as a representation of the construct, should be unidimensional and correlated. Changes in a reflective construct cause changes in the reflective indicators, but not vice versa. Meanwhile, dropping an indicator should not alter the conceptual domain of the reflective construct.

To specify formative constructs and reflective constructs, the causal relationships between the measures and their constructs should be carefully examined, even if the measures obtained are previously validated and used in other research studies. Construct misspecification is an often observed phenomenon. According to Jarvis and MacKenzie (2003), 28% of top-level marketing articles had used misspecified measurement models in structural equation modeling (SEM) applications. A substantial number of latent constructs in these studies were inappropriately specified by treating formative constructs as if they were reflective. Jarvis *et al.* (2003) stated *four primary decision rules* (Table 3.8) for determining whether a construct is reflective or formative. These four rules should be used in combination to identify a construct.

By checking these rules step by step, and based on insights obtained from the field research, we identified communication willingness as a reflective construct and all other constructs as formative constructs. The following section introduces the identification of these constructs.

'Communication willingness' is operationalized with two items, namely, 'we are willing to provide information to our most important customer/supplier if it is helpful for them', and 'we are expected to provide each other with information that may be of help'. First, the direction of causality is from the construct to its measures. When communication willingness is high, we can expect that the firm is willing to provide information to the partner, and they expect to provide each other with information that may be of help. Second, the two items are interchangeable; they have similar content and share the same theme, whereas dropping one of the two items does not alter the conceptual domain of the construct. Third, the two items are expected to covary with each other, and a change in one item is associated with a change in another item. Fourth, the nomological net for the two items is not different; they have similar antecedents (e.g. communication norm), and similar consequences (e.g. communication quality). Thus, we identify 'communication willingness' as a reflective and, actually, the only reflective construct in this research.

Conversely, other constructs show different traits. With regard to 'transaction specific investments', first, the direction of causality is from measures to constructs. The measures are defining characteristics of the

Table 3.8. Decision rules to identify formative constructs and reflective constructs (Jarvis et al., 2003).

Decision rules	Formative constructs	Reflective constructs
1. Direction of causality from constructs to measures implied by the conceptual definition.	Direction of causality is from measures to constructs.	Direction of causality is from constructs to their measures.
a. Are measures defining characteristics or manifestations of constructs?	a. Measures are defining characteristics of constructs.	a. Measures are manifestations of constructs.
b. Would changes in measures cause changes in constructs or not?	b. Yes.	b. Not.
c. Would changes in constructs cause changes in measures?	c. No.	c. Yes.
2. Interchangeability of measures.	Measures need not be interchangeable.	Measures should be interchangeable.
a. Should measures have similar content and share the same theme?	a. No, need not.	a. Yes, should.
b. Would dropping one measure alter the conceptual domain of the construct?	b. Yes, it might.	b. No, should not.
3. Covariation among measures.	Not necessary for measures to covary with each other.	Measures are expected to covary with each other.
a. Should a change in one of the measures be associated with changes in the other measures?	a. Not necessarily.	a. Yes.
4. Nomological net of the construct measures.	Nomological net for the measures may differ.	Nomological net for measures should not differ.
a. Are measures expected to have the same antecedents and consequences?	a. Not required.	a. Required.

construct: each of the three items represents one aspect of specific investments, namely, investment in sales/procurement, in quality control, and in knowledge. Meanwhile, changes in one item cause changes in the construct, but not necessarily vice versa. For example, an increase in TSI may not necessary lead to an increased investment in quality control, but may be caused by an increased investment in sales. Second, the three items are not interchangeable, they have different themes, namely, three different types of investments. Third, the three items do not necessarily covary. For example, investment in sales/procurement can be high when investment in quality control is low or even zero. Fourth, we can expect that the three items have different antecedents and consequences. High profit margins could be a driving force for investments in sales/procurement, while long-term competitive edge could be a driving force for investments in quality control.

As for other constructs used in this research, a common trait is that their items/measures do not necessarily covary:

- 'Environmental uncertainty': the market price could be quite volatile while the quality of products is more or less stable, or vice versa.
- 'Trust': the inter-organizational trust and inter-personal trust do not necessarily covary with each other.
- 'Contractual governance': price and transaction volume can be negotiable during the transaction according to the latest price fluctuation, while transaction time and place, and quality are pre-agreed.
- 'Communication frequency': companies may negotiate frequently on product price, but discuss problem resolution only when there is a problem, whilst setting more or less stable times and requirements for delivery.
- 'Multi-functional staff involvement': cross-functional teams may be employed in frequent communication between organizations, but without or with relatively few senior level managers interacting.
- 'Information quality': information can be timely, but less adequate or credible.
- 'Knowledge on each other's requirements and expectations': a focal company may be well aware of the expectations and requirements of its partner, but deem that its partner is not clear enough with its requirements.
- 'Perceived communication benefits for customers' and 'perceived communication benefits for suppliers': communication with business partners may benefit a company more in timely and accurate delivery, but less in quality control.
- 'Logistics compliance': a company may deliver timely and accurately but with unsatisfactory packaging.
- 'Quality compliance': a company may provide products that meet the quality requirements of its customer, but may not necessarily be of even higher quality than its counterparts.
- 'Efficiency': an efficient transaction could cost less time, but may not necessarily cost less money for a company.
- 'Satisfaction': a company could be satisfied with the quality but not with the price, or vice versa.
- 'Profit & competitive edge': a company may achieve an increased competitive edge at the cost of profitability, compared to its main competitors.

3.3.2 Construct validity and construct reliability

In the long history of the philosophy of science, validation of positivist research instruments is simply a late twentieth century effort of academic disciplines to understand the basic principles of the scientific method for discovering truth (Nunnally, 1978). The purpose of validation is to give researchers, their peers, and society as a whole a high degree of confidence that positivist methods selected are useful in the quest for scientific truth (Nunnally, 1978). It is paramount to ensure that the data being gathered in a science is as objective as possible, and is a relatively accurate representation of the underlying phenomenon (Straub *et al.*, 2004).

Construct validity is a type of validity that focuses on the extent to which the answer to a question is a true measure and a true reflection of the operational definition. Literature indicates that, for formative constructs, important validity procedures are: content validity, nomological validity, and item multicollinearity. For reflective constructs, important validity procedures are: content validity, nomological validity, convergent validity, discriminant validity, and construct reliability (Van Plaggenhoef, 2007). Table 3.9 summarizes these important components of construct validity and reliability that are examined in this study, as well as their level of importance, and the applicable type of constructs. The following paragraphs specify the validity and reliability of those constructs employed in this research.

Content validity is the adequacy with which the domain of a concept is captured by the measure (Churchill, 1979). Although it is not easy to assess content validity, the key lies in the procedures that are used to develop the measurement instrument of a construct, as discussed by Gefen and Straub (1989). Following them, we employed two ways jointly to approach content validity. First, the primary source was the relevant literature on Transaction Cost Economics, Management Information Systems, and Supply Chain Management. We looked at the *history* of the scales. If a measurement scale performed well in previous studies, this supports the scale validity. This is a common method used within social sciences (Van Plaggenhoef, 2007). Second, concomitant with the literature review, we asked comments from relevant experts and professionals, and employed a pre-test, to screen the questionnaire carefully in order to find possible inconsistencies.

Nomological validity, namely criterion validity, is concerned with the 'behavior' of the construct, or, how well it relates to other theoretically related constructs (Churchill, 1999). To assess the nomological validity of a formative construct, we need to examine other variables that are effects of the focal formative construct. In contrast, to assess the nomological validity of a reflective construct, we need to check other constructs that affect the focal construct (Bollen and Lennox, 1991). We checked the nomological validity by testing the hypotheses about the relationships between the constructs of interest and other constructs, as suggested by Steenkamp and van Trijp (1991), and Churchill (1979). The results provide evidence of the nomological validity of the formative and the reflective constructs (see Section 4.1.1).

Table 3.9. Construct validity and reliability, the assessed constructs, and the level of importance (Adapted from Straub, 2004 and Claro, 2004).

Validity component	Constructs implied[1]	Level of importance	Sources
Content validity	F / R	Highly recommended	Lawshe (1975); Churchill (1979)
Nomological validity	F / R	Highly recommended	Bollen and Lennox (1991); Steenkamp and van Trijp (1991)
Item multicollinearity	F	Highly recommended	Malhorta (1999); Diamantopoulos and Winklhofer (2001)
Convergent validity	R	Mandatory	Hair *et al.* (1998); Thompson *et al.* (1995); Chin (1998); Segars (1997); Gefen *et al.* (2000)
Discriminant validity	R	Mandatory	Capbell and Fiske (1959); Churchill (1979); Bagozzi (1980); Hair *et al.* (1998); Segars (1997); Gefen *et al.* (2000)
Construct reliability	R	Mandatory	Nunnally (1978); Claro (2004); Straub *et al.* (2004)

[1] F – formative constructs; R – reflective constructs.

Item multicollinearity, raised by Diamantopoulos and Winklhofer (2001) for formative constructs, refers to the correlation between items of a construct. Excessive item multicollinearity among indicators makes it difficult to separate the distinct influence of the individual indicators on the formative constructs. To examine item multicollinearity, we examined the Pearson correlation[5] between pairs of indicators of each formative construct. It is suggested that correlations that lie below 0.80 are not considered to exhibit a problem of multicollinearity (Hair *et al.*, 1998; Malhortra *et al.*, 1999). The results in Section 4.1.1 show that, there is no problem of item multicollinearity with all other items that precludes their use, except with the two items of 'market share' and 'overall competitive edge'. Thus, the item of 'market share' has been dropped in this research.

Convergent validity measures the extent to which items correlate positively with other items of the same construct (Churchill, 1979). In other words, convergent validity is shown when each measure correlates strongly with its assumed theoretical construct (Gefen and Straub, 2005). To assess convergent validity of the reflective construct in this research, item-total correlation[6], explorative factor analysis (EFA), and confirmatory factor analysis (CFA) were employed. The threshold level for item-total correlation is 0.5, because items with lower values do not share a substantial part of the variance with the other items constituting a construct (Steenkamp and Trijp, 1991). Meanwhile, we took 0.6 as the threshold level for the loadings for EFA, and 0.7 as the threshold level for the loadings for CFA (Straub *et al.*, 2004). To further increase convergent validity, the explained variances were assessed, which are preferably greater than 60%. Finally, the variance extracted (higher than 0.5) from the CFA was employed as the last measure to verify convergent validity of the reflective construct used in this research (see Section 4.1.1).

Discriminant validity[7] assesses the extent to which a construct and its items differ from other constructs and their items (Churchill, 1979). To assess discriminant validity of the reflective construct, two methods can be employed: first, in a correlations matrix of the constructs, the square root of the average variances extracted (AVE) should be greater than all correlations of the constructs; second, in a factor structure matrix of loadings and cross-loadings, all items should load higher to its associated construct than to other constructs (Fornell and Larcker, 1981). There is only one reflective construct (communication willingness) in this research. Thus, it is not necessary to examine the discriminant validity herein, whereas the validity of the reflective construct was proved by content validity, nomological validity, convergent validity (see above), as well as construct reliability (see below) jointly.

---

[5] *Pearson correlation* presents the magnitude and direction of the association between two variables in a data set (Malhorta, 1999). It is an index used to determine whether a linear or straight-line relationship exists between the two variables. The interpretation of the significant correlation coefficients are based on two-tailed *t* values of a 1% significance level ($t > 2.58$), or of a 5% significance level ($t > 1.96$).

[6] *Item-total correlation* is the correlation of one item with the average of all other items of a certain construct.

[7] With regard to *discriminant validity*, when the correlation between two conceptually different items is too high, they will probably measure the same phenomenon (or, the same reflective construct), rather than different ones. In other words, discriminant validity is shown when each item correlates weakly with all other constructs except for the one to which it is theoretically associated (Heeler and Ray, 1972).

Construct reliability[8] refers to the extent to which respondents in comparable situations will answer the questions in similar ways. To assess reliability, this study examined three criteria: Cronbach's alpha[9], composite reliability[10], and average variance extracted (AVE)[11]. First, for Cronbach's alpha, though reported recommended reliability levels differ, generally accepted levels are 0.60 for explorative studies, and 0.70 for confirmatory studies (Hair *et al.*, 1998; Straub *et al.*, 2004). Second, following Nunnally (1988), we took 0.70 as the threshold level for composite reliability. Third, it is recommended that AVE should be greater than 0.50, meaning that 50% or more variance of the indicators should be accounted for (Fornell and Larcker, 1981; Hair *et al.*, 1998). Furthermore, we also checked whether the square root of the AVE of the latent constructs is greater than the correlation coefficients among the latent constructs as it should be, which indicates that more variance is shared between the latent constructs items than with other constructs. The results presented in Section 4.1.1 have verified the reliability of the reflective construct used in this study. Table 3.10 summarizes the threshold levels of the statistical evaluation criteria of the validity and reliability of reflective constructs.

3.4 Data analyses

3.4.1 Partial least squares (PLS) modeling

As introduced in Chapter 2, we first proposed the relationships between the concepts after extensively reviewing the existing literature. Then, partial least squares (PLS) modeling technique was employed to test whether these hypothesized relations and causalities do occur in practice. This section describes this analysis technique.

PLS path modeling is a type of structural equation modeling (SEM) technique. The advent of SEM techniques allowed social scientists to perform path analytic modeling with latent variables (LV), and to simultaneously examine theory and measures. This in turn has led some to describe this approach as an example of 'a second generation of multivariate analysis' (Fornell, 1987: 408). Nowadays, SEM tools are the most applied and consolidated means of testing relations and causality in the field of management information systems (e.g. Pavlou and Chai, 2002; Dibbern *et al.*, 2004), buyer-supplier relationships (e.g. Claro, 2004), and marketing research (e.g. Steenkamp and Trijp, 1991; Malhotra *et al.*, 1999; Steenkamp and Baumgartner, 2000).

---

[8] Nunnally (1978: 206) defined *reliability* as 'the extent to which measurements are repeatable and that any random influence which tends to make measurements different from occasion to occasion is a source of measurement error'.

[9] *Cronbach's alpha* is typically employed to evaluate construct reliability or internal consistence of measurement scales of a construct (Devilles, 1991). Cortina (1993) suggested applying different lower levels for the alpha coefficient depending on the number of items and the level of inter-item correlation.

[10] *Composite reliability* was developed by Werts *et al.* (1974) to measure internal consistency. They argue that this measure is superior to Cronbach's alpha. Despite Cronbach's alpha, it does not assume equivalency among the measures with its assumption that all indicators are equally weighted, and it is less sensitive to the number of items of the construct. It also uses the item loadings obtained within the nomological network (or cause model).

[11] *AVE* was developed by Fornell and Larcker (1981), in an attempt to measure the amount of variance that a latent construct (LV) component captures from its indicators relative to the amount due to measurement error. It is suggested that this measure can also be interpreted as a measure of reliability for the LV component score and tends to be more conservative than composite reliability.

Table 3.10. Overview of the statistical evaluation criteria for reflective constructs (Adapted from Anderson and Gerbing, 1988; Straub et al. 2004; Claro, 2004; and Henseler et al., 2009).

Evaluation criteria	Threshold
Validity of constructs	
Corrected item-total correlation	≥0.50
Exploratory factor analysis (EFA)	
Extracted variance	≥0.60
Factor loadings	≥0.60[a]
Confirmatory factor analysis (CFA)	
Standardized loadings (λ, outer loading)	≥0.70
t-value of the standardized loadings	* ≥1.96; ** ≥2.58
Reliability of constructs	
Cronbach's α for EFA	≥0.60
Cronbach's α for CFA	≥0.70
Composite reliability	≥0.70
AVE (average variance extracted)	≥0.50

[a] Straub *et al.* (2004) suggested a threshold of 0.40 for EFA loading, and no cross-loading of items above 0.40, though some references suggest a higher cutoff. They suggested that Cronbach's alpha for EFA should be above 0.60.
* Significant at 5% level; ** significant at 1% level.

There are two distinct families of SEM techniques: (1) the covariance-based SEM techniques, as represented by LISREL and AMOS; and (2) the component-based SEM techniques, also known as variance-based techniques, of which PLS modeling is the most prominent representative (Chin, 1998b; Henseler *et al.*, 2009). Researchers and practitioners should note the substantial link between covariance-based SEM and PLS modeling, and also realize that they constitute two complementary, yet distinctive, statistical techniques for estimating parameters of conceptual models.

Applying PLS modeling has some advantages over covariance-based SEM tools so as to appear in diversified business disciplines (Chin, 1998b; Hulland, 1999; Brown and Chin, 2004). For example, Management Information Systems as a field often selects PLS modeling as a tool along with LISREL and standard regression (Gefen and Straub, 2005). In addition, a critical review of the PLS application in international marketing reveals that this methodology has increased in popularity, especially for multi-group analyses of PLS results for different nations (Henseler *et al.*, 2009). PLS modeling has also been used by a growing number of researchers in other disciplines such as strategic management (e.g. Hulland, 1999), organizational behavior (e.g. Higgins *et al.*, 1992), marketing (Zinkhan *et al.*, 1987), and consumer behavior (e.g. Fornell and Robinson, 1983). The following section briefly describes PLS modeling method and its advantages.

The PLS method was designed by (Wold, 1974, 1982, 1985) for the analysis of high dimensional data in a low-structure environment and has undergone various extensions and modifications (Henseler *et al.*, 2009). PLS path models are formally defined by two sets of linear equations: the inner model (structural model) and the outer model (manifest model). The inner model specifies the relationships between latent constructs (unobserved variables), whereas the outer model specifies the relationships between a latent construct and its manifest indicators (observed indicators). The PLS algorithm is essentially a sequence of regressions in terms of weight vectors. A detailed introduction on basic algorithmic design and some extensions can be found in Wold (1982), Lohmöller (1989), Tenenhaus (2005) and Wang (1999).

The main characteristics of PLS path modeling, which have increased its popularity within the research community, include (Henseler *et al.*, 2009):
1. PLS path modeling delivers latent variable (LV) scores, i.e. proxies of the constructs, which are measured by one or several indicators, namely, manifest variables (MV).
2. PLS path modeling avoids small sample size problems and can therefore be applied in some situations when other methods cannot (Chin and Newsted, 1999). For example, 'there can be more variables than observations and there may be a small amount of data that are missing completely at random' (Tenenhaus *et al.*, 2005: 202).
3. PLS path modeling can estimate very complex models (i.e. models consisting of many LV and MV) without leading to estimation problems (Wold, 1985).
4. PLS path modeling makes less stringent assumptions about the distribution of variables and error terms (Fornell, 1982: 443; Bagozzi, 1994); however, it is noteworthy that PLS modeling does not make less stringent assumptions about the representativeness of the sample.
5. PLS path modeling can handle both formative measurement models and reflective ones (Chin, 1998a; Diamantopoulos and Winklhofer, 2001). Although the inclusion of formative measures in covariance-based SEM has been well documented (e.g. Jöreskog and Goldberger, 1975; MacCallum and Browne, 1993; Jöreskog and Sörbom, 1996), analysts usually encounter identification problems.
6. PLS path modeling is methodologically advantageous to covariance-based SEM whenever improper or non-convergent results are likely to occur (i.e. Heywood cases; see (Krijnen *et al.*, 1998)).
7. PLS path modeling is recommended at an early stage of theoretical development in order to test and validate exploratory models.
8. PLS path modeling is suitable for prediction-oriented research; PLS modeling thereby assists researchers who are focusing on the explanation of endogenous constructs.

These characteristics and advantages of PLS modeling have promoted our decision to employ this technique for empirical estimation. Following (Chin, 1998b), bootstrapping with 500× resampling has been run to show the precision of the PLS estimates.

3.4.2 Control variables

This research has included a number of company characteristics as control variables, which are: company size, company age, company type, quality standard implemented, and administrative level of a location. *Company size* is distinguished according to the criteria described in Appendix 3.2. *Company age* is a scale variable. *Company type* is modeled as a dummy variable: with 1 for companies having trading activities as main functions, being closer to end markets, and with more market power; and 0 for companies having production activities as main functions, being farther from end markets, and with less market power. Meanwhile, *quality standard* is represented by the highest quality standard adopted by a company. Standard quality systems are considered as facilitators available for communicating quality performance requirements to suppliers and customers (Van Plaggenhoef, 2007). *Administrative level of a location* is an ordinal variable: with 1 for town or county, 2 for other cities, and 3 for national or provincial capital cities.

It is suggested in the literature that buyer-supplier relationships and company performance in supply chains might be affected by company characteristics. Kim (2006) reported that the level of supply chain integration is likely to be influenced by different company sizes in different ways. Arana (2010) found that company characteristics, such as producer age, property size and quality standard, turned out to significantly affect some performance indicators of avocado producers, such as total sale, yield increase, and actual/perceived product quality. Wollni and Zeller (2007) found that coffee farms' characteristics such as property size and product quality could explain producer performance in the context of market channel choice. Stanford (1998) emphasized that property size could affect producer performance, because producers with large property may be able to purchase inputs at a lower price, to use them more intensively, and thereby increase product yield compared to producers with small property. Although Van Plaggenhoef (2007) reported that most control variables had no effect on the dependent variables, he found that integration of quality management with the customer by the focal firm was positively related to customer satisfaction. And the presence of a quality manager in the focal firm was found to positively influence revenue growth. In addition, firm size was found to be negatively related to the integration of quality management with customers. By analyzing sub-groups (primary producers, and traders and processors in agri-business), Van Plaggenhoef (2007) also found that some relationships are significant with one group of companies, but not significant with another type of company.

3.4.3 Dealing with missing data

As described in Section 3.1.1, we called and/or visited the respondents to confirm their opinions, if certain returned questionnaires were incomplete or if we were confused by certain answers. Thus, there are just a few missing values in the final returned questionnaires (Table 3.11). Even so, we should be careful about the results with regard to the three measures (Staff1, Staff2, and Trust3), which have more missing data compared to the others.

For missing value analysis, several methods are applied commonly, including: (1) deleting cases with missing data; (2) replacing missing values with a mean; (3) replacing the missing value by the Expectation-Maximization (EM) estimation technique. Following Hair *et al.* (1998), the EM approach was selected for this research, because it has not the pitfalls of other methods such as their influence on the data distribution, and thus increases the reliability of multivariate analysis based on these data. The EM approach belongs to the model-based missing data analysis techniques, which replace the missing

Table 3.11. Missing values for items in the total sample[1,2].

Missing values	Staff1	Staff2	Trust3
Count	14	15	13
Percentage	8.5	9.1	7.9

[1] See Appendix 3.1 for the detailed questions for these three items.
[2] Indicator variables (items) with less than 5% missing are not displayed.

data either through a specifically designed procedure or as an integral portion of multivariate analysis (Hair *et al.*, 1998). The EM method is an iterative two-stage method (the E and the M stages) in which the E-stage makes the best possible estimates of the missing data, then the M-stage makes estimates of the parameters (means, standard deviations, or correlations) assuming the missing data were replaced. The E-step finds the conditional expectation of the 'missing data' given the observed data and current estimated parameters, and then substitutes these expectations for the 'missing data'. The EM process has an iterative character and continues re-estimating parameters until a convergence is reached (Little and Rubin, 1987; Hendriks-Gusc, 2007).

It is noteworthy that, considering diverse companies have been involved in this chain research, we performed missing value analysis separately for each type of company. Besides, there are no missing values with the three focal firms classified as 'others'.

3.5 Concluding remarks

A triangular approach including interviews, pre-test, and survey was employed in this research. The face-to-face interviews helped capture the relevant dimensions for prospective measures of transaction attributes, governance structures, inter-organizational communication, supply chain compliance, and comparative company performance. Furthermore, the interviews also helped to identify areas and potential companies for the survey. In addition, the respondents in the pre-test helped to identify ambiguous or other problematic scale measures. In total, the triangular approaches contributed jointly to identifying the convergence of themes and patterns, and to ensuring the validity and reliability of the concepts in this research.

Although PLS modeling has been applied to analyze data in this research, it is noteworthy that, as pointed out by Henseler *et al.* (2009), both the covariance-based SEM (CBSEM) method and the component-based PLS method provide a powerful framework to estimate causal models with latent variables and systems of simultaneous equations with measurement errors. They constitute two complementary, yet distinctive rather than competitive, statistical techniques for estimating parameters of a conceptual model. 'CBSEM method is theory-oriented, and emphasizes the transition from exploratory to confirmatory analysis. PLS method is primarily intended for causal-predictive analysis in situations of high complexity but low theoretical information' (Jöreskog, 1982: 270). The philosophical distinction between these approaches is whether to use CBSEM for theory testing and development, or PLS path modeling for predictive applications. Although the application of CBSEM in social sciences started earlier, a critical review of the PLS application in international marketing reveals that this method has increased in popularity.

Chapter 4

Antecedents of Inter-Organizational Communication

This chapter discusses antecedents of inter-organizational communication (IOC). It aims to answer Research Question A: '*What is the impact of transaction attributes and governance structure on inter-organizational communication?*' This chapter starts in Section 4.1 with the assessment of the validity and reliability of constructs employed in this research. Then, it displays the baseline statistics of constructs on transaction attributes, governance structure, communication willingness and behavior. Section 4.2 reports the outcomes of the (revised) Communication Antecedents Models, for companies in relationships with their most important suppliers, and with their most important customers, respectively. It also discusses the influences of company characteristics on transaction attributes and governance structure. In addition, section 4.2 makes some general suggestions for future research. The chapter ends with some concluding remarks in Section 4.3.

4.1 Construct validity, construct reliability, and baseline statistics

4.1.1 Validity and reliability of constructs used in this research

This section examines the validity and reliability of constructs employed in this research, including constructs for transaction attributes, governance structure, communication willingness and behavior, communication quality, perceived communication benefits, supply chain compliance, and company performance.

As introduced in Section 3.3.2, the *content validity* of the formative and reflective constructs is first based on prior literature, and further confirmed by experts, officers, and practitioners during interviews and the pre-test.

The *nomological validity* of the formative and reflective constructs has been confirmed by estimating the structural equations in our theoretical models, following (Churchill, 1979; Steenkamp and Trijp, 1991). Section 4.2.1, 4.2.2, 4.2.3 and 4.2.4 present the estimated model for companies in relationships with their most important suppliers (the company-supplier sample), and with their most important customers (the company-customer sample). A number of significant relationships have been found between the focal formative constructs and their affected constructs, and between the focal reflective construct and its affecting construct as they should be (Bollen and Lennox, 1991).

To assess *item multicollinearity* of the formative constructs, Pearson correlation has been applied to pairs of items of each formative construct. The only problem found was that the correlation coefficients between 'market share' and 'overall competitive edge' (see Section 3.2.3 and Appendix 3.1) for both the company-supplier and the company-customer samples are slightly higher than the threshold value of 0.80. Thus, the item of 'market share' has been dropped. As for all other constructs, the correlation coefficients lie well below the threshold of 0.80, which exhibit no problem of item multicollinearity (Malhotra *et al.*, 1999; Diamantopoulos and Winklhofer, 2001).

Convergent validity of the reflective construct, correlated item-total correlation, explorative factor analysis (EFA), and confirmatory factor analysis (CFA) have been employed. The results in Table 4.1 show that for both samples, the values of item-total correlations are well above the threshold of 0.50 (Doll and Torkzadeh, 1988). Meanwhile, the EFA loadings are much greater than the threshold of 0.60^{12}. In addition, the CFA loadings are well greater than the threshold of 0.70, and each of the items loads significantly on its latent construct at 1% level (Straub *et al.,* 2004; Claro, 2004). These results jointly confirm convergent validity of the reflective construct.

To assess reliability of the reflective construct, three criteria, namely Cronbach's alpha, composite reliability, and average variance extracted (AVE), have been checked (Table 4.2). The composite reliability is much greater than the threshold of 0.70. Cronbach's alpha for EFA (see Table 3.6 in Section 3.2.2) is greater than the threshold of 0.60, and Cronbach's alpha for CFA is greater than the threshold of 0.70 (Straub *et al.,* 2004: 411). AVE is greater than the cutoff of 0.50 as it should be. These results reflect satisfactory internal consistency reliability (Nunnally and Bernstein, 1994).

Table 4.1. Analysis of the reflective construct for the company-supplier sample and the company-customer sample.

Construct	Items	Companies with suppliers (N=165)			Companies with customers (N=96)		
		Item-total correlation[3]	EFA loading[1]	CFA loading[2]	Item-total correlation[3]	EFA loading[1]	CFA loading[2]
Communication	W1	0.59	0.89	0.86	0.63	0.90	0.91
willingness	W2	0.59	0.89	0.92	0.63	0.90	0.89

[1] EFA – exploratory factor analysis.
[2] CFA – confirmatory factor analysis.
[3] For a construct with two items, the coefficients of corrected item-total correlation and the loadings for EFA of the two items are the same.

4.1.2 Baseline statistics

This section presents the baseline description of constructs, including environmental uncertainty, transaction specific investments (TSI), trust (relational governance), contractual governance (pre-agreement), communication willingness, media modernity, communication frequency, and multi-functional staff involvement. The unweighted score of each construct is calculated with related manifest indicators. The means, standard deviations, and correlation coefficients have been calculated and shown for companies in relationships with their most important suppliers, and with their most important customers, respectively, in Table 4.3 and 4.4.

---

[12] Straub and Boudreau *et al.* (2004) suggested a threshold of 0.40 for EFA loading, and no cross-loading of items above 0.40, whereas some references suggest a higher cutoff as 0.6.

Table 4.2. Reliability of the reflective construct for the company-supplier sample and the company-customer sample.

Constructs	Companies with suppliers (N=165)			Companies with customers (N=96)		
	AVE[1]	Composite Reliability	Cronbach's α	AVE	Composite Reliability	Cronbach's α
Communication willingness	0.79	0.88	0.74	0.81	0.90	0.77

[1] Average variance extracted.

Table 4.3. Construct mean, standard deviations (S.D.) and correlation matrix[1] for the company-supplier sample (N=165).

Constructs[2]	Mean	S.D.	1	2	3	4	5	6	7
1. Environmental uncertainty	3.88	0.80							
2. Transaction specific investments	*3.31*	1.34	**0.29**						
3. Trust (relational governance)	4.23	0.65	*0.11*	**0.25**					
4. Contractual governance (pre-agreement)	4.27	0.64	**0.19**	**0.23**	**0.58**				
5. Communication willingness	4.12	0.77	**0.29**	**0.54**	**0.40**	**0.28**			
6. Media modernity	1.61	0.79	*0.05*	**0.28**	*0.10*	*0.04*	**0.21**		
7. Communication frequency	3.69	0.66	*0.02*	**0.37**	*0.08*	*0.09*	**0.24**	*0.09*	
8. Multi-functional staff involvement	3.57	1.07	**0.24**	**0.48**	**0.18**	**0.16**	**0.51**	**0.31**	**0.22**

[1] In this correlation matrix, the mean of transaction specific investments (**bold** and *italics*) is significantly different from that of the company-customer sample; correlation coefficients with a value of at least 0.16 (**bold**) are significant at 5%; non-significant coefficients are shown in *italics*.
[2] Media modernity is measured with a 3-point Likert scale, the other contructs with a 5-point Likert scale (see Appendix 3.1).

Comparing means of each construct between the company-supplier and the company-customer samples reveal that the respondent companies in relationships with their most important suppliers, and those in relationships with their most important customers, have reported similar scores for all constructs, except for TSI. Meanwhile, standard deviations (0.5 ~ 0.8) are relatively low, except for TSI (1.1 ~ 1.3) and multi-functional staff involvement (1.1). These results seem to reflect that all of the respondent companies, either in their relationships with their main suppliers or with their main customers, and regardless of which stage they are at the supply chains, have adopted similar opinions and/or actions on issues concerning environmental uncertainty, governance structures, communication willingness, and communication behavior, except on specific investments and multi-functional staff involvement.

Table 4.4. Construct means, standard deviations (S.D.) and correlation matrix[1] for the company-customer sample (N=96).

Constructs[2]	Mean	S.D.	1	2	3	4	5	6	7
1. Environmental uncertainty	3.96	.80							
2. Transaction specific investments	**3.66**	1.05	**.30**						
3. Trust (relational governance)	4.24	0.64	-0.02	**0.31**					
4. Contractual governance (pre-agreement)	4.35	0.54	0.17	**0.45**	**0.57**				
5. Communication willingness	4.13	0.76	0.18	**0.54**	**0.52**	**0.43**			
6. Media modernity	1.61	0.75	-0.03	**0.32**	0.17	**0.24**	**0.22**		
7. Communication frequency	3.62	0.77	-0.02	0.11	0.16	**0.29**	**0.31**	**0.23**	
8. Multi-functional staff involvement	3.76	1.08	**0.22**	**0.65**	**0.31**	**0.32**	**0.52**	**0.41**	0.15

[1] In this correlation matrix, the mean of transaction specific investments (**bold** and *italics*) is significantly different from that of the company-supplier sample; correlation coefficients with a value of at least 0.22 (**bold**) are significant at 5%; non-significant coefficients are shown in *italics*.
[2] Media modernity is a one-item construct measured with a 3-point Likert scale, other constructs are measured with a 5-point scale (see Appendix 3.1).

Recalling that all observed indicators, except that for media modernity, are measured by 5-point Likert scales ranging between 1 for 'not agree at all' and 5 for 'totally agree', a mean above 3 indicates that the respondents agree with the statement. The results in Table 4.3 and 4.4 show that most of the constructs in this study have a positive response (i.e. agree with the statements). Furthermore, the relatively high means for contractual governance (4.3 ~ 4.4), trust (4.2), and communication willingness (4.1) might reflect that, in general, a company is likely to employ trust and contractual governance to jointly safeguard transactions with its main customers and suppliers, and is highly willing to communicate with its main customers and suppliers.

The item of *media modernity* is measured by a 3-point Likert scale ranging as 1 for 'traditional communication tools', 2 for 'middle advanced tools', and 3 for 'modern tools'. Thus, a mean of at least 2 or above 2 indicates that the respondents make use of moderately advanced tools to modern tools. The means of both samples (1.6) reflect that most respondent companies applied traditional media to moderately advanced media to communicate with their most important suppliers and customers. More advanced media, such as Electronic Data Interchange (EDI), are at an early stage, and not yet widely used.

It is noteworthy that the only significantly different means between the two samples is for *specific investments*. It is shown that the companies in relationships with their main customers (3.7) reported a higher level of TSI than the companies in relationships with their main suppliers (3.3). This might reflect that while a company is likely to invest more for specific transactions with its main customers, so as to safeguard its sales and markets, it nonetheless tends to invest comparatively less in specific transactions with its main suppliers, and prefers to flexibility concerning purchasing sources. It would be valuable to investigate in future research into the suitable level of specific investments for main customers and suppliers, respectively.

'*TSI*' and '*multi-functional staff involvement*' have standard deviations above 1, indicating that: (1) diverse levels of investments have been made by the respondent companies through the chains, to safeguard transactions with their main suppliers and customers; (2) diverse staff arrangements, for instance, the use of senior and non-senior managers, and staff from single and different functions, have been made by the different companies throughout the chains, to communicate with their main suppliers and customers. In addition, we suppose that the comparatively high standard deviations for 'TSI' and 'multi-functional staff involvement' might be the result of diverse firm size and firm type. In other words, it might reflect that: (1) diverse sizes and types of companies exist throughout the chains, which lead to diverse levels of specific investments; (2) diverse staff arrangements are applied by companies of different sizes and types to communicate with their main suppliers and customers. Senior managers and staff from different functions might be employed more in a large company. Instead, in a small company an employee in general has to perform diverse functions. We discuss such influence of company characteristics on communication and its antecedents in more detail in Section 4.3.

The correlation matrices in Table 4.3 and 4.4 show that certain associations exist among the constructs as expected. It is shown that *TSI*, *communication willingness*, and *multi-functional staff involvement* are significantly (and often strongly) linked to most other constructs. This might reflect that: (1) TSI is a critical indicator for governance structure, and for communication willingness and behavior. This might hold true for a company in relationships with its main suppliers, and with its main customers; (2) communication willingness, as well as multi-functional staff involvement in chain communication, could be forecasted well by looking at transaction attributes and governance structure. This also stands true for a company in relationships with its main suppliers, and with is main customers.

Adversely, *environmental uncertainty*, *media* modernity, and *communication frequency* were linked to fewer constructs, and these links were less strong, though significant. This might reflect that: (1) environmental uncertainty might affect communication willingness and behavior through other factor(s). For example, the correlation results show that environmental uncertainty is highly correlated with TSI. According to this finding and the results of PLS modeling of the Communication Antecedents Model shown in Section 4.2.1 and 4.2.3, a revised Communication Antecedents Model is examined in Section 4.2.3 and 4.2.4. (2) Media modernity and communication frequency appears to be less well explained by transaction attributes and governance structure, compared to communication willingness and multi-functional staff involvement. There might be other factors that better indicate media modernity and communication frequency. It would be valuable to look for other potential indicators for media modernity and communication frequency in future research.

The high associations between *trust* and *contractual governance* appear to prove again that companies are likely to employ these two types of governance structure to jointly safeguard transactions with their main suppliers and customers. Thus, we proposed an extra hypothesis (H_{iC2}) that trust (relational governance) is positively associated with contractual governance (pre-agreement). This hypothesis has also been tested in the (revised) Communication Antecedents Model. Interestingly, the correlation coefficient between *contractual governance* and *communication willingness* for companies in relationships with their main customers (0.4) is much higher than that for companies in relationships with their main suppliers (0.3). This might imply that comparatively, a company in relationships with its main *customers* is likely to be more willing to communicate with its contractual customers than with non-contractual customers. Adversely, a company in relationships with its main *suppliers* is more or less equally willing to communicate with contractual and non-contractual suppliers. A likely explanation is that a company prefers to safeguard markets with contracts, whereas it tends to be open to flexibility as regards purchasing sources. Meanwhile, the high correlation coefficients between *trust* and *communication willingness* for both companies in relationships with their suppliers and customers might indicate that trust is a reliable antecedent of communication willingness for a company in relationships with its main suppliers and customers. When trust is higher, a company is likely to be more willing to communicate with its main suppliers and customers.

As mentioned above, *environmental uncertainty* was not significantly correlated with most other constructs for the two samples. And it is noteworthy that environmental uncertainty was negatively, though not significantly, correlated with trust, media modernity, and communication frequency for companies in relationships with their main customers, but not for companies in relationships with their main suppliers. This might imply that in relationships with its main customers and in marketing activities, a company is more sensitive to environmental uncertainty than when it is in relationships with its main suppliers and in purchasing activities. Or, a company's trust and communication relationships with its main customers are likely to be affected more by environmental uncertainty than its trust and communication relationships with its main suppliers. When environmental uncertainty is higher, in relationships with its main *customers*, a company might trust its customers slightly less, communicate slightly less often with the customers, and employ less advanced tools for communication. Adversely, in relationships with its main *suppliers* a company might not necessarily change its trust and communication behavior towards its main suppliers.

In addition, *media modernity* is linked to specific investments and multi-functional staff involvement, but is less linked or not linked to other constructs. This is probably because media modernity, as well as TSI and multi-functional staff involvement, are all linked to company sizes and firm types. Meanwhile, *communication frequency* was linked to communication willingness, multi-functional staff involvement, TSI (for companies in relationships with their main suppliers), and contractual governance (for companies in relationships with their main customers).

We also checked the possible multicollinearity problem for these constructs. A cut-off of 0.80 is commonly used for correlations among variables for dismissing multicollinearity problems (Hair *et al.*, 1998; Malhotra *et al.*, 1999). It is shown that all the correlation coefficients herein are well below 0.8, therefore, the individual magnitude of the correlations between the constructs does not suggest obvious problem of pairwise collinearity. This proves the discriminant validity of the constructs. Thus, we can employ all of these listed constructs in one model.

4.2 Antecedents of inter-organizational communication

4.2.1 Results of the (revised) Communication Antecedents Model for the company-supplier sample

By partial least squares (PLS) modeling, the proposed hypotheses on communication antecedents were examined with the company-suppliers sample. The results are presented in Appendix 4.1. It is shown that the expected significant relationship between environmental uncertainty and contractual governance was not supported, though it was argued in the literature (Williamson, 1991) and reported in some empirical studies (Barthélemy and Quélin, 2006; Arana, 2010). Recalling that environmental uncertainty is highly correlated with specific investments (see Table 4.3 and 4.4), we pondered over:

does this imply that environmental uncertainty affect governance structures indirectly rather than directly, i.e. through other mediating factors, such as specific investments? Thus, we proposed one more hypothesis: 'when the level of environment uncertainty is higher, the level of transaction specific investments is higher' (H_{iA2}). Then, we revised the Communication Antecedents Model by adding an extra pass from environmental uncertainty to transaction specific investments (TSI). Other parts of the model remained the same as the original Communication Antecedents Model. Following Chin (1998b), we ran bootstrapping with 500× resampling.

The results of the revised Communication Antecedents Model for companies in relationships with their most important suppliers are presented in Figure 4.1 and Appendix 4.2. The values of R square in this model range as 0.09 for 'transaction specific investments', 0.06 for 'trust', 0.37 for 'contractual governance', 0.17 for 'communication willingness', 0.01 for 'media modernity', 0.01 for 'communication frequency', and 0.05 for 'multi-functional staff involvement'. The low R square for 'trust' and 'communication behavior' might be partly a result of the comparatively small size of the sample. In addition, it might imply that more potential antecedent factors should be foraged for communication willingness and behavior in future research. The overall model explains about 10.7% of the variance of the endogenous latent variables.

The results reveal that *environmental uncertainty* here is positively and directly associated with TSI, and indirectly associated with trust and contractual governance. Other relationships in the revised model remained the same as in the original model.

It is shown that when environmental uncertainty is higher, a company is likely to invest more in specific transactions with its main suppliers, and in this way to safeguard its main purchasing sources. Moreover, owing to the increased TSI, a higher level of environmental uncertainty is likely indirectly lead to greater trust and stronger contractual governance between the company and its main suppliers. Thus,

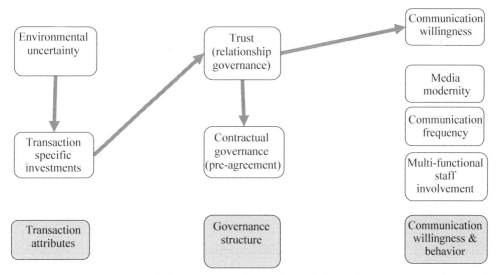

Figure 4.1. Results of the revised Communication Antecedents Model for the company-supplier sample.
━━━: Path coefficient is significant at P<0.01.

by comparing the original and the revised Communication Antecedent Models, a noteworthy finding is that: environmental uncertainty does not seem to affect trust and contractual governance directly, but indirectly through increased TSI; adversely, TSI directly affects trust and contractual governance between a company and its main suppliers.

It is also shown that *transaction specific investments* (*TSI*) are positively and strongly associated with trust, but not with contractual governance. This might reflect that for a company investing more in facilities and skilled knowledge specifically for the transactions with the suppliers, the level of trust between the company and its main suppliers is greater. However, it does not necessarily employ stronger contractual governance to safeguard the transactions with the suppliers.

Appendix 4.2 presents path coefficients, total effects, and *t*-values of the PLS modeling of the revised Communication Antecedents Model for companies in relationships with their suppliers. The results of *total effects* reflect that both *TSI* and *environmental uncertainty* are not significantly associated with communication willingness and behavior at 5% level. Thus, when environmental uncertainty is higher, or when a company invests more in the specific transactions with its main suppliers, the communication willingness, media modernity, communication frequency do not necessarily be higher, and the company and its main suppliers do not necessarily involve senior managers or staff from different functions in the communication.

The results of total effects also indicate that specific investments are positively and significantly linked to contractual governance, though the link is indirect rather than direct. A likely explanation is that when transaction specific investments are higher, the company and its main suppliers hold greater trust on each other. And such greater trust leads to stronger contractual governance.

When looking at the relationships between governance structure, and communication willingness and behavior, the results show that *trust* is positively and strongly associated with communication willingness, but not significantly with communication behavior. When the trust between a company and its main suppliers is greater, they are more willing to communicate with each other, but do not necessarily communicate more frequently, or employ more advanced media, senior managers, and staff from different functions.

Meanwhile, the hypothesized relationships between *contractual governance* and communication willingness and behavior are not significant at 5% level. Thus, for a company in relationships with its main suppliers, a higher level of contractual governance does not necessarily lead to a higher level of communication willingness, media modernity, communication frequency, and multi-functional staff involvement in its communication with its main suppliers.

In addition, it is shown that trust is positively and highly associated with contractual governance. A likely explanation is that when the trust between a company and its main suppliers is greater, they tend to invest in contracts to safeguard their transactions.

Table 4.5 summarizes the hypothesized relationships and results of the revised Communication Antecedents Model for companies in relationships with their most important suppliers. Five out of the seven hypothesized relationships are significant at 5% or 1% level. One is partly significant at 1% level and one is not significant at 5% level.

Table 4.5. Results of the hypotheses of the revised Communication Antecedents Model for the company-supplier sample.

		Path coefficient significant?	Sign of coefficient as expected?	Hypothesis
H_{iA1}	The level of environmental uncertainty is positively associated with the level of contractual governance.	No	Yes	Supported by total effects
H_{iA2}	The level of environmental uncertainty is positively associated with the level of transaction specific investments (TSI).	Yes	Yes	Supported
H_{iB1}	The level of TSI is positively associated with the level of trust.	Yes	Yes	Supported
H_{iB2}	The level of TSI is positively associated with the level of contractual governance.	No	Yes	Supported by total effects
H_{iC1}	The level of trust is positively associated with the level of communication willingness and communication behavior (media modernity, communication frequency, and multi-functional staff involvement).	Yes with Willingness	Yes with Willingness & Behavior	Supported with Willingness
H_{iC2}	The level of trust is positively associated with the level of contractual governance.	Yes	Yes	Supported
H_{iD}	The level of contractual governance is positively associated with the level of communication willingness and behavior.	No	Yes	Not supported

These hypotheses are proposed in Section 2.4, 4.1.2 and 4.2.1.

4.2.2 Results of the (revised) Communication Antecedents Model for the company-customer sample

By partial least squares (PLS) modeling, the proposed hypotheses on communication antecedents were examined with the company-customer sample. The results are presented in Appendix 4.3. The expected significant relationship between environmental uncertainty and contractual governance was again not supported. Thus, we revised again the Communication Antecedents Model by adding an extra pass from environmental uncertainty to transaction specific investments (TSI). Other parts of the model remained the same as the original Communication Antecedents Model. Following Chin (1998b), we ran bootstrapping with 500 resampling again.

Figure 4.2 and Appendix 4.4 present the results of the revised model for companies in relationships with their most important customers. The values of R square in this model range as 0.10 for 'transaction specific investments', 0.11 for 'trust', 0.45 for 'contractual governance', 0.31 for 'communication willingness', 0.07 for 'media modernity', 0.10 for 'communication frequency', and 0.16 for 'multi-functional staff

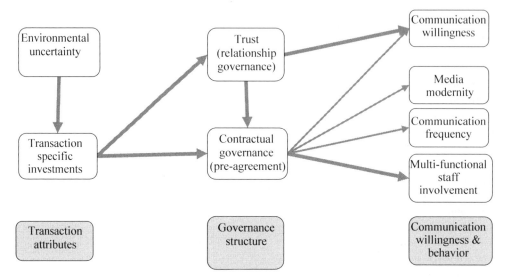

Figure 4.2. Results of the revised Communication Antecedents Model for the company-customer sample.
──────: *Path coefficient is significant at P<0.01;*
──────: *Path coefficient is significant at P<0.05.*

involvement'. The overall model explains about 18.5% of the variance of the endogenous latent variables. The increased variance explained might reflect that this model explains better the antecedents of inter-organizational communication of a company with its main customers, than with its main suppliers.

The results of PLS modeling show that '*environmental uncertainty*' here is positively and directly associated with TSI, and indirectly associated with trust and contractual by increased specific investments. Other relationships in the revised model remained the same as the original model.

Specifically, when environmental uncertainty is higher, a company is likely to invest more in specific transactions with its main customers to safeguard its markets. Moreover, owing to the increased specific investments, higher environmental uncertainty is likely to lead indirectly to greater trust and stronger contractual governance. This trend for a company in relationships with its main customers is similar to that for a company in relationships with its main suppliers. Thus, by comparing the original and the revised models for both the company-supplier and the company-customer samples, a noteworthy finding is that: environmental uncertainty does not directly affect trust and contractual governance, but appears to indirectly affect them through increased specific investments; whereas specific investments directly affect trust and contractual governance. This holds true for a company in relationships with its main suppliers and customers. Barthelemy and Quelin (2006) and Arana (2010) also reported empirical findings of the positively relationships between environmental uncertainty and contractual governance.

As for *specific investments*, an important finding is that TSI here appears to be an extremely important indicator for governance structure, communication willingness, and communication behavior for a company in relationships with its main customers. The results of path coefficients show that 'TSI' is positively and strongly associated with both 'contractual governance' and 'trust'. A likely explanation is that when a company invests specifically more in its main customers, it sends a powerful sign to the customers. And this sign causes them to be more confident in the company's compliance. Thus, the trust between the company and its main customers is likely to be higher. Meanwhile, with weaker negotiating power than its customers, the company is likely to invest in contracts to safeguard its specific investments and markets. As introduced in Section 2.4.1, recent relevant studies in the Chinese context reported similar findings, regarding the positive relationship between TSI and contractual governance (Lu, 2007; Han, 2009), and between TSI and trust (Han, 2009).

Appendix 4.4 presents path coefficients, total effects, and *t*-values of the PLS modeling of the revised Communication Antecedents Model for companies in relationships with their customers. The results of *total effects* indicate that 'environment uncertainty' here is positively and significantly associated with 'communication willingness' and 'multi-functional staff involvement', indirectly through specific investments and governance structure. A likely explanation is that when environment uncertainty is higher, a company is likely to invest more in specific transactions with its main customers, and in this way, to guard against uncertainty and to safeguard its markets. Correspondingly, it tends to make use of trust and contractual governance to jointly safeguard its investments and transactions. With greater trust and stronger contractual governance, the company and its main customers are more willing, and tend to make use of senior managers and staff from different functions to communicate with each other.

In addition, the results of total effects also reflect that TSI here is also positively and significantly associated with communication willingness and behavior. Thus, when a company invests more in specific transactions with its main customers, the company and its main customers are likely to communicate more willingly and more frequently with each other, and they tend to make use of more advanced information tools, senior managers, and staff from different functions to communicate with each other.

When looking at the relationships between governance structure and communication willingness and behavior, we can see that, similar to the results for the company-supplier sample shown above, '*trust*' here is again positively and strongly associated with communication willingness, but again not with communication behavior. In other words, for a company in relationships with its main suppliers or customers, trust appears to be key to improving communication willingness. When trust is greater, companies are likely to communicate with each other more willingly; however, they do not necessarily communicate more frequently, or employ more advanced information tools, senior managers, or staff from different functions in the communicate.

However, it was reported empirically in the literature that trust was associated with communication behavior. It was found that trading partners' level of trust in the client positively influenced their information exchange behavior, and in turn, information communication positively affected client customizations (Klein *et al.*, 2007). Trust was also found to be an important factor influencing the adoption and use of inter-organizational information systems (Hart and Saunders, 1997, 1998; Gang *et al.*, 2006). A higher level of trust in an apple chain in South Africa led to improved communication (Hardman *et al.*, 2002). In addition, Li and Lin (2006) reported that trust in chain partners positively influenced both information communication and information quality. Recalling that Son *et al.* (2005) reported only an indirect effect of trust on EDI usage, we assume that trust here might be indirectly linked to communication behavior. Thus, it would be valuable to look for mediator factors between trust and communication behavior in future research. By checking the results of total effects, we can see that 'trust' is positively and strongly associated with 'multi-functional staff involvement', indirectly through improved 'contractual governance'. Furthermore, trust might also influence communication behavior through improved communication willingness. This would be meaningful to be examined in future research.

Similar to the results of the company-supplier sample, here 'trust' is again positively and strongly associated with 'contractual governance'. A likely explanation is that a company in relationships with its main suppliers and customers tends to make use of trust and contractual governance to jointly safeguard its transactions.

A remarkable difference from the results of the company-supplier sample is that '*contractual governance*' here is positively and significantly associated with communication willingness and behavior. When contractual governance between a company and its main customers is higher, the company is likely to communicate more willingly and more frequently with its main customers, by making use of more advanced information tools, senior managers, and staff from different functions. This might imply that on the one hand, a company in relationships with its main customers and in marketing activities is likely to pay more attention to contractual customers than to non-contractual customers. It tends to communicate more willingly and frequently with contractual customers, by making use of modern media, senior managers, and staff from different functions. On the other hand, a company in relationships with its main suppliers and in purchasing activities is likely to be open to flexibility regarding sources, and treats contractual and non-contractual suppliers more or less equally, regarding communication willingness and behavior. In other words, contractual governance might indicate the willingness and behavior of a company's communication with its main customers, but might not with its main suppliers. This finding is noteworthy, because we did not find direct empirical evidence in the literature on the relationship between contractual governance and communication willingness and behavior, though it is argued in theory that contracts are explicitly drafted with provisions against asymmetric information (Bogetoft and Olesen, 2004), and coordination devices specified by contract may foster more frequent communication and a greater flow of information (Zhou and Poppo, 2010).

Table 4.6 summarizes the hypothesized relationships and the results of the revised Communication Antecedents Model for companies in relationships with their most important customers. Six out of the seven hypothesized relationships are significant at 5% or 1% level. One is partly significant at 1% level.

4.2.3 Results of the revised Communication Antecedents Model: similarity and confrontation of the company-supplier and the company-customer samples

Based on the empirical results of the revised Communication Antecedents Model for companies in relationships with their most important suppliers (see Section 4.2.1 and 4.2.2), and with their most important customers (see Section 4.2.3 and 4.2.4), we can summarize the relationships among transaction attributes, governance structure, and communication willingness and behavior as follow.

Similar findings for the company-supplier and the company-customer samples

It is shown that when the level of *environmental uncertainty* is higher, a company is likely to invest more in specific transactions with its main suppliers and customers, in order to guard against uncertainty

Table 4.6. Results for the hypotheses of the revised Communication Antecedents Model for the company-customer sample.

		Path coefficient significant?	Sign of coefficient as expected?	Hypothesis
H_{iA1}	The level of environmental uncertainty is positively associated with the level of contractual governance.	No	Yes	Supported by total effects
H_{iA2}	The level of environmental uncertainty is positively associated with the level of transaction specific investments (TSI).	Yes	Yes	Supported
H_{iB1}	The level of TSI is positively associated with the level of trust.	Yes	Yes	Supported
H_{iB2}	The level of TSI is positively associated with the level of contractual governance.	Yes	Yes	Supported
H_{iC1}	The level of trust is positively associated with the level of communication willingness and communication behavior (media modernity, communication frequency, and multi-functional staff involvement).	Yes with Willingness	Yes with Willingness & Behavior	Supported with Willingness
H_{iC2}	The level of trust is positively associated with the level of contractual governance.	Yes	Yes	Supported
H_D	The level of contractual governance is positively associated with the level of communication willingness and behavior.	Yes	Yes	Supported

These hypotheses are proposed in Section 2.4, 4.1.2 and 4.2.1.

and safeguard its purchasing sources and markets. In addition, an important finding is that higher environmental uncertainty appears to lead not directly, but indirectly, to improved trust and contractual governance, through increased specific investments, in order to guard against uncertainty and safeguard the investments.

Meanwhile, when a company invests more in specific transactions with its main suppliers and customers, they are likely to trust each other more. A likely reason is that the increased specific investments send a powerful signal, so that its suppliers and customers are more confident in the company's compliance. Another likely explanation is that the company tends to build up trust with its main suppliers and customers to safeguard its investments.

It is shown that higher specific investments are also linked to higher contractual governance, indirectly for a company in relationships with its main suppliers, or directly for a company in relationships with its main customers. This might imply that when a company invests more in specific transactions, it tends to build up trust and make use of contractual governance to jointly safeguard its investments.

Trust appears to be a reliable indicator for communication willingness, but not necessarily for communication behavior. When trust is higher between a company and its main suppliers and customers, they tend to be more willing to communicate with each other. However, they might not communicate more frequently, or make use of more advance information media, senior managers, or staff from different functions to communicate with each other.

Meanwhile, trust seems to be a reliable indicator for contractual governance. When trust is higher between a company and its main suppliers, and its main customers, the contractual governance is stronger. A likely explanation is that companies tend to build up trust and adopt contractual governance to jointly safeguard their purchasing sources and their markets.

Confrontation between the company-supplier and the company-customer samples

The results reveal two major differences between the two samples. First, '*transaction specific investments*' are not directly associated with 'contractual governance' for a company in relationships with its main suppliers, but are for a company in relationships with its main customers. A likely explanation is that a company in relationships with its main suppliers has relatively strong market power, thus it does not necessarily need to invest in contract governance in order to safeguard its specific investments in its suppliers and the purchasing sources. Adversely, faced with relatively powerful customers, a company in relationships with its main customers tends to invest in contract governance, and make use of contracts to safeguard its specific investments in its customers and the markets.

Contractual governance' is not significantly associated with communication willingness and behavior for a company in relationships with its main suppliers, but is for a company in relationships with its main customers. A likely explanation is that a company in relationships with its main suppliers prefers to be open to flexibility regarding purchasing sources, and therefore tends to treat its contractual and non-contractual suppliers more or less equally. When contracts are implemented to govern the transactions between a company and its main suppliers, the company does not necessarily communicate more willingly or more frequently with the contractual suppliers, or make use of modern media, senior managers, and staff from different functions to communicate with the contractual suppliers. Adversely, a company in relationships with its main customers might draw up a contract as a sign of reliable markets. Therefore, it tends to pay more attention to its contractual customers than non-contractual customers, and is more willing to communicate with its contractual customers frequently, by making use of modern media, senior managers, and staff from different function.

Conclusion

In conclusion, the most important findings are as follows:

For a company in relationships with its main suppliers and customers, environmental uncertainty appears to *directly* and strongly affect specific investments, and *indirectly* affect trust and contractual governance, through specific investment. In contrast, specific investments (TSI) *directly* affect trust and contractual governance.

Contractual governance does not appear to affect communication willingness and behavior of a company with its main suppliers, but is likely to affect communication willingness and behavior of a company with its main customers.

For a company in relationships with its main suppliers and customers, trust appears to be key to improving communication willingness, but does not necessarily affect communication media modernity, communication frequency, or multi-functional staff involvement.

All in all, communication among chain partners is one broad issue covering diverse aspects. It is useful to examine communication in detail by looking at its diverse aspects. Moreover, these diverse aspects might be affected by distinct factors, such as environment uncertainty, transaction specific investment, trust and contractual governance. An efficient way to *improve the communication among chain partners is to examine each aspect of the communication, then to target those main problem areas, and further, improve these aspects jointly through their specific antecedents.*

4.3 Influence of company characteristics on communication antecedents

4.3.1 Influence of company characteristics on antecedents of IOC for the company-supplier sample

In this section, to explore the influences of company characteristics on the relationships between communication and its antecedents for companies in relationships with their most important suppliers (the company-supplier sample), five company characteristics have been added as control variables to each dependent construct in the revised Communication Antecedents Model. Other parts and paths of the model remained the same as the revised Communication Antecedents Model tested in Section 4.2. Following Chin (1998), we ran bootstrapping with 500× resampling again.

These five control variables are: company size, company age, company type, quality standard applied, and the administrative level of a location (see Section 3.4.2). *Company size* is distinguished according to the criteria described in Appendix 3.2. *Company age* is a scale variable. *Company type* is modeled as a dummy variable, with 1 for companies with trading as main function, being closer to end markets, and with higher market power; and 0 for companies with production as main function, being less close to end markets and with lower market power. Meanwhile, *product quality* is represented by the highest quality standard adopted by a company, ranging between 1 for no specific quality standard and 5 for Green AA or similar level of standards. *The administrative level of a company's location* is an ordinal variable herein, with 1 for town or county, 2 for medium-sized cities, and 3 for national or provincial capital cities.

The overall model explains about 20.3% of the variance of the endogenous latent variables. The results are shown in Table 4.7 and Appendix 4.5. It is shown that one out of the five company characteristics (company type) turns out to have certain significant effects on the level of a company's specific investments in its most important suppliers. However, these five company characteristics do not necessarily change the significance of the relationships between transaction attributes, governance structure, and communication willingness and behavior, which is presented in Section 4.2.1. In other words, the result of each hypothesis for the company-supplier sample remains the same after adding

Table 4.7. The significant *influences of company characteristics on communication antecedents for the* company-supplier *sample.*

	Path coefficient significant?	Sign of coefficient
CV_3: Firm type →Transaction specific investments	**Yes***	-

The same significant paths for both the company-supplier and the company-customer (see Table 4.8) samples are shown in **bold** and *italics*.
* Significant at 5%.

these control variables to the research model. Thus, for a company in relationships with its main suppliers, the results presented in Figure 4.1 and Appendix 4.5 reflect the interrelationships between transaction attributes, governance structure, and communication willingness and behavior, with OR without taking into account company characteristics.

Table 4.7 shows the significant influence of company type on transaction specific investments of a company in relationships with its most important suppliers. Other non-significant influences of the five company characteristics on transaction attributes or governance structure are omitted here, but shown in Appendix 4.5. It is shown that company type is negatively and significantly associated with the level of transaction specific investments. A company with trading as its main function and being closer to end markets, and with more market power, such as a supermarket or a trader, is likely to invest less in specific transactions with its main suppliers. Adversely, a company with production as its main function, farther away from end markets and with less market power, such as a commercial farm or a processor, is likely to invest more in specific transactions with its main suppliers.

It is noteworthy that all of these five company characteristics do not necessarily influence the level of trust and contractual governance between a company and its most important suppliers.

In addition, the five company characteristics are likely to influence the level of communication willingness and behavior of a company with its most important suppliers in one way or the other. These are discussed later in Section 5.3.1.

4.3.2 Influence of company characteristics on antecedents of IOC for the company-customer sample

In this section, in order to explore the influences of company characteristics on the relationships between communication and its antecedents for companies in relationships with their most important customers (the company-customer sample), the five company characteristics have been added again as control variables to each dependent construct in the revised Communication Antecedents Model. Other parts and paths of the model remained the same as the revised model tested in Section 4.2. Following Chin (1998), we ran bootstrapping with 500× resampling again.

The overall model explains about 30.3% of the variance of the endogenous latent variables. The results are shown in Table 4.8 and Appendix 4.6. It is again shown that one out of the five company characteristics (company type) turns out to have significant effects on the level of a company's specific investments in its most important customers. However, these five company characteristics do not necessarily change the significance of the relationships between transaction attributes, governance structure, and communication willingness and behavior, which are presented in Section 4.2.4. In other words, the result of each hypothesis for the company-customer sample remains the same after adding these control variables to the research model. Thus, the results presented in Figure 4.2 and Appendix 4.6 reflect the relationships between transaction attributes, governance structure, and communication willingness and behavior, with OR without taking into account company characteristics.

Table 4.8 shows the significant influence of company type on transaction specific investments of a company in relationships with its most important customers. Other non-significant influences of the five company characteristics on transaction attributes or governance structure are omitted here, but shown in Appendix 4.6. It is shown that company type is again negatively and significantly associated with the level of transaction specific investments. A company with trading as its main function, closer to end markets, and with more market power, such as a supermarket or a trader, is likely to invest less in specific transactions with its main customers. Adversely, a company with production as its main function, being farther away from end markets, and with less market power, such as a commercial farm or a processor, is likely to invest more in specific transactions with its main customers.

It is noteworthy that all of these five company characteristics do not necessarily influence the level of trust and contractual governance between a company and its most important customers.

In addition, the five company characteristics are again likely to influence the level of communication willingness and behavior of a company with its most important customers in one way or the other. These are discussed later in Section 5.3.2.

Table 4.8. The significant influences of the company characteristics on communication antecedents for the company-customer sample.

	Path coefficient significant?	**Sign of coefficient**
CV_3: Firm type → Transaction specific investments	**Yes****	-

The same significant paths for both the company-supplier (see Table 4.7) and the company-customer samples are shown in **bold** and *italics*.
** Significant at 1%.

4.3.3 Influence of company characteristics on antecedents of IOC: similarity and confrontation of the company-supplier and the company-customer samples

In general, the five company characteristics have shown *similar* significant and non-significant influences on the level of transaction attributes and governance structure, for a company in relationships with its most important suppliers and customers. In other words, there is not much difference between the two samples, regarding the influence of company characteristics on the level of transaction attributes and governance structure.

Specifically, company type is likely to influence the level of a company's investments in specific transactions with its most important suppliers and customers. Companies with trading as their main functions tend to invest less in their main suppliers and customers; whereas companies with production as their main functions tend to invest more in their main suppliers and customers. A likely explanation is that production functions are comparatively more complex, thus the investments of a production company have greater specificity, and it is more difficult for the production company to switch its investments to its other suppliers or customers. Adversely, trading functions are comparatively less complex, thus the investments of a trading company have less specificity, and it is less difficult for the trading company to switch its investments to other suppliers or customers.

In addition, the other four company characteristics do not necessarily influence the level of trust and contractual governance of a company with its main suppliers and customers.

The most important finding is that company characteristics do not necessarily influence the relationships between transaction attributes, governance structure, and communication willingness and behavior, though they are likely to influence the level of certain constructs. Therefore, we can conclude that the results of the hypothesized relationships between transaction attributes, governance structure, and communication willingness and behavior, which are described in this research, are likely to be tenable for different companies with different characteristics.

4.4 Concluding remarks

This chapter aims to analyze antecedents of inter-organizational communication (IOC) of a company with its main suppliers, and with its main customers. It displays empirical results regarding construct validity and construct reliability, baseline statistics, and the Communication Antecedents Model proposed in this research. The chapter starts by assessing the validity and reliability of constructs employed in this research. The results support the content validity, nomological validity, being free of the problem of item multicollinearity for the formative constructs, as well as content validity, nomological validity, convergent validity, and construct reliability for the reflective construct.

Subsequently, this chapter presents baseline statistics regarding expected antecedents of communication willingness and behavior, which have been gleaned from the literature on Transaction Cost Economics. It is shown that the respondent companies in relationships with their most important suppliers, and with their most important customers, have reported similar opinions and activities (by similar average scores) regarding environmental uncertainty, governance structure, communication willingness and behavior. Specifically, companies tend to take the view that environment uncertainty in the Chinese poultry chain is relatively high, regarding market, product price, and product quality. Regarding governance structure, they tend to make use of trust and contractual governance to jointly safeguard transactions with their most important suppliers and customers. As for communication willingness and behavior, these companies tend to have a relatively high willingness to communicate frequently with business partners; and most companies make use of traditional to moderately advanced information tools, senior managers, and staff from different functions to communicate with their most important suppliers and customers.

The significant difference between companies in relationships with their main suppliers, and with their main customers, is shown with transaction specific investments. Comparatively, companies in relationships with their main suppliers reported lower specific investments, than companies in relationships with their main customers. Importantly, this might reflect that a company is likely to invest more in specific transactions with its main customers, and in this way to increase its rent from the markets; it is likely to invest less in specific transactions with its main suppliers, because there is less need to invest in purchasing sources in a market-oriented and buyer-dominant economy. Furthermore, the correlation coefficients show that the constructs are nicely associated with most other constructs, as expected. This provides evidence for nomological validity of these constructs.

Furthermore, this chapter displays the results of PLS modeling of the (revised) Communication Antecedents Model, for a company in relationships with its most important suppliers (the company-supplier sample), and with its most important customers (the company-customer sample), respectively. A valuable finding is that for both samples, a higher level of specific investments leads *directly* to a higher level of trust and contractual governance, whereas a higher level of environmental uncertainty *indirectly* affects trust and contractual governance through its direct effect on specific investments.

Thus, though higher environment uncertainty is a negative factor in general, it could be regarded as a positive opportunity, if a company makes good use of this 'tough' environment by focusing on strengthening the business relationships with its important customers and suppliers. An environment of higher uncertainty for some companies' purchasing sources could be an environment of lower uncertainty for their suppliers' marketing. Correspondingly, an environment of higher uncertainty for some companies' marketing could be an environment of lower uncertainty for their customers' purchasing sources. Thus, if a company intends to strengthen its relationships with targeted customers or suppliers, it should try its best to help them reduce the uncertainty, when the targeted customers or suppliers face a more uncertain environment. It might then be less difficult for the company to persuade its targeted customers or suppliers to increase specific investments in it, and in this way, safeguard its markets or purchasing sources in the long run. Furthermore, this might imply that the way in which a company behaves in a relatively less uncertain environment for itself but a more uncertain environment for its business partners, might determine, to a certain extent, how successful it will be later on in a more uncertain environment for itself and a less uncertain environment for its partners.

Trust has been shown to have similar positive effects on communication willingness and behavior for companies in relationships with their most important suppliers and customers. Adversely, contractual governance does not necessarily influence communication willingness and behavior for a company in relationships with its main suppliers, but is likely to influence these for a company in relationships with its main customers.

Thus, another valuable finding is that there might be certain common factors, but also certain distinct factors, which influence the communication willingness and behavior of a company with its main suppliers, and with its main customers. Therefore, to improve communication willingness and behavior, a company should not only focus on issues of interest to itself, but also on issues of interest to its communication partner. When communicating with its main suppliers, a company should pay attention to the interests of the suppliers; when communicating with its main customers, a company should pay attention to the interests of the customers. Correspondingly, a company may have different interests in its relationships with its suppliers to those in its relationships with its main customers. Therefore, its main suppliers should pay attention to its interests as a customer, whereas its main customers should pay attention to its interests as a supplier. In addition, we suggest that an efficient way of improving the communication with chain partners is to examine each aspect of communication, target main problematic areas, and then improve these aspects jointly though their specific antecedents, such as environment uncertainty, specific investments, trust and contractual governance.

Subsequently, this chapter examines the potential influence of company characteristics on communication and its antecedents. It is shown that company characteristics are likely to influence the level (namely, magnitude) of specific investments, and communication willingness and behavior between a company and its main suppliers and customers. However, company characteristics do not necessarily affect the relationships between these constructs. Therefore, we can conclude that the relationships between transaction attributes, governance structure, and communication willingness and behavior, which are analyzed in this research, are likely to be tenable for different companies with different characteristics. As such, this research has helped to extend the scientific research concerning the impact of company characteristics on the relationships between transaction attributes, governance structure, and communication willingness and behavior.

Chapter 5

Elements of Inter-Organizational Communication

This chapter is about the interrelationships of different aspects of communication between a company and its most important suppliers, and its most important customers. By revealing such interrelationships, this chapter aims to answer Research Question B: *'What are the relationships between communication willingness, communication behavior, communication quality, and perceived communication benefits? And how can inter-organizational communication to be used to provide more benefits for companies?'*. Section 5.1 starts by displaying the baseline statistics. Then, Section 5.2 reports the outcomes of the estimated Communication Elements Models for companies in relationships with their most important suppliers, and with their most important customers, respectively. Section 5.3 discusses the influences of company characteristics on inter-organizational communication (IOC). In addition, Section 5.2 and 5.3 make general suggestions for future research. The chapter ends with some concluding remarks in Section 5.4.

5.1 Baseline statistics

This section presents the baseline description of constructs, including communication willingness, media modernity, communication frequency, multi-functional staff involvement, knowledge of each other's requirements and expectations, information quality, perceived communication benefits for companies in relationships with their main suppliers, and perceived communication benefits for companies in relationships with their main customers. The unweighted score of each construct has been calculated with the related manifest indicators. The means, standard deviations, and correlation coefficients have been calculated and shown for companies in relationships with their most important suppliers (the company-supplier sample), and with their most important customers (the company-customer sample), respectively, in Table 5.1 and 5.2.

Comparing means of each construct between the company-supplier and the company-customer samples revealed that the respondent companies reported similar scores for all of these constructs. This seems to reflect that, in general, most surveyed companies have adopted similar opinions and/or actions on issues concerning the communication of a company with its main customers, and with its main suppliers.

Recalling that all observed indicators, except those for media modernity, are measured by 5-point Likert scales ranging between 1 for 'not agree at all' and 5 for 'totally agree', a mean above 3 indicates that the respondents tended to agree with the statement. The results in Table 5.1 and 5.2 show that most of the constructs of inter-organizational communication (IOC) in this study had a positive response (i.e. agreed with the statements).

Furthermore, for both samples, the means above 4 for communication willingness (4.1), knowledge of each other's requirements and expectations (4.1-4.2), information quality (4.1), perceived communication benefits for companies in relationships with their main suppliers (4.1-4.2), and perceived communication benefits for companies in relationships with their main customers (4.2) might reflect that, in general:

Table 5.1. Construct mean, standard deviations (S.D.) and correlation matrix[1] for the company-supplier sample (N=165).

Constructs[2]	Mean	S.D.	1	2	3	4	5	6	7
1. Communication willingness	4.12	0.77							
2. Media modernity	1.61	0.79	**0.22**						
3. Communication frequency	3.65	0.66	**0.25**	*0.12*					
4. Multi-functional staff involvement	3.58	10.06	**0.50**	**0.30**	**0.23**				
5. Knowledge of each other's requirement / expectations	4.05	0.85	**0.61**	**0.18**	**0.32**	**0.41**			
6. Information quality	4.07	0.73	**0.59**	*0.11*	**0.25**	**0.45**	**0.54**		
7. Perceived communication benefits for the companies	4.08	0.70	**0.37**	**0.16**	**0.24**	**0.26**	**0.44**	**0.45**	
8. Perceived communication benefits for suppliers	4.18	0.67	**0.51**	**0.17**	**0.25**	**0.28**	**0.55**	**0.51**	**0.77**

[1] In this correlation matrix, correlation coefficients with a value of at least 0.16 (**bold**) are significant at 5%; non-significant coefficients are shown in *italics*.
[2] Media modernity is measured with a 3-point Likert scale. Other constructs are measured with a 5-point Likert scale (see Appendix 3.1).

Table 5.2. Construct mean, standard deviations (S.D.) and correlation matrix[1] for the company-customer sample (N=96).

Constructs[2]	Mean	S.D.	1	2	3	4	5	6	7
1. Communication willingness	4.13	0.76							
2. Media modernity	1.61	0.75	**0.22**						
3. Communication frequency	3.60	0.77	**0.32**	**0.23**					
4. Multi-functional staff involvement	3.76	10.08	**0.52**	**0.41**	*0.16*				
5. Knowledge of each other's requirements/ expectations	4.15	0.76	**0.69**	**0.22**	**0.38**	**0.49**			
6. Information quality	4.07	0.71	**0.48**	*0.13*	**0.29**	**0.47**	**0.53**		
7. Perceived communication benefits for customers	4.18	0.71	**0.45**	**0.22**	**0.30**	**0.23**	**0.48**	**0.46**	
8. Perceived communication benefits for the companies	4.16	0.58	**0.48**	*0.13*	**0.33**	**0.27**	**0.54**	**0.57**	**0.72**

[1] In this correlation matrix, correlation coefficients with a value of at least 0.16 (**bold**) are significant at 5%; non-significant coefficients are shown in *italics*.
[2] Media modernity is measured with a 3-point Likert scale. Other constructs are measured with a 5-point Likert scale (see Appendix 3.1).

1. The companies were willing to communicate with their main customers and suppliers.
2. They tended to be of the opinion that they were well aware of the requirements and expectations of their main customers and suppliers; and their main customers and suppliers were also well aware of their requirements and expectations.
3. They considered that the quality of information communicated with their main customers, and with their main suppliers, was high.
4. Of particular interest is that these companies tended to believe that their communication with their main suppliers had produced high and almost equal (!) benefits for themselves and for their main suppliers. Meanwhile, their communication with their main customers had produced high and almost equal (!) benefits for themselves and for their main customers. In the literature, there has been a lively debate about the extent to which a company should invest in information exchange, compared to its customers or its suppliers. The results of this research appear to support that it might be advantageous for both a company and its main customers, and both a company and its suppliers, to invest heavily and more or less equally in information exchange with each other.

The item of *media modernity* is measured by a 3-point Likert scale ranging as 1 for 'traditional communication tools', 2 for 'middle advanced tools', and 3 for 'modern tools'. As explained in Section 4.1.2, the means of 'media modernity' for both the customers (1.6) and the suppliers (1.6) reflect that most respondent companies made use of traditional media (face-to-face and phone) and moderately advanced media (e-mail) to communicate with their main customers, and with their main suppliers. More advanced media, such as EDI, were at an introductory stage, and not yet widely used.

It is noteworthy that '*multi-functional staff involvement*' is with standard deviations of being above 1. As explained in Section 4.1.2, this might indicate that diverse staff arrangements coexisted throughout the chain, and were used by different companies to communicate with their main business partners. Some companies adopted senior managers and staff from different functions, while others adopted non-senior managers and staff from single functions to communicate with their main customers and suppliers. In addition, we suppose that the comparatively high standard deviations for 'multi-functional staff involvement' might be the result of the diversity of company characteristics, such as firm size and firm type. Staff from different functions might be employed more in a large company, whereas there is often a lack of so-called multi-functional teams or senior managers (except firms' owners) in a mini or small company. Instead, an employee in a small company often has to perform diverse functions. The influences of company characteristics on 'multi-functional staff involvement' have been checked and are confirmed in Section 5.3, by adding company characteristics (represented by five control variables) to the research model.

The correlation matrices in Table 5.1 and 5.2 show certain associations among the constructs of IOC, as expected. Specifically, it is shown that *communication willingness, communication behavior* (except media modernity), *communication quality*, and *perceived communication benefits* were significantly, and often strongly correlated with all other constructs or most other constructs. This might reflect that, in general: (1) communication willingness and communication behavior (except media modernity) are critical indicators for communication quality between a company and its main customers and suppliers; (2) communication quality, including both knowledge of each other's requirements and expectations, and information quality, are critical indicators for perceived communication benefits for both a company and its main customers, and for both a company and its main suppliers; (3) communication willingness and communication behavior (except media modernity) may not only indirectly, through communication quality, but also directly make a certain contribution to perceived communication benefits for a company, for its main customers, and for its main suppliers.

Comparatively, *media modernity* was correlated with fewer constructs, and these correlations are less strong (except with multi-functional staff involvement). These might reflect that: (1) media modernity *here* did not appear to contribute much to the improvement of information quality; (2) media modernity here had shown to make a limited contribution to perceived communication benefits for the companies. A likely reason is that there is limited use of modern media, and the adoption of modern media is still in its early stages in the Chinese poultry chain. This is in line with mean results shown above. Combining the results of the research model tested in Section 5.2, we discuss the potential reasons in more detail later on.

In addition, it is interesting that media modernity was comparatively strongly correlated with multi-functional staff involvement. A likely explanation is that both them are linked to company characteristics such as firm size. A larger company is likely to be able to invest more in advanced media, and is likely to adopt senior manager(s) and staff from different functions to communicate with their main business partners.

It is shown that '*knowledge of each other's requirements and expectations*' was highly correlated with 'information quality'. Thus, to examine the relationship between these two aspects of communication quality, we herein propose one more hypothesis, besides others proposed in Section 2.5: the more aware companies are of each other's requirements and expectations, the higher the information quality (H_{iiD}). Then, this hypothesis, together with others on IOC (H_{iiA}, H_{iiB}, H_{iiC}, see Section 2.5), is examined in Section 5.2, and the results are presented in Table 5.3 and 5.4.

It is worth noting the positive and strong correlation ($0.7 \sim 0.77$) between 'perceived communication benefits for companies in relationships with their main suppliers' and 'perceived communication benefits for companies in relationships with their main customers'. This might imply that when a company benefits more from the communication with its main customers, or with its main suppliers, its main customers or suppliers also (therefore) benefit more from the mutual communication with the company. This is in line with the above results of (high) mean ($4.1 \sim 4.2$) and (low) standard deviation ($0.6 \sim 0.7$) of these two constructs. These results indicate an important finding that companies should help their main business partners to realize the potential benefits of information exchange, because such action turns out to be a kind of self-help.

We also checked the possible multicollinearity problem for these constructs. A cut-off of 0.80 is commonly used for correlations among variables for dismissing multicollinearity problems (Hair *et al.*, 1998; Malhotra *et al.*, 1999). It is shown that all the correlation coefficients herein are well below 0.8. Therefore, the individual magnitude of the correlations between the constructs does not suggest an obvious problem of pairwise collinearity. This proves the discriminant validity of the constructs. Thus, we can employ all of these listed constructs in one model.

5.2 Communication elements and their interrelationships

5.2.1 Results of the Communication Elements Model for the company-supplier sample

The results of the Communication Elements Model for companies in relationships with their most important suppliers are presented in Figure 5.1 and Appendix 5.1. Most of the paths are significant at 5% or 1%. The values of R square in this model range as 0.43 for 'knowledge of each other's requirements and expectations', 0.43 for 'information quality', 0.26 for 'perceived communication benefits for firms in relationships with suppliers', and 0.39 for 'perceived communication benefits for companies in relationships with customers'. The overall model explains about 37.5% of the variance of the endogenous latent variables, which indicates that a satisfactory model fit is obtained for companies in relationships with their most important suppliers (the company-supplier sample).

Figure 5.1 shows the significant relationships among communication elements between a company and its main suppliers, based on the results of PLS path modeling. The results show that *'communication willingness'* is positively and strongly associated with 'communication quality', specifically, with both 'knowledge of each other's requirements and expectations', and with 'information quality'. These might reflect that communication willingness is key for improving communication quality between a company and its most important suppliers. When a company and its main suppliers are more willing to communicate with each other, they are likely to be more aware of the requirements and expectations of each other. Moreover, the quality of the communicated information is likely to be higher.

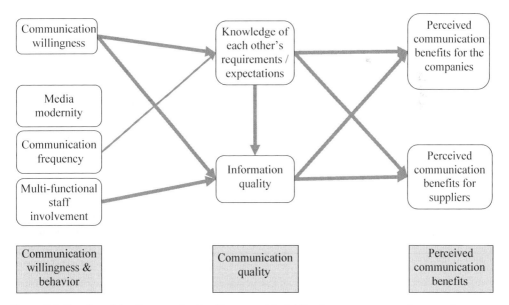

Figure 5.1. Results of the Communication Elements Model for the company-supplier sample.
━━━: Path coefficient is significant at P<0.01;
─────: Path coefficient is significant at P<0.05.

As for the relationships between *communication behavior* and 'communication quality', the hypothesized relationship is partly supported here. First, in contrast to our expectations, but in line with the correlation results in Section 5.1, applying *modern media* here does not seem to lead automatically to a higher level of communication quality between a company and its main suppliers. Combined with the similar result of the company-customer sample shown below in Section 5.2.2, we discuss the possible reasons later in this section. Second, 'communication frequency' is positively associated with 'knowledge of each other's requirements and expectations', but not with 'information quality'. A likely reason is that the more frequently a company communicates with its main suppliers, the more opportunities it might gain to understand the requirements and expectations of its suppliers; but this might not necessarily lead to a higher level of information quality. Third, 'multi-functional staff involvement' is positively associated with 'information quality', but not with 'knowledge of each other's requirements and expectations'. This might imply that when senior managers and staff from different functions are involved in the communication between a company and its main suppliers, the (regular) information quality is likely to be improved, but it does not necessarily help the companies better understand each other's (changing) requirements and expectations.

Appendix 5.1 presents the path coefficients, total effects, and *t*-values of the PLS modeling of the Communication Elements Model shown in Figure 5.1. Of particular interest are the results of *total effects*, which reflect that 'communication willingness' is positively and strongly associated with 'perceived communication benefits for the companies' and 'perceived communication benefits for its main suppliers'. Thus, when a company and its main suppliers are more willing to communicate with each other, both the company and its main suppliers are likely to realize more benefits from the communication, which helps them to resolve problem and control quality. Therefore, in summary, for the communication between a company and its main suppliers, *communication willingness* appears to be critical, since it not only greatly helps a company and its main suppliers to improve communication quality, but also significantly helps them to realize more potential benefits of the communication.

The results of total effects in Appendix 5.1 also reflect that, *'communication behavior'* is partly associated with 'perceived communication benefits'. First, *'media modernity'* here is not significantly associated with either 'perceived communication benefits for the companies', or 'perceived communication benefits for suppliers'. Thus, for a company that employs modern media to communicate with its main suppliers, both the company and its suppliers do not necessarily benefit more from the communication. A potential reason is discussed later when the results of the company-customer sample are combined.

Second, *'communication frequency'* is positively and significantly associated with 'perceived communication benefits for the companies', but not with 'perceived communication benefits for suppliers'. This might imply that when a company and its main suppliers communicate more frequently with each other, the company does not necessarily benefit more, but its main *suppliers* are likely to benefit more in obtaining direct support for problem resolution, quality control, delivery, and product pricing decisions.

Third, *'multi-functional staff involvement'* is positively and strongly associated with both 'perceived communication benefits for the companies' and 'perceived communication benefits for their suppliers'. This might imply that when a company and its main suppliers adopt senior manager(s) and staff from different functions (rather than a single function) to communicate with each other, both the company and its suppliers are likely to benefit more and receive more direct support for problem resolution, quality control, delivery, and product pricing decisions. Thus, we can conclude that, for the communication between a company and its main suppliers, multi-functional staff involvement appears to be another critical factor that greatly helps to improve not only information quality, but also perceived communication benefits for a company and for its main suppliers.

When looking at the relationships between '*communication quality*' and '*perceived communication benefits*', we can see that both '*knowledge of each other's requirements and expectations*' and '*information quality*', as expected, are positively and strongly associated with 'perceived communication benefits for the companies', and 'perceived communication benefits for suppliers'. This implies that: (1) when a company and its main suppliers are more aware of the requirements and expectations of each other, both of the company and its suppliers could realize more benefits from the communication; (2) when the quality of information communicated between a company and its main suppliers is higher, both the company and its suppliers could realize more benefits from the communication. Thus, we could also summarize that: (3) when communication quality between a company and its main suppliers is higher, both the company and its main suppliers are likely to realize more potential benefits from the communication.

It is shown that '*knowledge of each other's requirements and expectations*' is positively and significantly associated with *information quality*. This reflects the fact that when a company and its main suppliers catch better the requirements and expectations of each other, the company tends to believe that the information quality is higher.

Table 5.3 summarizes the hypothesized relationships and results of the Communication Elements Model for companies in relationships with their most important suppliers. Three out of the four hypothesized relationships are significant at 1% level. One out of the four hypothesized relationships is partly significant at 5% level and at 1% level (H_{iiB}).

5.2.2 Results of the Communication Elements Model for the company-customer sample

The results of the Communication Elements Model for companies in relationships with their most important customers are presented in Figure 5.2 and Appendix 5.2. Most of the paths are significant at 5% or 1%. The values of R square in this model range as 0.53 for 'knowledge of each other's requirements and expectations', 0.38 for 'information quality', 0.30 for 'perceived communication benefits for customers', and 0.43 for 'perceived communication benefits for suppliers'. The overall model explains about 41.1% of the variance of the endogenous latent variables, which indicates that a satisfactory model fit is obtained for companies in relationships with their most important customers (the company-customer sample).

Figure 5.2 shows the significant relationships between communication aspects between a company and its most important customers, based on the results of PLS path modeling.

It is shown that '*communication willingness*' is again positively and significantly associated with 'knowledge of each other's requirements and expectations'; but not with 'information quality' here. Thus, when a company and its main customers are more willing to communicate with each other, they

Table 5.3. Results of the hypotheses of the Communication Elements Model for the company-supplier sample.

		Path coefficient significant?	Sign of coefficient as expected?	Hypothesis
H$_{iiA}$	The level of communication willingness is positively associated with the level of communication quality.	Yes	Yes	Supported
H$_{iiB}$	The level of communication behavior (media modernity, communication frequency, and multi-functional staff involvement) is positively associated with the level of communication quality.	Yes (except media modernity)	Yes (except media modernity)	Supported (except media modernity)
H$_{iiC}$	The level of communication quality is positively associated with the level of perceived communication benefits.	Yes	Yes	Supported
H$_{iiD}$	The level of knowledge of each other is positively associated with the level of information quality.	Yes	Yes	Supported

These hypotheses are proposed in Section 2.5 and 5.1.

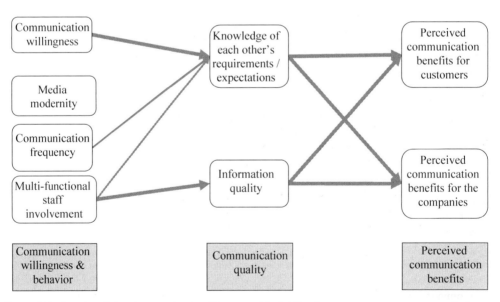

Figure 5.2. Results of the Communication Elements Model for the company-customer sample.l
━━━: Path coefficient is significant at P<0.01;
────: Path coefficient is significant at P<0.05.

are likely to better understand each other's requirements and expectations, but the information quality is not necessarily higher in the opinion of companies in relationships with their main customers.

As for the relationship between '*communication behavior*' and 'communication quality', the hypothesized relationship is partly supported here. First, in contrast to our expectations, *media modernity* again appears not to lead automatically to a higher level of communication quality between a company and its main customers. Combined with the results of total effects presented below, the potential reason is discussed later in this section.

Second, '*communication frequency*' is again positively and significantly associated with 'knowledge of each other's requirements and expectations', but again not with 'information quality'. These appear again to reflect the fact that the more frequently a company communicates with its main customers, the more likely it is to understand the changing requirements and expectations of the customers, but the quality of the regular information it obtains will not necessarily be higher.

Third, '*multi-functional staff involvement*' is again positively and significantly associated with 'information quality', but different from the company-supplier sample, also with 'knowledge of each other's requirements and expectations'. This seems to imply that when a company adopts senior manager(s) and staff from different functions to communicate with its main suppliers, and with its main customers, the company and the suppliers do not necessarily enrich their knowledge of each other; however, the company and the customers are likely to be more aware of each other's changing requirements and expectations. In other words, while making use of multi-functional staff in communication is useful for improving the (regular) information quality for a company and its main customers and its main suppliers, it appears to be more important to understand business partners' changing requirements and expectations for a company in relationships with its main customers than for a company in relationships with its suppliers. A likely explanation is that supply activities are more complex than purchasing activities, thus, it makes sense for a company in relationships with its customers to use senior manager(s) and staff from different functions to communicate with the customers. In this way, the company can better understand the changing markets.

Combined with the results of the company-supplier and the company-customer samples, these results of multi-functional staff involvement might imply that when senior manager(s) and staff from different functions are employed in the communication between a company and its main customers and suppliers, the information quality is likely to be improved. In addition, the company and its main customers are likely to become more aware of each other's requirements and expectations. These findings are partly in conflict with the study of (Li and Lin, 2006). They surveyed 196 organizations from different industries in the USA, and reported that top managers had shown a positive impact on information sharing but no impact on information quality. Thus, we assume that adopting senior manager(s) only for the communication with chain partners is not a good enough staffing strategy. Instead, companies should arrange both senior manager(s) and staff from different functions to communicate with their business partners. These multi-dimensional staff arrangements would jointly help to improve the information quality and knowledge of each other's requirements and expectations, thus improve the total communication quality, and finally help a company and its main customers and its main suppliers to realize more potential benefits from communication.

Appendix 5.2 presents path coefficients, total effects, and *t*-values of the PLS modeling of the Communication Elements Model for companies in relationships with their most important customers. Of particular interest are the results of total effects, which reflect that *'communication willingness'* is again positively and significantly associated with both 'perceived benefits of communication for customers' and with 'perceived benefits of communication for the companies'. Thus, when a company and its main customers are more willing to communicate with each other, both the company and its main customers are likely to realize more benefits from the communication. Therefore, combining the results of the company-supplier and the company-customer samples, we could summarize as follows: (1) for the communication between a company and its main suppliers, communication willingness appears to be a critical factor that greatly helps not only to improve communication quality, but also to realize potential communication benefits for the company and its main suppliers. Correspondingly, (2) for the communication between a company and its main customers, communication willingness appears to be a critical factor that greatly helps not only to improve communication quality, but also to realize potential communication benefits for the company and its main customers.

The results of total effects in Appendix 5.2 also reflect that *'communication behavior'* (except media modernity) is positively and significant associated with perceived communication benefits. First, *'communication frequency'* is positively and significantly associated with 'perceived communication benefits for customers', and with 'perceived communication benefits for the companies'. It might imply that, when a company and its main customers communicate more frequently with each other, both the company and its customers are likely to benefit more from the communication for problem resolution, quality control, delivery, and product price decision. As discussed above, a likely explanation is that, when they communicate more frequently with each other, they might gain more opportunities to better understand each other's changing requirements and expectations, and thus to enrich their knowledge of each other.

Second, *'multi-functional staff involvement'* is again positively and strongly associated with 'perceived communication benefit for customers', and with 'perceived communication benefits for the companies'. This might imply that, when a company and its main customers use senior manager(s) and staff from different functions (rather than a single function) to communicate with each other, both the company and its customers are likely to improve their knowledge of each other, and the information quality is likely to be improved. Thus, adopting senior managers and staff from different functions could jointly help the companies and their main customers to realize more potential communication benefits. In addition, making use of senior managers and staff from different functions could be regarded as a sign that the companies pay great attention to relationships with the customers involved in the communication.

'Media modernity' here is again not significantly associated with 'perceived communication benefits for customers', or 'perceived communication benefits for the companies'. Recalling the relatively low means for 'media modernity' and the researcher's experience in the field research, this might reflect that modern media have limited implementation in the Chinese poultry chains, and have not yet shown their potential value.

The results of media modernity are in line with the studies of (Chen and Luo, 2003; Li and Lin, 2006; Han, 2009; and Hsu *et al.*, 2009). Li and Lin (2006) surveyed 196 manufacturing and logistics companies in the USA. They reported that information technology (IT) enablers[13] did not show an impact on information sharing and information quality. Hsu *et al.* (2009) interviewed eight selected companies from different industries in Taiwan. They reported that information technology dynamics showed no impact on information transparency and information visibility. In a recent study in the Chinese context, Han (2009) reported that integrated information technology did not show a significant contribution to company performance in the pork processing industry. And a similar finding was reported by Chen and Luo (2003) based on their study on the processed meat products chain in China.

These findings on IT might reflect that, first, small companies and traditional communication media are still dominant in the chains in China, though the Chinese economy is in rapid development, and the poultry sector is one of its most integrated perishable sectors. In the field research, the researcher noticed that the most frequently used media between chain partners are traditional media to moderately modern media (including face-to-face contact, mobile/phone, fax, and e-mail). Every member of staff has a cell phone, and the staff within or between business partners call each other immediately or frequently as needed. More advanced media such as electronic data interchange (EDI) are not yet widely used in the Chinese poultry chain. In addition, as the researcher noticed, making a call by mobile or phone seems to show more amity and respect to a Chinese business partner than simply sending an e-mail, even though e-mail might be quicker and less costly. Second, though modern media have been employed by some companies in the chain, they might not yet be used to their full advantage, since most business partners of these companies do not yet employ more advanced media. Third, this might also reflect the fact that modern technology is not always essential for all types of companies to obtain high communication benefits. Companies are possible to obtain high communication benefits by selecting the most suitable media in terms of firm scale, tool investment, social economic development level, and local culture. In addition, Media Richness Theory states that traditional media, such as face-to-face contact and phone, are the richest medium in terms of resolving ambiguity, negotiating varying interpretations, and facilitating understanding, with the highest wealth of information.

A company should not depend solely on modern communication media; on the contrary, for those who can afford modern media, a multiple media strategy, which combines both traditional and modern media and matches the firm scale, product attributes, function attributes, and social-economic/cultural conditions, should be employed jointly. By making full use of both traditional and suitable modern media, it is possible for a company to approach the optimal benefit of the communication with its main customers and suppliers. Thus, these findings lead to a valuable management implication: on the one hand, a company should commit to improving media modernity, and endeavor to approach maximum usage of these modern media for communication; on the other hand, companies should build a communication system of diverse tools, in order to improve communication quality and to realize the potential communication benefits in the dynamic environment.

When looking at the relationships between *communication quality* and *perceived communication benefits*, we can again see that both 'knowledge of each other's requirements and expectations' and

---

[13] Here the IT enablers are: Electronic Data Interchange (EDI), Electronic Fund Transfer, Internet, Intranet, and Extranet. According to the literature, these five IT enablers are identified as influencing information sharing and information quality in supply chain management (Li and Lin, 2006: 1645).

'information quality' are positively and strongly associated with 'perceived communication benefits for customers' and 'perceived communication benefits for the companies'. These similar results of the company-supplier and the company-customer samples might show that by improving knowledge of business partners' changing requirements and expectations and by improving regular information quality, the companies and their main customers and main suppliers could realize more potential communication benefits. Thus, communication quality is multi-dimensional, and it is valuable to distinguish between the two dimensions, 'knowledge of each other's requirements and expectations' and 'information quality'. The findings in (Raghunathan, 2001) reported that information sharing is of no benefit if the supplier is intelligent enough to retrieve all of the demand information from the order history, and it concluded that only sharing information about unexpected events, e.g. promotion, is beneficial. 'Knowledge of each other's requirements and expectations' might be valuable because it leads to potential opportunities of capitalizing on unexpected events and creating joint knowledge. In addition, when companies are more aware of each other's requirements and expectations, they are likely to comply better with each other's requirements. These results might also imply that to improve communication quality and to approach optimal communication benefits, chain partners should not only focus on the quality of regular information, but also pay more attention to understanding each other's (changing) demands, requirements, and expectations in the dynamic business environment.

In contrast to the results of the company-supplier sample, here 'knowledge of each other's requirements and expectations' with the company-customer sample is not significantly associated with 'information quality', though the path coefficient is also positive. This brings to mind a proverb: 'the more one learns, the less one knows'. It is vital for a company to have precise and timely knowledge of its main customers' activities. Such knowledge might be complicated and involve many aspects. When a company learns more about its customers' activities, it might realize that there is more that it needs to know. Therefore, it might think the information communicated with the customers is not as adequate and precise as it could be. However, because it has less negotiating power than its main customers, the company cannot obtain all of the information as it wishes, and thus tends to make a conservative assessment about the information quality. This appears to be a likely explanation for the non-significant relationships between 'knowledge of each other's requirements and expectations' and 'information quality' for companies in relationships with their main customers. However, considering that this is the first study proposing and empirically examining the new construct of 'knowledge of each other's requirements and expectations', it would be valuable and interesting to check its relationship with 'information quality' in different contexts in future research.

Table 5.4 summarizes the hypothesized relationships and the results of the Communication Elements Model for companies in relationships with their most important customers. One out of the four hypothesized relationships is significant at 1% level. Two out of the four are partly significant at 1% or 5% level. And one out of the four is not significant at 5% level, though the path coefficient is positive as expected.

5.2.3 Results of the Communication Elements Model: similarity and confrontation of the company-supplier and the company-customer samples

Based on the empirical results of the Communication Elements Models for companies in relationships with their most important suppliers (see Section 5.2.1), and for companies in relationships with their

Table 5.4. Results for the hypotheses of the Communication Elements Model for the company-customer sample.

		Path coefficient significant?	Sign of coefficient as expected?	Hypothesis
H_{iiA}	The level of communication willingness is positively associated with the level of communication quality.	Yes	Yes	Supported
H_{iiB}	The level of communication behavior (media modernity, communication frequency, and multi-functional staff involvement) is positively associated with the level of communication quality.	Yes (except media modernity)	Yes (except media modernity)	Supported (except media modernity)
H_{iiC}	The level of communication quality is positively associated with the level of perceived communication benefits.	Yes	Yes	Supported
H_{iiD}	The level of knowledge of each other's requirements and expectations is positively associated with the level of information quality.	No	Yes	Not supported

These hypotheses are proposed in Section 2.5 and 5.1.

most important customers (see Section 5.2.2), we summarize the relationships between communication willingness, communication behavior, communication quality, and perceived communication benefits in this section.

Similar findings for the company-supplier and the company-customer samples

The results of this research on *communication willingness* are in line with the findings in (Fawcett *et al.*, 2007), which strongly support the critical role of a company's communication willingness in developing its external communication capability and realizing the potential benefits of information exchange for the company, and for its main customers and suppliers. Communication willingness here significantly contributes not only to communication quality, especially to knowledge of each other's requirements and expectations, but also to perceived communication benefits for a company, and for its main customers and main suppliers. This empirical evidence leads to a management implication: it is worthwhile for a company, and its main customers and suppliers, to jointly improve their own communication willingness, and that of their main business partners. As warned by Fawcett *et al.* (2007), those overlooking their own communication willingness or that of their partners, are likely to have problems with information quality and benefit less from chain communication.

Though *communication frequency* does not necessarily help to improve information quality, it is likely to improve the chain partners' knowledge of each other's requirements and expectations. The more frequently companies communicate with their main customers and main suppliers, the more likely they are to better understand each other's changing requirements and expectations; furthermore, with such improved knowledge of each other, the companies are likely to realize more potential benefits from the frequent communication. This empirical evidence leads to the second implication for practitioners: companies should encourage their staff to communicate frequently with their main customers and suppliers.

Adopting *senior managers* and *staff from different functions* to communicate with main customers and suppliers is likely to improve communication quality, especially information quality and help a company, as well as its main customers and main suppliers, to realize more potential benefits from the communication. These findings lead to the third management implication: it is valuable for a company to arrange for senior manager(s) and staff from different functions to communicate with its main customers and suppliers. In this way, the companies could improve the communication quality and realize more potential benefits from the communication.

Remarkably, media modernity appears to be associated with neither communication quality, nor perceived communication benefits. Even so, the respondent companies have reported comparatively high communication quality and have perceived high communication benefits. The likely explanation for these results are, on the one hand, that modern media is not yet widely used, as reflected by the relatively low mean of 'media modernity' (see Table 5.1 and 5.2); on the other hand, traditional communication tools, such as face-to-face contact and phone, are dominant in the chain. According to Media Richness Theory, traditional media are the richest medium in terms of resolving ambiguity, negotiating varying interpretations, and facilitating understanding. These findings of the present research alert us to the fact that there is still a long way to go for companies in the China poultry chain to improve their media modernity. This might also hold true for other chains in other developing and transitional countries. Meanwhile, these findings also lead to the fourth management implication that a company should not only depend on modern information media, but also focus on the use of traditional communication tools, even in this so-called information age.

Companies should build communication systems with diverse information tools. For those that can afford modern media, a multiple media strategy, which combines both traditional and modern media and fits the firm scale, product attributes, function attributes, and social-economic/cultural conditions, should be employed jointly. Those small companies that are unable to afford modern media immediately, should not necessarily lose confidence in their competitive advantage in this so-called information age. Instead, it might be a realistic and positive information competence strategy, to confidently endeavor to make full use of traditional information tools at hand, while constructively accumulating knowledge and skills relating to advanced information technology for future development.

Of particular interest is that both 'knowledge of each other's requirements and expectations' and 'information quality' are found to be positively as well as strongly associated with 'perceived communication benefits for companies in relationships with their main suppliers', and 'perceived communication benefits for companies in relationships with their main customers'. It was reported by Raghunathan (2001) that information sharing might have zero benefit if the supplier is able to retrieve demand information from the order history, and that only sharing information about unexpected events is beneficial. Thus, we suppose that knowledge of each other's changing requirements and expectations might be valuable as a potential enabler, providing a company with an opportunity to capitalize on unexpected events and create joint knowledge. Therefore, the fifth management implication is that to approach optimal communication benefits, chain partners should not only focus on the quality of regular information, but also endeavor to understand the changing demands, requirements, and expectations of their main customers and suppliers.

Confrontation between the company-supplier and the company-customer samples

The model results show that there are three major communication differences between the two samples. First, 'communication willingness' is positively and significantly associated with 'information quality' for a company in relationships with its most important suppliers, but not for a company in relationships with its most important customers, though the path coefficient is also positive. A likely explanation is that a company normally has more negotiating power than its suppliers, but has less negotiating power than its customers. Therefore, the willingness of a company is likely to have more influence on information quality with its suppliers, but less on information quality with its customers.

Second, 'multi-functional staff involvement' is positively and significantly associated with 'knowledge of each other's requirements and expectations' for a company in relationships with its main customers, but not for a company in relationships with its main suppliers. As discussed above, a likely reason is that supply activities are more complex than purchasing activities in the market-oriented economy. Thus, it makes sense for a company in relationships with its main customers to use top manager(s) and staff from different functions to communicate with its most important customers, in order to better understand the changing markets. Therefore, we summarize our finding as follows: multiple staff input, combining both senior managers and staff from different functions, is likely to help a company to better understand its main customers' requirements and expectations, and thus better understand the changing markets; but such staff arrangements might not necessarily help the company to learn more about its suppliers' requirements and expectations.

Third, it is shown that 'knowledge of each other's requirements and expectations' is positively and significantly associated with 'information quality' for a company in relationships with its main suppliers, but not for a company in relationships with its main customers, though the path coefficient is also positive. As discussed in Section 5.2.2, a likely explanation is that a company normally needs more complicated information on its customers and the markets than on its suppliers. However, as the proverb says, 'the more one learns, the less one knows'. When a company learns more about its customers' events, it might realize that the information communicated with the customers is not as adequate and precise as it could be. Thus, the company tends to make a conservative assessment about the information quality. Considering that this is the first study proposing 'knowledge of each other's requirements and expectations' as a new dimension of communication quality, and no other study has checked this construct before, it would be meaningful to further check its relationships with information quality in future research.

Conclusion

In conclusion, the most important findings are as follows:
1. Communication quality appears to be key to approach optimal communication benefits, for a company in relationships with its main suppliers and customers.

2. The results show that it is valuable to assess 'communication quality' using the two dimensions jointly, which are 'knowledge of each other's requirements and expectations' and 'information quality'.

3. In order to improve communication quality and approach optimal communication benefits, a company should invest in its own communication willingness, and that of its most important customers and its most important suppliers; should communicate more frequently; and should use senior managers and staff from different functions to communicate with its main customers and suppliers.

4. Modern media are not yet widely used in the Chinese poultry chain. They have not yet shown their full potential in improving communication quality, or in realizing potential communication benefits. Comparatively, traditional communication tools are dominant in the chain, as noticed by the researcher in the field study, and appear to have contributed to (the high means of) communication quality and perceived communication benefits. In the future, developing diverse information systems that combine both traditional and modern media, and both formal and informal communication, might be the right strategy for most companies.

5.3 Influence of company characteristics on communication between companies

5.3.1 Influence of company characteristics on communication between companies and their most important suppliers

In this section, to explore the influences of company characteristics on inter-organizational communication, five control variables have been added to each construct in the Communication Elements Model. These five control variables are: company size, company age, company type (sorted by function and market power), quality standard applied, and the administrative level of a location (see Section 3.4.2). Other parts and paths of the model remained the same as the model that is tested in Section 5.2. Following Chin (1998b), we ran bootstrapping with 500× resampling again.

The overall model explains about 40.4% of the variance of the endogenous latent variables. The results are shown in Table 5.5 and Appendix 5.3. It is shown that three out of the five control variables, including company size, company type, and the administrative level of a location, turn out to have certain significant effects on the *level* (namely, magnitude) of each aspect of communication between a company and its main suppliers. But, these five control variables do not necessarily change the significance of the *relationships* among communication elements that are presented in Section 5.2.1. The result of each hypothesis for the company-supplier sample remains the same after adding these control variables to the research model. Thus, the results presented in Figure 5.1 and Appendix 5.1 reflect the interrelationships among communication elements between a company and its most important suppliers with OR without taking into account company characteristics.

In general, *company size* has shown positive and significant effects on communication willingness, media modernity, multi-functional staff involvement, information quality, and perceived communication benefits for the companies, and perceived communication benefits for their main suppliers. When a company is larger, the company and its main suppliers are more willing to communicate with each other. They prefer to make use of more advanced tools, senior managers, and staff from different functions for the communication. And the communication is likely to realize more benefits for the company and for

Table 5.5. The significant influences of company characteristics on communication for the company-supplier sample.

	Path coefficient significant?[1]	Sign of coefficient
CV$_1$: Firm size → Communication willingness	**Yes***	+
CV$_1$: Firm size → Media modernity	Yes*	+
CV$_1$: Firm size → Multi-functional staff involvement	Yes**	+
CV$_1$: Firm size → Information quality	Yes*	-
CV$_1$: Firm size → Perceived communication benefits for the companies	Yes*	+
CV$_1$: Firm size → Perceived communication benefits for suppliers	Yes*	+
CV$_3$: Firm type → multi-functional staff involvement	**Yes***	-
CV$_5$: Administrative level of the location → Media modernity	Yes*	-
CV$_5$: Administrative level of the location → Multi-functional staff involvement	Yes**	-

[1] The same significant paths for both the company-supplier and the company-customer samples (see Table 5.6) are shown in **bold** and *italics*.
* Significant at 5%; ** significant at 1% level.

its main suppliers. However, it is noteworthy that when a company is larger, the quality of information communicated between it and its main suppliers is likely to be lower. A likely explanation is that, a manager in a larger company normally focuses on specific rather than different functions. He or she may not necessarily be fully aware of activities and information involved with other functions, and therefore tends to make a conservative assessment about information quality. This is worth examining further in future research.

Company type is shown to be negatively and significantly associated with multi-functional staff involvement. A company with trading as a main activity, which is closer to the customers, and has higher market power, such as a supermarket or a trader, is likely to make use of non-senior manager(s) and staff from a single function to communicate with its main suppliers. Conversely, a company with production as a main activity, which is farther from end consumers, and has lower market power, such as a processor or a commercial farm, prefers to adopt senior manager(s) and staff from different functions to communicate with its main suppliers. Recalling the researcher's experience in the field research, some managers in trading companies professed that they had work experience in different sections of their companies, and were aware of both purchasing and marketing activities of the companies. So, a manager in one section is likely to be aware of the activities and requirements of other sections of the trading company. This might partly explain why trading companies adopted fewer senior managers and fewer staff from different functions to communicate with their suppliers, compared to production companies. Conversely, because of the higher complexity involved in the production function, it might be helpful for a production company to invest senior managers and staff from different functions in the communication with its main suppliers.

In contrast to our expectations, *the administrative level of a location* has shown negative and significant effects on media modernity and multi-functional staff involvement. To communicate with its main suppliers, a company located in a smaller city prefers to employ more advanced communication tools and to make use of senior managers and staff from different functions, whilst a company located in a larger city is likely to make use of less advanced media, non-senior managers, and staff from a single function to communicate with its main suppliers. A likely explanation is that most production companies, such as commercial farms and processors, are located in small towns to medium-sized cities, partly because of low land prices and their potential obstacle to environment quality. Comparatively, these production companies, especially the large ones, are likely to make use of modern media that match the complexity of production functions. Conversely, most trade companies are located in medium-sized to large cities, which are important end markets. Comparatively, trading companies are small to medium-sized. Most of them use phone, fax, and e-mail to facilitate their transactions, and cannot really afford more advanced media. In addition, trading functions are less complex than production functions. Therefore, trading companies have relatively less needs of modern tools to communicate with their suppliers. The negative (though, non-significant) relationships between company type and media modernity appears to be proof of this explanation. It would be valuable to examine the potential influence of the administrative level of a location on inter-organizational communication further in future research.

It is noteworthy that company age and quality standard here do not appear to necessarily affect any of these communication aspects. In addition, communication frequency and knowledge of each other's requirements and expectations do not appear to be necessarily influenced by any of these five company characteristics.

5.3.2 Influence of company characteristics on communication between companies and their most important customers

To explore the influences of company characteristics on communication between a company and its main customers, the five control variables are again added to each construct in the Communication Elements Model. Other parts and paths of the model remained the same as the Communication Elements Model that is tested in Section 5.2.

The overall model explains about 46.3% of the variance of the endogenous latent variables. The results are presented in Table 5.6 and Appendix 5.4. It is shown that three out of the five control variables (company size, company type, and quality standard) turn out to have certain significant effects on the *level* (namely, magnitude) of each aspect of communication between a company and its main customers. Again, these five control variables do not change the significance of the *relationships* among communication elements that are presented in Section 5.2.2. The result of each hypothesis for the company-customer sample remains as the same after adding these control variables to the research model. Thus, the results presented in Figure 5.2 and Appendix 5.2 reflect the interrelationships among communication elements between a company and its most important customers with OR without taking into account company characteristics.

Comparing the results of the company-supplier and the company-customer samples, it is shown that the size of a company seems to have more influence on the communication of the company with its main suppliers, than with its main customers. *Company size* here shows a positive and significant effect on communication willingness, but not on other communication elements as shown in the company-

Table 5.6. The significant *influences of company characteristics on communication for the company-customer sample.*

	Path coefficient significant?[1]	Sign of coefficient
CV$_1$: Firm size → Communication willingness	**Yes****	+
CV$_3$: Firm type → Multi-functional staff involvement	**Yes****	-
CV$_4$: Quality standard → Media modernity	Yes**	+
CV$_4$: Quality standard → Knowledge of each other's requirements and expectations	Yes*	+
CV$_4$: Quality standard → Perceived communication benefits for the companies	Yes*	-

[1] The same significant paths for both the company-supplier (see Table 5.5) and the company-customer samples are shown in **bold** and *italics*.
* Significant at 5%; ** significant at 1% level.

supplier sample. Combined with the results of the two samples, it can be summarized as follows: (1) for the communication between a company and its main *suppliers*, when the company is larger, it is likely to be more willing to communicate with its main suppliers; it prefers to make use of advanced tools (rather than traditional media), senior manager(s), and staff from different functions (rather than a single function) to communicate with the suppliers; it tends to believe that it benefits more, and tends to suppose the suppliers also benefit more from the mutual communication; but it appears to have a conservative assessment of the information quality, and tends to believe the information quality is less high, compared to the assessment of a smaller company. However, (2) for the communication between a company and its main *customers*, the size of the company appears to have no influence on other aspects of the communication, except the positive influence on communication willingness. A potential reason for these differences is that a company in relationships with its *suppliers* normally has higher market power, and is in a comparatively more powerful position than its suppliers; but a company in relationships with its *customers* normally has lower market power, and is in a less powerful position than its main customers.

Again, *company type* shows a negative and significant effect on multi-functional staff involvement. Thus, comparing the results of the two samples, we can summarize that the type of a company here has shown a similar influence on the communication of a company with its main suppliers, and with its main customers. A company with trading as a main activity, and which has more market power, such as a supermarket or a trader, is likely to make use of non-senior manager(s) and staff from a single function (rather than different functions) to communicate with its main suppliers and customers. One reason might be that a manager in a trading company, as the researcher noticed in the field research, often has work experience in different sections, and is therefore aware of activities and requirements of other sections of the company. So it is less important for a trading company to employ senior manager(s) and staff from different functions to communicate with its main customers and suppliers. Conversely, a company with production as a main activity, which is farther from its end customers and has less market power, such as a processor or a commercial farm, prefers to employ senior manager(s) and staff from different functions to communicate with its main suppliers and customers. A likely reason is the complexity of the production process. Because of the production complexity, in order to meet the requirements of its main customers and complete transactions with them, and in order to make sure its suppliers meet its requirements, it is more necessary for a production company, which is farther from its end customers, to employ senior manager(s) and staff from different functions to communicate with its main customers and suppliers. In this way, the different function sections of a production company could obtain relevant information and make use of the information for their specific functions.

In contrast to the results for the company-supplier sample, *quality standards* here have shown some influence on the communication between a company and its main customers. When a company adopts a higher level of quality standard, it is likely to employ more advanced tools (rather than traditional media) to communicate with its main customers, and the company and its main customers are likely to better understand each other's requirements and expectations. However, the company tends to believe it benefits less from the communication with its main customers. This result is in line with the finding in (Han, 2009). Han recently studied the Chinese pork processors, and reported that customer quality management of the pork processors is not positively linked to company performance.

A food company employing a higher quality standard often has higher or special requirements for quality control, and such quality control is often combined with special delivery control in food industry. To meet the requirements of a higher quality standard, extra investments in facilities and operations, such as cold chain facilities and specific sanitary operations, are often needed. A company often has more negotiating power over its suppliers than over its customers. Comparatively, it is less difficult for a company to persuade its main suppliers to make the necessary adjustments and comply with its logistics and quality requirements, but more difficult to make its main customers do so. Thus, the company is less likely to be satisfied with the operations supported by the communication with its customers. The increased quality requirements of a company and its lower negotiating power compared to that of its main customers might explain the negative relationship between the quality standard of a company and its scores on the perceived benefits of the communication with its main customers.

Nowadays, many quality standards are focused on the production stage (such as commercial farms and processors) rather than on trading stage. However, there are still many nodes in the trading stage of food chains, such as logistics and retailing nodes, which are in shortage of specific and valid quality standards. In addition, as noticed by the researcher in the field research, even some well-known international retailers do not pay as much attention to quality management in their new Chinese markets, as they do in the West. The evidence includes the increasing number of news reports on complaints from and conflicts with their suppliers and consumers, and the rising number of scandals on exactions on suppliers, poor quality products mixed with normal products, as well as price gouging on consumers. Recently, two top international supermarkets' 19 stores in China were fined 9.5 million Chinese Yuan for price gouging[14]. Therefore, it might be useful to create a suitable policy in support of setting quality standards that focus on food retailers, especially those in developing and transitional countries. In the face of very powerful retailers, production companies and logistics companies are likely to comply with the (increased) quality requirements of the retailers; thus, with the application of quality standards

---

[14] 'Carrefour and Wal-mart's parts of stores were severely punished for price fraud', news report issued on http://www.ndrc.gov.cn/xwfb/t20110222_396220.htm on 22-02-2011.

throughout the whole chain instead of only in the production parts of the chain, there would be a serious reduction in resistance to quality control among chain partners.

In contrast to the results for the company-supplier sample, *the administrative level of a location* does not show a significant effect on the communication between a company and its main customers. Thus, while the location of a company is likely to negatively influence media modernity and multi-functional staff involvement in the communication between the company and its main *suppliers*, it does not necessarily influence the communication between the company and its main customers. We fail to find similar findings or relevant argument in the literature. It would be valuable to examine this with other product chains in different contexts in future research.

Similar to the results for the company-supplier sample, company age again does not show a significant influence on communication willingness, communication behavior, communication quality, and perceived communication benefits. In general, we summarize that: company age does not necessarily influence the communication between a company and its main customers and suppliers.

Again, none of these control variables has shown a significant influence on *communication frequency*. Thus, we summarize that: the characteristics of a company do not necessarily influence the company's communication frequency with its main customers and suppliers.

In contrast to the results for the company-supplier sample, none of these control variables has shown an influence on *information quality*. Thus, the quality of information communicated between a company and its main *customers* is not necessarily affected by company characteristics in general, though the quality of information communicated between a company and main *suppliers* is likely to be negatively affected by the size of the company. According to the literature, beyond a certain size, a company has less control over the operation of each of its functions. This might explain the negative relationship between company size and information quality.

5.3.3 Influence of company characteristics on inter-organizational communication: similarity and confrontation of the company-supplier and the company-customer samples

In general, a company's characteristics are likely to influence the level of each aspect of its communication with main customers and suppliers, in one way or the other. It appears that certain characteristics, such as size and location, might have more influence on the level of its communication with main *suppliers*, whilst others, such as quality standard, might have more influence on the level of its communication with main *customers*. Table 5.7 summarizes the relationships between the characteristics of a company and the level of its communication with its main customers and suppliers.

Comparing the empirical results for the two samples presented in Section 5.3.1 and 5.3.2, and Table 5.7, we can summarize the main findings as follows:
1. The *size of a company* appears to have more effect on the communication of the company with its main suppliers, than with its main customers. A likely reason is that a company normally has more negotiating power over its suppliers, but less negotiating power over its customers. Therefore, the size of the company is likely to have more influence on its communication with its suppliers, than with its customers.

Table 5.7. Influence of company characteristics on communication for the company-supplier sample and the company-customer sample[1,2].

	Companies with suppliers				Companies with customers			
	Size	Type	Quality	Location	Size	Type	Quality	Location
Communication willingness	+				+			
Media modernity	+			-			+	
Communication frequency						-		
Multi-functional staff involvement	+	-		-				
Knowledge of each other's requirements and expectations							+	
Information quality	-							
Perceived communication benefits for the companies	+							-
Perceived communication benefits for customers	n.a.[3]	n.a.	n.a.	n.a.				
Perceived communication benefits for suppliers	+				n.a.	n.a.	n.a.	n.a.

[1] The five company characteristics examined are: company size, company age, company type, quality standard applied, and the administrative level of a location. Specifically, company type: 0 = production firms with lower market power; 1 = trading firms with higher market power. Administrative level of a location: 1 = town or county; 2 = medium-sized city; 3 = national or provincial capital city.
[2] Firm age does not necessarily affect any aspect of communication.
[3] n.a. = not applicable.

2. The *business age of a company* does not necessarily affect the communication of the company with its main customers and suppliers, in terms of communication willingness, communication behavior, communication quality, and perceived communication benefits. Companies with a longer business history are not necessarily distinct from companies with a shorter business history in communication with their main customers, and with their main suppliers.
3. *Company type* has shown similar influence on staff arrangements regarding the communication of a company with its main suppliers and customers. A company with trading as its main activity and with more market power, such as a supermarket or a trader, is likely to make use of non-senior manager(s) and staff from a single function to communicate with its main suppliers and customers. Conversely, a company with production as its main function and with less market power, such as a commercial farm or a processor, is likely to adopt senior manager(s) and staff from different functions for the communication with its main suppliers and customers. This difference might be explained by the comparatively more complex nature of production activities than trading activities. Company type does not necessarily affect other communication aspects of the company with its main customers, and with its main suppliers.
4. The level of *quality standard* adopted by a company does not necessarily affect its communication with main suppliers, but is likely to affect its communication with main customers, in terms of

media modernity, knowledge of each other's requirements and expectations, and perceived communication benefits for the companies. The negative association between the quality standard adopted by a supplier and communication benefits obtained by the supplier could be explained by the increased prices and costs resulted from a higher quality standard, and its lower negotiating power as a supplier, compared to its main customers.

5. *The administrative level of the location* of a company is likely to affect its communication with main suppliers, but does not necessarily affect its communication with main customers. A company located in a smaller city is likely to make use of more advanced media (rather than traditional media), senior manager(s), and staff from different functions (rather than a single function) to communicate with its main suppliers. A likely explanation is that, most production companies are located in small towns or medium-sized cities, because of lower land prices and their potential obstacle to environment quality. Conversely, most trading companies are located in medium-sized or large cities that are important end markets. Comparatively, there is more complexity involved in production functions, especially those of large production companies; whereas the trading function is far less complex. Thus, large production companies tend to invest in modern tools, whereas trading companies tend to take use of traditional or moderately advanced tools, to communicate with their suppliers.

6. All of the above five characteristics of a company do not necessarily influence how frequently it communicates with main customers and main suppliers.

Based on these findings, we can further conclude in general that: (1) firm characteristics are likely to influence, in one way or the other, the level (namely, magnitude) of the communication of a company with its main customers and suppliers, in terms of communication willingness, communication behavior, communication quality, and perceived communication benefits. However, there are the following exceptions. Specifically, (2) company age does not necessarily influence the level of communication of a company with its main customers and suppliers; and (3) all company characteristics do not necessarily influence how frequently a company communicates with its main customers and suppliers. Meanwhile, the most important finding is that, (4) all of the above company characteristics do not necessarily influence the interrelationships among the communication elements. Therefore, we can conclude that the results of the hypothesized relationships on inter-organizational communication, which are presented in Table 5.3 and 5.4, are likely to be tenable for different companies with different characteristics.

5.4 Concluding remarks

This chapter attempted to answer Research Question B by revealing the interrelationships among important aspects of a company's communication with its main customers and its main suppliers. It displayed empirical results about baseline statistics and the Communication Elements Model that is proposed in this research.

First, this chapter presented the results of baseline statistics. The similar average scores for each item showed that the respondent companies from different stages of the chain reported similar opinions and activities regarding their communication with their main customers and their main suppliers, in terms of communication willingness, communication behavior, communication quality, and perceived communication benefits. Of particular interest, they tend to believe that their communication with main *suppliers* has led to high and almost equal (!) benefits for themselves and for their main suppliers; and their communication with main *customers* has led to high and almost equal (!) benefits for themselves and for their main customers. In addition, the correlation coefficients showed that the constructs are well correlated with several or even all of the other constructs as expected. This not only provides evidence for the nomological validity of these constructs, but also further proof of the above finding that the communication of a company with its main suppliers is likely to benefit the company and the suppliers; and the communication of a company with its main customers is likely to benefit the company and the customers. These empirical findings are valuable in response to a commonly debated conundrum, namely 'to what extent a company should invest in inter-organizational information exchange, compared to its chain partners.'

Subsequently, this chapter displayed the results of partial least squares (PLS) modeling of the Communication Elements Model, for the companies in relationships with their main suppliers and for the companies in relationships with their main customers, respectively. The Communication Elements Model was composed of four main parts: communication willingness, communication behavior, communication quality, and perceived communication benefits. This model can be used to understand, examine, assess, and improve the communication of a company with its main customers and suppliers in the real world. Previous studies often take inter-organizational communication (IOC) as an aspect of a broad concept, or only typically examined limited aspects of IOC. However, IOC itself is a broad issue covering diverse aspects. The interrelationships between different aspects of IOC have remained more or less like a 'black box'. We are aware that this is the first empirical study to examine the diverse 'inside figure' of IOC in a Chinese food chain.

In addition, this research proposed and empirically checked for the first time the three constructs: 'knowledge of each other's requirements and expectations', 'perceived communication benefits for companies in relationships with their suppliers' and 'perceived communication benefits for companies in relationships with their customers'. With the first construct, we drew attention to the need to measure communication quality by using multiple dimensions, rather than the typically used one dimension of 'information quality'. Specifically, the results of this research suggest that it is better to measure communication quality by using knowledge of (the often changing) requirements and expectations of business partners', and 'the quality of regular information' jointly. With the latter two constructs, this research aimed to examine the direct benefit of communication (for problem resolution and quality control, and so on), rather than the indirect and further benefits of communication (e.g. profitability and competitive age) as previous studies have normally done; it also tried to distinguish such communication benefits for customers and for suppliers, rather than for only customers or suppliers as most previous studies have done.

In conclusion, the most important findings are as follows:
1. Communication quality is key to approach optimal communication benefits for a company, its main suppliers and customers.
2. It is valuable to assess communication quality by the two dimensions jointly: 'knowledge of each other's requirements and expectations' and 'information quality'. Knowledge about the (changing) requirements and expectations of business partners here has proved to be at least as important as the quality of (regular) information.
3. In order to improve communication quality and to realize potential communication benefits, a company should invest in its own communication willingness, and that of its main customers and

its main suppliers; should communicate frequently; and should make use of senior manager(s) and staff from different functions to communicate with its main customers and suppliers.

4. Modern media are not widely used in the Chinese poultry chain. They have not yet shown their full potential in improving communication quality and realizing potential communication benefits. However, the respondent companies still score highly on communication quality, and reported that they perceived high communication benefits. These might reflect the high value of traditional communication media, such as face-to-face contact and phone, in improving communication quality and realizing communication benefits. For those companies that can afford modern information facilities, it would make sense to build diverse information systems combining both modern and traditional communication media. Companies should pay attention not only to setting up and making use of modern information facilities, but also to the value of traditional communication tools and informal communication.

Finally, this chapter examined the potential influence of company characteristics on communication between chain partners. The results showed that company characteristics tend to influence the level (namely, magnitude) of each aspect of the communication of a company with its main suppliers, and with its main customers. However, company characteristics do not necessarily impact the interrelationships of communication willingness and behavior, communication quality, and perceived communication benefits. Therefore, their interrelationships revealed in this research are likely to be tenable for different companies with different characteristics. We fail to find similar studies in the literature. As such, this research extends the scientific research regarding relationships between company characteristics and the communication between chain partners. Meanwhile, this research provides a nice initiation of the discussion on 'why some company characteristics have influences on the level of some communication aspects, while others have not'.

Chapter 6

Influence of Inter-Organizational Communication on performance

This chapter is concerned with the relationships between inter-organizational communication, supply chain compliance, and company performance. It aims to answer Research Question C: '*what is the potential influence of inter-organizational communication on company performance?*'. Section 6.1 displays the baseline statistics and is followed by Section 6.2 that reports the outcomes of the estimated Communication-Chain compliance-Performance Models, for companies in relationships with their most important suppliers, and with their most important customers, respectively. Section 6.3 discusses the influences of company characteristics on supply chain compliance and company performance. In addition, Section 6.2 and 6.3 make general suggestions for future research. The chapter ends with concluding remarks in Section 6.4.

6.1 Baseline statistics

This section presents the baseline description of constructs, including perceived communication benefits for companies in relationships with their suppliers, perceived communication benefits for companies in relationships with their customers, logistics compliance, quality compliance, satisfaction, efficiency, and profit & competitive edge. The unweighted score of each construct has been calculated with the related manifest indicators. The means, standard deviations, and correlation coefficients have been calculated and shown for the companies in relationships with their most important suppliers (the company-supplier sample), and with their most important customers (the company-customer sample), respectively, in Table 6.1 and 6.2.

Recalling that the observed indicators of perceived communication benefits and of supply chain compliance are measured using a 5-point Likert scale, ranging between 1 for 'not agree at all' and 5 for 'totally agree', a mean above 3 indicates that the respondents agree with the relevant statements.

Table 6.1. Construct mean, standard deviations (S.D.) and correlation matrix[1] for the company-supplier sample (N=165).

Constructs	Mean	S.D.	1	2	3	4	5	6
1. Perceived communication benefits for companies	4.08	0.70						
2. Perceived communication benefits for suppliers	4.18	0.67	**0.77**					
3. Logistics compliance	4.30	0.65	**0.32**	**0.36**				
4. Quality compliance	*4.17*	0.63	**0.43**	**0.51**	**0.54**			
5. Satisfaction	5.93	0.91	**0.33**	**0.40**	**0.40**	**0.62**		
6. Efficiency	5.44	1.23	**0.46**	**0.57**	**0.33**	**0.50**	**0.54**	
7. Profit & competitive edge	5.42	1.23	**0.35**	**0.38**	**0.34**	**0.43**	**0.50**	**0.60**

[1] In this correlation matrix, the mean of quality compliance (**bold** and *italics*) is significantly different from that of the company-customer sample; correlation coefficients (**bold**) are all significant at 1% level.

Table 6.2. Construct mean, standard deviations (S.D.) and correlation matrix[1] for the company-customer sample (N=96).

Constructs	Mean	S.D.	1	2	3	4	5	6
1. Perceived communication benefits for customers	4.18	0.71						
2. Perceived communication benefits for the companies	4.16	0.59	**0.71**					
3. Logistics compliance	4.57	0.49	**0.32**	**0.39**				
4. Quality compliance	**4.46**	0.56	**0.47**	**0.49**	**0.66**			
5. Satisfaction	5.96	0.82	**0.30**	**0.42**	**0.34**	**0.41**		
6. Efficiency	5.50	1.27	**0.53**	**0.46**	*0.18*	**0.33**	**0.46**	
7. Competitive edge	5.43	1.23	**0.28**	**0.28**	**0.28**	**0.46**	**0.49**	**0.56**

[1] In this correlation matrix, the mean of quality compliance (**bold** and *italics*) is significantly different from that with the company-supplier sample; correlation coefficients with a value of at least 0.28 (**bold**) are significant at 1%; the non-significant coefficient at 5% level is shown in *italics*.

Meanwhile, the observed indicators of company performance are measured using a 7-point Likert scale, ranging between 1 for 'not agree at all' and 7 for 'totally agree', thus a mean above 4 for company performance indicates that the respondents agree with the relevant statements.

The results in Table 6.1 and 6.2 show that all of the constructs in this research have a positive response (agreements) with the statements. For both the company-supplier and the company-customer samples, the means for 'perceived communication benefits' and 'supply chain compliance' are above 4, and the means for 'company performance' are above 5. In addition, the respondent companies of the two samples have reported similar scores for most of the constructs except for 'quality compliance'. And the standard deviations (0.56 ~ 0.82) are relatively low, except for 'efficiency' and 'profit & competitive edge'. These results seem to reflect that the surveyed companies have similar opinions concerning perceived communication benefits for themselves, perceive communication benefits for their suppliers and customers, logistics compliance, and satisfaction. Thus, we can summarize that in general:

1. The respondent companies tended to believe that the communication with their most important *suppliers* had produced high and almost equal benefits for themselves and for their main suppliers. Meanwhile, they tended to believe that the communication with their most important *customers* had also produced high and almost equal benefits for themselves and for their main customers. These benefits obtained from communication had supported them in different aspects, including problem resolution, quality control, delivery, and pricing decisions. As discussed in Section 5.1 and 5.4, these results seem to prove that it might be advantageous for both a company and its main customers, and both a company and its main suppliers, to invest heavily, and more or less equally, in information exchange with each other.
2. The respondent companies were of the opinion that their main suppliers had complied well with their logistics and quality requirements. Meanwhile, the respondent companies tended to believe that they themselves had also complied well with their customers' logistics and quality requirements.
3. Companies in the chain were satisfied with their performance, compared to their main competitors in the last twelve years. Specifically, they were satisfied with the product quality of, and the prices paid to, their suppliers. They had paid less money and had taken less time, thus they had realized

higher (external) efficiency in the transactions with their main suppliers and customers. Further, they tended to believe that they had achieved better performance, compared to their main competitors in the last twelve months, in terms of profitability, sales growth rate, and overall competitive edge.

Of particular interest is that, the company-supplier sample has scored significantly lower than the company-customer sample for suppliers' compliance with customers' quality requirements. This might reflect that, although the companies have complied well with customers' quality requirements in general, they do not comply as well as their customers think they should have. This finding is a valuable warning for companies in the Chinese poultry chain to pay more attention to improving their chain quality compliance, and to make sure that they meet their customers' quality requirements and expectations.

It is noteworthy that the standard deviations for '*efficiency*' (1.2 ~ 1.3) and '*profitability & competitive edge*' (1.1 ~1.2) were relatively high compared to those of other constructs. This might indicate that the companies in the chain have achieved discordant performance in terms of efficiency, profitability, and competitive edge. Some companies suffer worse performance, whilst others have perceived better efficiency, profitability, and competitive edge than their main competitors in the last twelve months. We suppose that the comparatively high standard deviations for 'efficiency' and 'profit & competitive edge' might be the result of diverse company characteristics. In other words, it might reflect that different companies with different characters in the chain may achieve different levels of performance in terms of efficiency, profitability, and competitive edge. This is further examined and discussed in Section 6.3, when company characteristics are added as control variables to the research model.

The *correlation* matrices in Table 6.1 and 6.2 show strong correlations between the majorities of the constructs, as expected. These results appear to reflect that, in general: (1) The benefits obtained by a company from the communication with its main customers are likely to help the company comply better with its customers' logistics and quality requirements. (2) A company's compliance with its main customers' quality requirements contributes to better performance for the company and for its main customers. (3) The communication benefits obtained by a company are likely to contribute to higher performance for itself, its main customers, and its main suppliers. These correlation results, which correspond to the mean results shown above, seem to prove once more that it might be advantageous for both a company and its main customers, and both a company and its main suppliers, to invest more or less equally in information exchange with each other.

It is noteworthy that, though 'logistics compliance' is correlated with 'efficiency' for the company-supplier sample, this is not the case for the company-customer sample. This might imply that, when a company's main suppliers comply better with its delivery requirements, the company is likely to achieve higher external efficiency, but the suppliers themselves may not necessarily achieve improved efficiency.

We also checked the possible multicollinearity problem for these constructs. A cut-off of 0.80 is commonly used for correlations among variables for dismissing multicollinearity problems (Hair *et al.*, 1998; Malhotra *et al.*, 1999). All the correlation coefficients here are below 0.8. Therefore, the individual magnitude of the correlations between the constructs does not suggest obvious problems of pairwise collinearity. This proves the discriminant validity of the constructs. Thus, we can employ all of these listed constructs in one model.

6.2 Performance results of inter-organizational communication

6.2.1 Results of the Communication-Chain compliance-Performance Model for the company-supplier sample

The results of partial least squares (PLS) modeling of the Communication-Chain compliance-Performance Model for companies in relationships with their most important suppliers are presented in Figure 6.1 and Table 6.3. The values of R square in this model range as 0.14 for 'logistics compliance', 0.28 for 'quality compliance', 0.39 for 'satisfaction', 0.27 for 'efficiency', and 0.21 for 'profit & competitive edge'. The overall model explains about 25.7% of the variance of the endogenous latent variables, which indicates that a satisfactory model fit is obtained for companies in relationships with their most important suppliers (the company-supplier sample).

Figure 6.1 shows the significant relationships between perceived communication benefits, supply chain compliance, and company performance, based on PLS path modeling results of the company-supplier sample.

It is shown that 'perceived communication benefits for *the companies*' and 'perceived communication benefits for *suppliers*', appear to have different impacts on supply chain compliance. Communication benefits obtained by the respondent companies were not significantly associated with their suppliers' compliance with their requirements. But communication benefits obtained by their *suppliers* were positively and significantly associated with the suppliers' compliance with their logistics and quality requirements. These results reflect the fact that when a company communicates with its main suppliers, the benefits obtained by its suppliers are likely to help these suppliers to comply well with its logistics and quality requirements. Thus, it leads to a valuable finding, i.e. that it makes sense for a company that

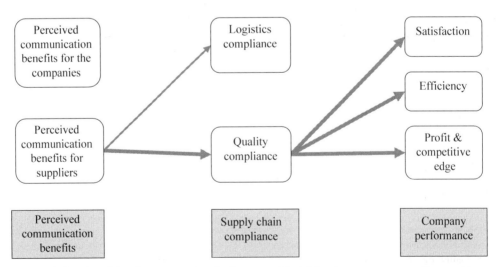

Figure 6.1. Results of the Communication-Performance Model for the company-supplier sample.
▬▬▬: Path coefficient is significant at P<0.01;
─────: Path coefficient is significant at P<0.05.

intends to improve its suppliers' compliance with its requirements, to help its main suppliers (!) to really benefit from the information exchange.

Appendix 6.1 presents path coefficients, total effects, and *t*-values of PLS modeling of the Communication-Chain compliance-Performance Model shown in Figure 6.1. The results of *total effects* show that, communication benefits obtained by the companies are not significantly associated with company performance of the companies, whereas communication benefits obtained by their main suppliers are positively and significantly associated with company performance of the companies. This might reflect the fact that when a company communicates with its main suppliers, the benefits obtained by the company do not necessarily help this company stand out from its main competitors. However, the benefits obtained by its main suppliers are likely to make the company stand out from its main competitors. These results are in line with the above results, which provide noteworthy proof that it appears to be advantageous for a company to invest in helping its main suppliers (!) to benefit from the information exchange.

When looking at the relationships between *'supply chain compliance'* and *'company performance'*, we can see that logistics compliance is not significantly associated with company performance, but quality compliance is positively and strongly associated with each aspect of company performance. This might reflect the fact that for a company in relationships with its main suppliers, (1) its main suppliers' compliance with its *logistics* requirements do not necessarily help to improve its performance ultimately; (2) however, its main suppliers' compliance with its *quality* requirements is likely to improve each aspect of its performance, in terms of customer satisfaction, external efficiency, profitability, and overall competitive edge. In other words, it is the main suppliers' quality compliance in quality control, rather than logistics compliance, that helps a company stand out from its main competitors.

Thus, based on the above findings, we may conclude that, to improve and approach optimal company performance, a company should communicate well with its main suppliers, and invest in helping these suppliers really benefit from the communication for operations such as problem resolution, quality control, delivery control, and pricing decisions. Such benefits obtained by the suppliers are likely to help them comply better with the company's logistics and quality requirements, and help to improve the company's performance ultimately. It is noteworthy that it is the benefits obtained by its suppliers (rather than by the company itself), and it is the suppliers' compliance with quality control (rather than with logistics operations), that make the company stand out from its main competitor, in terms of each aspect of performance.

Table 6.3 summarizes the hypothesized relationships and results of the Communication-Chain compliance-Performance Model for the company-supplier sample. The two hypothesized relationships are partly significant at 5% or 1% level, and the path coefficients are all positive as expected.

6.2.2 Results of the Communication-Chain compliance-Performance Model for the company-customer sample

The results of the Communication-Chain compliance-Performance Model for companies in relationships with their most important customers are presented in Figure 6.2 and Table 6.4. The values of R square in this model range as 0.17 for 'logistics compliance', 0.32 for 'quality compliance', 0.20 for 'satisfaction', 0.12 for 'efficiency', and 0.24 for 'profit & competitive edge'. The overall model explains

Table 6.3. Results of hypotheses of the Communication-Chain compliance-Performance Model for the company-supplier sample.

		Path coefficient significant?	Sign of coefficient as expected?	Hypothesis
H$_{iiiA}$	The level of perceived communication benefits is positively associated with the level of supply chain compliance.	Yes	Yes	Supported
H$_{iiiB}$	The level of supply chain compliance is positively associated with the level of company performance.	Yes (with quality compliance)	Yes	Supported (with quality compliance)

The hypotheses have been proposed in Section 2.6.

about 20.9% of the variance of the endogenous latent variables, which indicates that a satisfactory model fit is obtained for companies in relationships with their most important customers (the company-customer sample).

Figure 6.2 shows the significant relationships between perceived communication benefits, supply chain compliance, and company performance, based on PLS path modeling results of the company-customer sample.

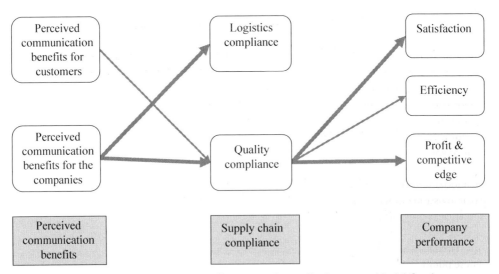

Figure 6.2. Results of the Communication-Chain compliance-Performance Model for the company-customer sample.
━━━: *Path coefficient is significant at P<0.01;*
────: *Path coefficient is significant at P<0.05.*

It is shown that, 'perceived communication benefits for *customers*' and 'perceived communication benefits for *the companies*' appear to have different impacts on supply chain compliance. On the one hand, communication benefits obtained by *customers* of the respondent companies are not significantly associated with these companies' *logistics* compliance, but are positively and significantly associated with these companies' *quality* compliance. On the other hand, communication benefits obtained by these respondent companies are again positively and significantly associated with their own logistics compliance and quality compliance. This reflects the fact that when a company communicates with its main customers, the communication benefits obtained by its customers do not necessarily help the company to comply well with the customers' *logistics* requirements, however, they are likely to help the company to comply well with the customers' *quality* requirements. Meanwhile, the communication benefits obtained by the company itself are likely to help it to comply better with the customers' logistics and quality requirements. Thus, these results lead to a valuable finding, i.e. that it makes sense for a company that intends to improve its compliance with customers' requirements, to ensure that not only itself, but also its main customers (!) really benefit from the information exchange.

Appendix 6.2 presents path coefficients, total effects, and *t*-values of PLS modeling of the Communication-Chain compliance-Performance Model shown in Figure 6.2. The results of *total effects* show that communication benefits obtained by *customers* of the respondent companies are positively and significantly associated with these companies' performance in terms of profitability and competitive edge. Meanwhile, communication benefits obtained by these respondent companies are also positively and significantly associated with these companies' performance, in terms of satisfaction, profitability, and competitive edge.

Thus, it provides valuable proof that it makes sense for a company to ensure that not only itself, but also its main customers (!), truly benefit from the information exchange. The reason is that the communication benefits obtained by its main customers are likely to improve its supply chain compliance, especially its quality compliance, and ultimately help it stand out from its main competitors.

Thus, combining the empirical results of the company-supplier and the company-customer samples, we summarize a valuable finding as follows: *regarding information exchange of a company with its main customers and suppliers, helping others is a kind of self-help. A company should commit to making sure that not only itself, but also its main suppliers and customers, truly realize the potential benefits of information exchange.* In this way, communication benefits obtained by the main suppliers and customers of a company are likely to help the company to improve supply chain compliance, and furthermore, achieve a performance that stands out from its main competitors.

When looking at the relationships between *supply chain compliance* and *company performance*, we can see that logistics compliance is again not significantly associated with company performance, but quality compliance is again positively and significantly associated with each aspect of company performance. There are two likely explanations for these results. One is that there is still limited implementation of logistics compliance, and the practice of supply chain management is still in its early stage in the Chinese poultry chain. Another likely explanation is that, although a company's logistics compliance helps a company to achieve a certain level of performance, it does not necessarily make it stand out from its main competitors. Instead, it is a company's compliance with the quality requirements of its main customers that leads to the major difference in the company's performance, and distinguishes it from its main competitors.

It is noteworthy that, although the practices of logistics compliance did not yet appear to show its potential impact on company performance, the respondent companies had scored highly on their suppliers' logistics compliance (mean = 4.3, S.D. = 0.7) or on their own logistics compliance (mean = 4.6, S.D. = 0.5). This might imply that, on the one hand, these managers tend to believe that logistics compliance is critical for a company; on the other hand, they have limited knowledge on and experience in logistics management, and do not really know what is logistics compliance. Thus, to realize the potential values and to approach the optimal benefits of logistics management, the first and most urgent step for most managers in the Chinese poultry chain might be to broaden their knowledge of logistics management, as well as gain experience in logistics practices.

By examining some recent relevant studies in the Chinese context, these findings of the present research are shown to be in line with the findings of Han (2009), but in conflict with the findings of Lu (2007). Han (2009) studied the pork processing industry in China, and found that quality management practices are likely to improve company performance, whereas integrated logistics management does not. Conversely, Lu (2007) studied the Chinese vegetable chain, and found that vegetable companies' compliance with customers' delivery requirements appears to contribute to quality, price satisfaction and profitability; whereas companies' compliance with quality requirements did not show a significant effect on any of these aspects of performance.

This present study (on poultry) and Han's study (on pork) are all about meat chains, whilst Lu's study concerns the vegetable chain. Quality control involving food safety is often more sensitive and critical for the value of meat products than for the value of vegetables. Failures in quality control of meat products might lead to serious health problems, and loss of market share and reputation. Meanwhile, delivery control is often important for the value of vegetables in terms of appearance and freshness. This might reflect the fact that, for different products, each aspect of supply chain compliance (for instance, logistics compliance and quality compliance) is likely to show different influences on company performance. Thus, for different companies producing different products, the key contents of their supply chain compliance are not fixed. Furthermore, managers should adjust their supply chain practices based on attributes of specific products.

Table 6.4 summarizes the hypothesized relationships[15] and the results of the Communication-Chain compliance-Performance Model for the company-customer sample. The two hypothesized relationships are partly significant at 5% or 1% level.

6.2.3 Results of the Communication-Chain compliance-Performance Model: similarity and confrontation of the company-supplier and the company-customer samples

Based on the empirical results of the Communication-Chain compliance-Performance Model for the companies in relationships with their most important suppliers (see Section 6.2.1) and for companies in relationships with their most important customers (see Section 6.2.2), we summarize the relationships between perceived communication benefits, supply chain compliance, and company performance in this section.

---

[15] The hypotheses have been proposed in Section 2.6.

Table 6.4. Results of hypotheses of the Communication-Chain compliance-Performance Model for the company-customer sample.

	Path coefficient significant?	Sign of coefficient as expected?	Hypothesis
H_{iiiA} The level of perceived communication benefits is positively associated with the level of supply chain compliance.	Yes	Yes	Supported
H_{iiiB} The level of supply chain compliance is positively associated with the level of company performance.	Yes (with quality compliance)	Yes (with quality compliance)	Supported (with quality compliance)

These hypotheses have been proposed in Section 2.6.

Similar findings for the company-supplier and the company-customer samples

Perceived communication benefits for companies in relationships with customers' are positively and significantly associated with both logistics compliance and quality compliance for the two samples. Therefore, it makes sense for a company to realize the potential benefits of communication with its main customers, because such benefits are likely to help the company comply better with its customers' logistics and quality requirements. Meanwhile, it is also meaningful for a company to help its main suppliers to realize the potential benefits of communication, because such benefits obtained by its main suppliers are likely to help these suppliers to comply better with its logistics and quality requirements.

It is shown that '*quality compliance*' is positively and significantly associated with each aspect of company performance, for a company in relationships with its most important suppliers and customers. In other words, when a company complies better with its main customers' quality requirements, both the company and its main customers are likely to stand out from their main competitors. This indicates the critical role of quality compliance in improving companies' performance, compared to their main competitors.

It is noteworthy that '*logistics compliance*' here is not significantly associated with each aspect of company performance for a company in relationships with its most important suppliers and customers. As we discussed above, one likely reason is that there is still limited implementation of logistics compliance in the Chinese poultry chain. Another potential reason is that, though logistics compliance helps a company to improve its performance to a certain extent, it may not necessarily help a company distinguish itself from its main competitor. It would be valuable to examine this further in future research.

Confrontation between the company-supplier and the company-customer samples

By comparing Figure 6.1 and 6.2, we find one major difference between the two samples, regarding the relationships between perceived communication benefits, supply chain compliance, and company performance. Specifically, 'perceived communication benefits for companies in relationships with their main suppliers' are not significantly associated with 'quality compliance' for the company-supplier sample, but are for the company-customer. We have failed to find a reasonable explanation for this result from the existing literature. It would be useful to further examine this relationship in future research.

Conclusion

In conclusion, the most important findings are as follows:

1. Communication benefits obtained by companies are valuable for improving their compliance with their customers' logistics and quality requirements. Therefore, in order to improve logistics and quality compliance in a supply chain, it is useful for companies to help themselves and their main suppliers to realize the potential benefits of communication. In this way, they can better comply with their customers' requirements, and their main suppliers can better comply with their own requirements.

2. Suppliers' quality compliance appears to be key, for the suppliers and also for their main customers, to stand out from their main competitors. Thus, companies should invest in complying well with their main customers' quality requirements; meanwhile, companies should also help their main suppliers to comply well with their own quality requirements.

3. It is shown that suppliers' logistics compliance is not significantly associated with company performance, thus, does not yet show its potential value in improving company performance. A likely reason is that there is limited implementation of logistics management in the Chinese poultry chain. Thus, these companies in the chain should invest in improving their knowledge and practice of logistics management, in order to realize its full potential and value. Another possible reason is that logistics compliance does not necessarily make a company stand out from its main competitor, though it might contribute to the improvement of its company performance to a certain extent. This would be worth examining in future research.

4. The results of total effects (see Appendix 6.1 and 6.2) show that communication benefits obtained by suppliers are likely to make them, and their main customers, stand out from their main competitors. Strangely, communication benefits obtained by customers do not necessarily make them or their main suppliers stand out from their main competitors, though such benefits might help to improve their own and their main suppliers' performance to a certain extent. It would be useful to examine the relationship between 'perceived communication benefits for customers' and 'company performance' in different contexts in future research.

6.3 Influence of company characteristics on supply chain compliance and company performance

6.3.1 Influence of company characteristics for companies in relationships with their most important suppliers

In this section, to explore the influences of company characteristics on the Communication-Chain compliance-Performance Model for companies in relationships with their most important suppliers, five control variables are added to each construct in the model. These five control variables are: company size, company age, company type (assorted by functions and market power), quality standard implemented, and the administrative level of a location (see Section 3.4.2). Other parts and paths of the model remain the same as the Communication-Chain compliance-Performance Model that has been tested in Section 6.2. Following Chin (1998b), we ran bootstrapping with 500× resampling again.

The overall model explains about 31.1% of the variance of the endogenous latent variables. The results are shown in Table 6.5 and Appendix 6.3. It is shown that, three out of the five control variables (including company type, quality standard, and administrative level of a location) turn out to have certain significant effects on the level of supply chain compliance and company performance. However, they do not necessarily change the significance of the relationships among the constructs in the model that is presented in Section 6.2.1. The result of each hypothesis for the company-supplier sample remains the same after adding these control variables to the research model. Thus, the results presented in Figure 6.1 and Appendix 6.1 on the relationships between the communication of a company with its main *suppliers*, supply chain compliance, and the company's performance are likely to be tenable for different companies with different characteristics.

It is shown that *company type* (sorted by functions and market power) has negative and significant effects on 'profit & competitive edge'. A commercial farm or a processor is likely to report a higher level, whilst a trader or a retailer is likely to report a lower level of profitability and competitive edge, compared to their main competitors for the last twelve months. Similar results have been found with the company-customer sample and the potential reason is discussed later on in Section 6.3.2.

In contrast to our expectations, quality standard here is negatively associated with quality compliance. A likely explanation is that when a company implements a higher quality standard, it might apply more strict quality controls, tends to feel unsatisfied with its main suppliers' compliance with its quality requirements, and is therefore likely to score lower for their suppliers' quality compliance.

Strangely, *the administrative level of a location* has shown a negative influence on satisfaction and efficiency. This might imply that a company located in a smaller city is likely to be more satisfied with the product quality of, and the price paid to, their main suppliers, and is likely to pay less money and take less time, thus, be more efficient in the transactions with its main suppliers.

It is noteworthy that all of the five control variables do not show a significant influence on logistics compliance. Thus, the characteristics of a company do not necessarily influence how well its suppliers comply with its logistics requirements and expectations. This result is compared with the relevant result of the company-customer sample and discussed in Section 6.3.2.

Table 6.5. The significant influences of company characteristics on supply chain compliance and company performance for the company-supplier sample.

	Path coefficient significant?[1]	Sign of coefficient
CV_3: Firm type → Profit & competitive edge	**Yes****	-
CV_4: Quality standard → Quality compliance	Yes*	-
CV_5: Administrative level of a location → Satisfaction	**Yes***	-
CV_5: Administrative level of a location → Efficiency	**Yes****	-

[1] The same significant paths for both the company-supplier and the company-customer (see Table 6.6) samples are shown in **bold** and *italics*.

* Significant at 5%; ** significant at 1% level.

It is worth noting that company size and age here have shown no significant influence on supply chain compliance or on company performance. Meanwhile, quality standard here does not show a significant influence on company performance. However, it is reported in the literature that company size (Stanford, 1998; Wollni and Zeller, 2007; Arana, 2010) and quality standard (Van Plaggenhoef, 2007; Arana, 2010) are likely to have a positive influence on company performance.

6.3.2 Influence of company characteristics for companies in relationships with their most important customers

In this section, to explore the influences of company characteristics on the Communication-Chain compliance-Performance Model for companies in relationships with their most important customers, the five control variables are again added to each construct in the model. These five control variables are: company size, company age, company type (sorted by functions and market power), quality standard implemented, and the administrative level of a location (see Section 3.4.2). Other parts and paths of the model remain the same as the Communication-Chain compliance-Performance Model that is tested by PLS modeling in Section 6.2.

The overall model explains about 34.0% of the variance of the endogenous latent variables. The results are shown in Table 6.6 and Appendix 6.4. It appears that the five company characteristics have a slightly greater effect on the Communication-Chain compliance-Performance Model for companies in relationships with their most important customers (the company-customer sample) than for companies in relationships with their most important suppliers (the company-supplier sample). A likely reason is that here we examine the mediating role of companies' complying with their *customers'* requirements. It would be interesting and valuable to check the mediating role of companies' complying with their *suppliers'* requirements in future research.

All of the five company characteristics turn out to have certain significant influences on supply chain compliance and/or company performance (Table 6.6). But, again, they do not necessarily change the significance of the relationships among the constructs in the model that is presented in Section 6.2.2. The results of each hypothesis for the company-customer sample remain the same after adding these control variables to the research model. Thus, the results presented in Figure 6.2 and Appendix 6.2 on the relationships between the communication of a company with its main *customers*, supply chain compliance, and the company performance are likely to be tenable for different companies with different characteristics.

It is shown that *company size* has a positive and significant effect on quality compliance, but not on logistics compliance. Thus, compared to a small company, a larger company is likely to comply better with the quality requirements of its main customers; but does not necessarily comply better with the logistics requirements of its main customers. A likely explanation for the positive and significant relationship between company size and *quality* compliance is that a larger company is able *and* willing to invest to comply better with its main customers' quality requirements, in order to safeguard its long-term reputation. Meanwhile, the likely explanation for the non-significant relationship between company size and *logistics* compliance is that logistics compliance has limited implementation and is still in its early stages. And this situation holds true for both small and large companies in the Chinese poultry chain.

Table 6.6. The significant influences of company characteristics on supply chain compliance and company performance for the company-customer sample.

	Path coefficient significant?[1]	Sign of coefficient
CV_1: Firm size → Quality compliance	Yes*	+
CV_2: Firm age → Logistics compliance	Yes*	-
CV_3: Firm type → Logistics compliance	Yes**	+
CV_3: Firm type → Profit & competitive edge	**Yes***	-
CV_4: Quality standard → Satisfaction	Yes*	-
CV_4: Quality standard → Efficiency	Yes*	-
CV_5: Administrative level of a location → Satisfaction	**Yes****	-
CV_5: Administrative level of a location → Efficiency	**Yes****	-

[1] The same significant paths for both the company-supplier (see Table 6.5) and the company-customer samples are shown in **bold** and *italic*.
* Significant at 5%; ** significant at 1% level.

In addition, the positive and significant relationship between company size and company performance had been expected, but strangely, is not supported here for both the company-supplier and the company-customer samples. It was reported in the literature that company size could affect producer performance positively, because larger companies have a larger power base, may be able to purchase inputs at a lower price, use them more intensively, and thereby increase product yield compared to companies with a smaller property (Stanford, 1998; Wollni and Zeller, 2007; Arana, 2010). A likely explanation for the results of this present research, which differ from the results in the literature, is that this research measures companies' 'comparative performance' compared to their competitors, whereas the studies of Arana (2010), and Wollni and Zeller (2007) measured companies' absolute performance, such as actual prices, total sales, and increased yields. Thus, the significant and positive influence of company size on performance might only exist among companies that vary greatly in size, but might not be tenable for companies with only a small variance in size, for instance, for companies and their main competitors.

Company age is shown to be negatively associated with logistics compliance. When a company is younger in terms of business age, it is likely to comply better with the logistics requirements of its main customers. A likely explanation is that chain logistics management is a relatively new practice in Chinese food chains. It might be hard for an old company to change its old operation habits.

Company type here is shown to be positively and significantly associated with logistics compliance. This might reflect the fact that a trader or retailer is likely to comply better, whilst a commercial farm or processor is likely to comply less well with its customers' logistics requirements. This finding is especially noteworthy for farms and processors, as producing and transporting products to customers are the main functions of these companies. They should commit to improving their knowledge and practices in logistics management, and in turn they might obtain huge development space and competitive advantage.

In addition, company type is negatively and significantly associated with *profit & competitive age*. A trader or a retailer is likely to report a lower level, whilst a commercial farm or a processor is likely to report a higher level of profitability and competitive age, compared to its main competitors in the last twelve months. The survey was conducted during the Financial Crisis (2008-2009) and the researcher heard complaints from some retailers about their reduced sales, especially those in the eastern and coastal advanced regions. This result might therefore reflect the fact that traders, and especially retailers, who normally sell multiple types of products, were confronted with major challenges in sales, and thus tended to have a negative opinion of their own performance. Conversely, commercial farms and processors of poultry products, a type of basic consumption product, experienced fewer challenges in sales, and thus tended to have a positive assessment of their own performance during the Financial Crisis.

In contrast to our expectations, *quality standard* here is negatively associated with *satisfaction* and *efficiency*. For a company implementing a higher level of quality standard, its main customers are likely to be less satisfied with it. This might be the result of the increased costs and prices involved with higher quality products. According to (Arana, 2010), adopted quality standards positively and significantly influence actual price. Meanwhile, a company adopting a higher quality standard might need to invest in specific facilities to safeguard quality, and might need to spend extra time on negotiation and transactions with its more powerful customers. These might be the reasons behind the negative relationship between quality standard adopted by a company and its external efficiency in transactions with its main customers.

These findings might imply that companies and consumers in the Chinese poultry chain are more sensitive to product price than product quality. When a company adopts a higher level of quality standard, its main customers might not think that the increased quality is worth the price premium, and are likely to become unsatisfied with the company. In addition, quality standard is also negatively, though not significantly, associated with profit & competitive edge.

Compared with the relevant results of the company-supplier sample, we can see that quality standards adopted by a company do not necessarily influence its satisfaction with its suppliers, or its external efficiency in transactions with its main suppliers, or its profit and competitive performance, but is likely to decrease its customers' satisfaction, and its external efficiency in transactions with its main customers. These negative or non-significant associations between quality standard and company performance might reflect and explain why there is so little motivation for players in the Chinese food chain to improve food quality. And these might also imply that the relevant administrative offices in China should question the effectiveness of the current policy on food quality control. How can food companies in a chain be motivated to improve and safeguard food quality? What would be the most efficient and effective policies? These appear to be critical questions for policy makers to think about when looking at food quality administration.

Similar to the results of the company-supplier sample, *the administrative level of a location* here again shows negative effects on company performance. A company located in a smaller city is likely to make its main customers feel more satisfied, and is likely to spend less money and less time, thus, be more externally efficient in transactions with its main customers. These results are in contrast to our expectations. A likely explanation is that, as discussed above, most production companies are located in small towns or cities because of lower costs and the environment protection policy. They deal with poultry product, a type of basic consumption product. Therefore, they have experienced fewer challenges even during the

Financial Crisis, and tend to make a positive assessment of their performance. However, most trading companies are located in middle or large cities that are important end markets. They normally deal with multiple types of products including luxury goods. Therefore, they faced more challenges in the financial crisis, and tend to have a negative assessment of their performance.

In addition, a company located in a smaller city often purchases from and also sells to local markets. The food miles (from farms to end markets) for a company in a smaller city are often less than the food miles for a company located in a larger city. Advocates of local food chains have suggested that expanded local food systems can improve performance along a number of dimensions (King *et al.*, 2010; Martinez *et al.*, 2010). A recent research (King *et al.*, 2010) examined five local food chains in the USA, and found that producers in local food supply chains provided rich information to, and normally had good relationships with, their customers. They tended to receive higher revenues per unit and retain a larger share of the retail price. And for nearly all of the local supply chains, revenues per unit retained by producers, net of marketing costs, are significantly higher in local supply chains than in national and international chains[16]. In addition, local food supply chains where product travels much shorter distances may be more efficient per unit of product delivered even when load sizes are smaller. These findings in the literature might go some way to explaining the significant and negative relationship between location and company performance. However, considering that the local chains in the USA are often advanced high quality chains, there might be other valuable reasons to be found in future research on the negative association between the administrative level of a location and company performance.

In Section 6.1, we discussed the potential reason for the comparatively high standard deviations for 'efficiency' and 'profit & competitive edge'. The results here supported the negative and significant influence of 'administrative level of a location' on efficiency, and of 'company type' on 'profit & competitive edge'. These might imply that companies located in a small town and those in a large city had realized significantly diverse efficiency, whilst different types of companies with different functions had achieved significantly different performance in terms of profitability and competitive edge.

A comparison of the results of the company-supplier and the company-customer samples shows that the characteristics of a company do not necessarily influence how well its suppliers might comply with its logistics requirements, but are likely to influence how well it might comply with its customers' logistics and quality requirements. In addition, some companies' characteristics, such as firm size and age, do not necessarily influence their company performance compared to their main competitor, whereas some other characteristics, such as company type, quality standard adopted, and location, are likely to influence their comparative performance.

6.3.3 Influence of company characteristics on supply chain compliance and company performance: similarity and confrontation of the company-supplier and the company-customer samples

In general, a company's characteristics are likely to influence the level of supply chain compliance and its comparative performance in one way or the other. Table 6.7 summarizes the relationships of

---

[16] National and international supply chains in the USA are characterized by distribution centres that receive products from many suppliers and efficiently distribute a wide array of products to supermarkets that offer consumers convenience and variety (King *et al.,* 2010).

companies' characteristics with supply chain compliance, and with their performance compared to their main competitors.

Comparing the empirical results for the company-supplier and the company-customer samples, presented in Section 6.3.1 and 6.3.2, and Table 6.7, the main findings are summarized below.
1. In general, the characteristics of a company are likely to affect, in one way or the other, how well it is likely to comply with the requirements of its main customers, and how well its company performance is likely to be achieved.
2. Specifically, the size, business age, and type of a company are likely to influence how well it is likely to comply with the logistics or quality requirements of its main customers, but do not necessarily affect how well its suppliers are likely to comply with its logistics or quality requirements. Meanwhile, the type, the highest quality standard employed, and the administrative level of a location of a company are likely to influence the level of each aspect of its company performance, compared to its main competitors.
3. Of particular interest, when a company employs a higher level of quality standard, it tends to be stricter and be unsatisfied with its suppliers' compliance with its quality requirement. Meanwhile, possibly due to increased costs, higher prices and more negotiation, it is likely to suffer a lower level of customer satisfaction and a lower level of external efficiency. This finding is a warning that new or adjusted policy on food quality control appears to be necessary and urgently needed, in order to motivate companies in the Chinese poultry chain to employ higher levels of quality standards.

6.4 Concluding remarks

By taking the perspective of Supply Chain Management, this chapter aimed to reveal the potential influence of inter-organizational communication on company performance and the mediating role

Table 6.7. The influences of company characteristics on supply chain compliance and company performance[1].

	Companies with their suppliers					Companies with their customers				
	Size	Age	Type	Quality	Location	Size	Age	Type	Quality	Location
Logistics compliance								-	+	
Quality compliance				-		+				
Satisfaction		-							-	-
Efficiency		-							-	-
Profit & competitive edge			-					-		

[1] The five company characteristics examined are: company *size*, company *age*, company *type*, *quality* standard implied, and the administrative level of a *location*. Specifically, company type: 0 = production firms with lower market power; 1 = trading firms with higher market power. Administrative level of a location: 1 = town or county; 2 = medium-sized city; 3 = national or provincial capital city.

of supply chain compliance. It displayed empirical results about baseline statistics and the results of partial least squares (PLS) modeling of the Communication-Chain compliance-Performance Model. The Communication-Chain compliance-Performance Model is proposed in this research.

First, this chapter presented the results of baseline statistics. Data were collected from each stage of the Chinese poultry chain, from commercial farms to supermarkets and restaurants. In general, the respondent companies in relationships with their most important suppliers and with their most important customers reported similar opinions and activities (with similar average scores) on perceived communication benefits and company performance. The significant difference between companies in relationships with their most important suppliers (the company-supplier sample) and companies in relationships with their most important customers (the company-customer samples) was shown with supply chain compliance. Comparatively, a company is likely to score slightly higher on its compliance with quality requirements of its main customers than their customers do. This might reflect that, although the companies and their main customers all appreciated these companies' compliance in general, these companies did not perform as well as their customers thought they should. In addition, the correlation coefficients showed that the constructs are correlated, and thus well related to each other, as expected. This provides evidence for the nomological validity of these constructs.

It is noteworthy that the results of means are in line with the results of correlation coefficients, which appears to imply that, in order to improve chain compliance and company performance, it might be advantageous for both a company and its main customers, and both a company and its main suppliers, to invest heavily and more or less equally in information exchange with each other. This empirical finding makes a valuable contribution to the critical discussion on 'to what extent a company should invest in information exchange, compared to its chain partners'.

Subsequently, this chapter displayed the results of PLS modeling of the Communication-Chain compliance-Performance Model, for the company-supplier and the company-customer samples, respectively. The Communication-Chain compliance-Performance Model is composed of three main parts: perceived communication benefits, supply chain compliance, and company performance. This model can be used to understand, examine, and assess how communication benefits obtained by companies lead to improved chain compliance, and further contribute to a higher level of company performance.

Previous studies examined the relationships of inter-organizational communication (IOC) with limited aspects of company performance, or typically take communication benefits as company performance. However, company performance itself is a broad concept covering diverse aspects, and we assume that company performance might not be a direct, but an indirect and additional result of IOC. Thus, here we checked the relationships between the direct benefits of IOC and company performance. Meanwhile, we examined the mediating role of chain compliance by taking the insights of Supply Chain Management. It is mentioned in the literature that companies, and their suppliers and customers, might obtain different levels of benefits from the information exchange. Thus, to measure and distinguish the direct communication benefits for customers and suppliers respectively, two constructs were proposed in this research. These are 'perceived communication benefits for companies in relationships with their main suppliers' and 'perceived communication benefits for companies in relationships with their main customers'. It is worth noting that this research supports the fact that companies have reported similar levels of benefits for themselves and for their main suppliers, and similar levels of benefits for themselves and for their main customers. Furthermore, this appears to be the first study to propose and empirically examine the direct benefits of communication for customers and suppliers, separately, and further to distinguish their different influence on different aspects of company performance, respectively. As such, a theoretical contribution of this research is its extension of existing research on the value of information exchange.

In general, we summarize the most important findings as follows: (1) the communication benefits obtained by a company are likely to help the company and its main suppliers to improve compliance in a chain; (2) the communication benefits obtained by a company and its improved quality compliance jointly lead to a higher level of performance for the company and for its main customers. Thus, in order to approach optimal performance, a company should endeavor to communicate well with its main customers, and with its main suppliers. It should make sure that it, as well as its main suppliers and customers, make good use of relevant information, and truly realize the potential benefits of information exchange; (3) suppliers' quality compliance is a key to improving the performance of suppliers themselves and of their customers. Meanwhile, for managers aiming to achieve higher company performance than their main competitors, learning to improve their own logistics compliance and that of their suppliers appears to be a great challenge, but a huge potential opportunity.

This chapter also examined the potential influence of company characteristics. The most important finding is that the five company characteristics do not necessarily change the interrelationship between perceived communication benefits, supply chain compliance, and comparative company performance. Thus, the interrelationships revealed in this research are likely to be tenable for different companies with different characteristics. As such, this research contributes to the extension of scientific research on the impact of company characteristics on the interrelationships between perceived communication benefits, supply chain compliance and company performance.

However, it was found that the characteristics of a company are likely to influence, in one way or another, how well it is likely to comply with the requirements of its main customers, and how well it is likely to achieve company performance, compared to its main competitors. Meanwhile, the unexpected negative relationship between quality standard and comparative performance provided a valuable warning about the urgent need for relevant policy in the area of food quality control, in order to motivate companies in the Chinese poultry chain to employ higher quality standards. This might also hold true and be significant for some other developing and transitional countries. No much research has discussed the relationship between company characteristics and supply chain compliance, though the relationship between company characteristics and company performance is often discussed. As such, this research extends the scientific research regarding the influence of company characteristics on the level of supply chain compliance and company performance. Meanwhile, this research also contributes to the discussion 'why certain company characteristics show influence on certain aspects of supply chain compliance and company performance but not on other aspects?'

Finally, it is worth remarking that this research examined the mediating role of *suppliers'* chain compliance, in the relationships between communication and company performance. It would also be valuable to examine the potential role of *customers'* chain compliance in future research.

Chapter 7

Synthesis

Communication between business partners has been accepted as an essential tool for approaching optimal company performance. The *main objective* of this book is therefore to investigate how to improve inter-organizational communication (IOC), in order to improve company performance ultimately. To achieve this objective, three lines of research were applied. The first line of research focused on potential antecedents of communication between a company and its main customers, and its main suppliers. The second focused on the interrelationships of important aspects of communication. The third line of research focused on the potential influence of IOC on companies' performance, compared to their main competitors. In this final chapter, the main results and conclusions of the present research are summarized in Section 7.1. The theoretical and methodological contributions are presented in Section 7.2. The most important managerial and policy implications are discussed in Section 7.3. The chapter ends with the limitations of this research and directions for future research in Section 7.4.

7.1 Summary and conclusions

To subsequently achieve the overall objective of this research, Chapter 4, 5, 6 each concentrates on one of the research questions proposed in Chapter 1.

> *Research Question A: What is the impact of transaction attributes and governance structure on inter-organizational communication (IOC)?*

To answer this research question, we adopted the perspective of Transaction Cost Economics, and examined the relationships between transaction attributes, governance structure, and communication willingness & behavior in Chapter 4. The research model (the Communication Antecedents Model) and the proposed relationships are presented in figure 7.1. Based on the results of basic statistics and partial least squares (PLS) modeling, some major findings are summarized here.

In general, the survey results supported positive and significant associations between transaction attributes and governance structure, and between governance structure and communication willingness and behavior. The results also supported significant and positive associations between 'environmental uncertainty' and 'transaction specific investments' (TSI), and between 'trust' and 'contractual governance' (pre-agreement). Thus, environmental uncertainty is likely to induce a higher level of TSI; both of them are likely to lead jointly to a higher level of trust and contractual governance; furthermore, a higher level of trust and contractual governance are likely to contribute jointly to improved communication willingness and behavior. Table 7.1 summarized these relationships between transaction attributes, governance structure, and communication willingness and behavior, based on the empirical results of this research.

The results indicated that when the level of *environmental uncertainty* was higher, a company was likely to increase specific investments and make use of contractual governance to safeguard the transactions with its main customers and main suppliers. These joint actions succeed in increasing the level of trust between the company and its main customers, and its main suppliers. In addition, when the level of environmental uncertainty is higher, a company is likely to be more willing to actively communicate

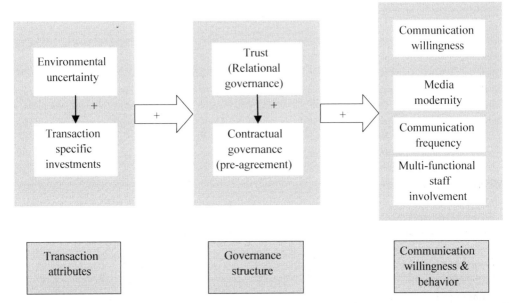

Figure 7.1. Proposed relationships between transaction attributes, governance structure, and communication willingness & behavior (the Communication Antecedents Model).

Table 7.1. Relationships between transaction attributes, governance structure, and communication willingness and behavior.

	Companies with their suppliers				Companies with their customers			
	Environmental uncertainty	Specific investments	Trust	Contractual governance	Environmental uncertainty	Specific investments	Trust	Contractual governance
Transaction specific investments	+				+			
Trust	+	+			+	+		
Contractual governance	+	+	+		+	+	+	
Communication willingness	n.s.	n.s.	+	n.s.	+	+	+	+
Media modernity	n.s.	n.s.	n.s.	n.s.	n.s.	+	n.s.	+
Communication frequency	n.s.	n.s.	n.s.	n.s.	n.s.	+	n.s.	+
Multi-functional staff involvement	n.s.	n.s.	+	n.s.	+	+	+	+

+: the relationship is supported at 5% level.

n.s.: the relationship is not supported at 5% level.

with its main *customers*, probably in order to obtain market information to counter the uncertainty and the induced risk. But it is likely to have a similar willingness and take similar action to communicate with its main *suppliers*, probably because safeguarding purchasing sources is not usually as urgent as safeguarding markets during a period of environmental uncertainty.

It appears that *specific investments* are reliable indicators for the level of trust between a company and its most important customers, and its most important suppliers. When a company has higher specific investments in the transactions with its main customers, and its main suppliers, the trust between it and the main customers, and its main suppliers is likely to be greater. In contrast, the association between specific investments and contractual governance is not supported by the sample of companies in relationships with their main suppliers (the company-supplier sample), but is supported by the sample of companies in relationships with their main customers (the company-customer sample). When a company has higher specific investments in the transactions with its main customers, it tends to employ contractual governance, as well as trust relationship governance, to jointly safeguard its investments. But this is not necessarily the case for a company when it invests specifically in its main suppliers. Moreover, the specific investments of a company appear to further influence its communication willingness and behavior with the specific customers, but may not necessarily influence its communication with the specific suppliers. Thus, a company's specific investments appear also to be useful indicators for its communication with the specific customers. A likely explanation for these findings is that in relationships with its main customers a company normally has less negotiating power, therefore, it tends to employ diverse means, which combine trust, contractual governance, and diverse communication activities, to jointly safeguard its specific investments in the customers. However, in relationships with its main suppliers a company normally has higher negotiating power, therefore, it is less necessary for it to invest in contractual governance to safeguard its specific investments in suppliers.

Trust here appears to be a reliable and positive indicator for contractual governance and for communication willingness between a company and its main customers, and its main suppliers. However, trust may not necessarily indicate the level of media modernity and communication frequency between a company and its main customers, and its main suppliers. As discussed in Section 5.2.3, a company should commit to improving the mutual trust with its main customers and suppliers, and thus broaden the potential communication scope with its main customers and suppliers.

Another noteworthy finding is that *contractual governance* appears to be an indicator for a company's communication with its main customers, but may not be for a company's communication with its main suppliers. When the level of contractual governance is higher, the level of communication willingness and behavior between a company and its main *suppliers* does not necessarily become higher, but that between a company and its main *customers* is likely to become higher. A likely explanation is that, on the one hand, in relationships with its main customers a company tends to pay more attention to contractual *customers* than to non-contractual customers; on the other hand, in relationships with its main suppliers a company refers to be open to flexibility in purchasing sources, and therefore tends to deal equally with contractual and non-contractual *suppliers* (regarding communication willingness and behavior). This finding is noteworthy, because we did not find direct empirical evidence in the literature on the relationship between contractual governance and communication (willingness and behavior), though it was argued in theories that contract was explicitly drafted with provisions against asymmetric information (Bogetoft and Olesen, 2004) and coordination devices specified by contract might foster more frequent communication and a greater flow of information (Zhou and Poppo, 2010). Thus, this finding in the present research provided empirical proof for the positive link between contractual governance and communication.

Thus, in answer to Research Question A, we further conclude that:

1. The communication between a company and its main customers, and its main suppliers, is a broad issue that covers diverse aspects; each of these aspects tends to be affected by distinct factors.
2. Specifically, first, improved *contractual governance* is likely to induce improved communication willingness and behavior between a company and its main customers, but not necessarily between the company and its main suppliers. Second, a higher level of *trust* is likely to lead to a higher level of contractual governance, communication willingness, and multi-functional staff involvement between a company and its main customers, and its main suppliers. Third, more *specific investments* are likely to contribute to greater trust between a company and its main customers, and its main suppliers, and a higher level of contractual governance between it and its main customers. In addition, more specific investments are likely to contribute to improved communication willingness and behavior of a company with its main customers. But more such investments might not necessarily improve a company' communication with its main suppliers. Fourth, a higher level of *environmental uncertainty* is likely to induce a higher level of specific investments and contractual governance, thus, induce more trust, but may not ultimately lead to improved communication willingness and behavior.
3. An efficient way to improve the communication of a company with its chain partners is to vet each aspect of its communication with its main customers, and its main suppliers, respectively, to target the main problem areas, and subsequently, to improve these aspects jointly through their specific antecedents.

We also examined the potential influence of a company's characteristics on its communication willingness and behavior with its main customers, and its main suppliers (see Table 4.11). The five company characteristics examined are: company size, company age, company type sorted by market power, quality standard implemented, and administrative level of a location. In general, a company's characteristics are likely to influence the level (namely, magnitude) of its communication with its main customers and suppliers in one way or another. However, they do not necessarily influence the relationships between transaction attributes, governance structure, and communication willingness and behavior. Thus, we conclude that the results of the hypothesized relationships (see Table 7.1) and our answers to Research Question A are likely to be tenable for different companies with different characteristics.

> *Research Question B: What are the main aspects of inter-organizational communication and what are their interrelationships? And how can inter-organizational communication be used to provide greater benefits for companies?*

We examined several communication aspects and their interrelationships in Chapter 5. The research model (the Communication Elements Model) and the proposed relationships are presented in Figure 7.2. Based on the results of basic statistics and PLS modeling, the major findings are summarized here.

In general, the survey results supported the significant and positive associations between communication willingness and communication quality, and between communication quality and perceived communication benefits. The results also partly supported the significant and positive

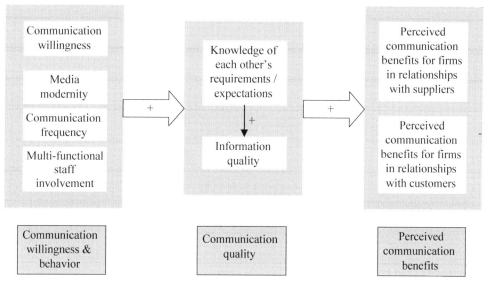

Figure 7.2. Proposed relationships between important aspects of inter-organizational communication (the Communication Elements Model).

association between communication behavior (media modernity, communication frequency, and multi-functional staff involvement) and communication quality[17]. Thus, it is communication willingness and communication behavior that jointly lead to improved communication quality, whilst improved communication quality further contributes to more communication benefits for the companies. Table 7.2 summarizes these relationships between communication willingness and behavior, communication quality, and perceived communication benefits, based on the empirical results of this research.

It is noteworthy that communication willingness not only significantly helps to improve communication quality, but also seriously contributes to a higher level of perceived (realized) communication benefits. This finding is in line with the results of Fawcett *et al.* (2007), which strongly support the critical role of a company's communication willingness in developing its external communication capability. Another finding of particular interest is that for each aspect of communication quality or of perceived communication benefits, the total effect of communication willingness is larger than the sum of the total effects of communication behavior. For example, regarding 'knowledge of each other's requirements and expectations', the total effect of communication willingness is 0.53, whilst the total effects of communication behavior are 0.28. This also appears to greatly support the extremely critical role of communication willingness in improving communication quality and in realizing the potential benefits of inter-organizational communication.

In contrast to our expectations, the adoption of more advanced media did not appear to lead automatically to a higher level of communication quality or perceived (realized) communication benefits. A likely reason is the fact that there was only limited implementation of modern media in the companies in the Chinese poultry chain. Most of the companies made use of traditional to moderately advanced media

---

[17] The hypothesized relationship between media modernity and communication quality is not supported.

Table 7.2. *Relationships between communication willingness, communication behavior, communication quality, and perceived communication benefits.*

	Companies with their suppliers						Companies with their customers					
	Communication willingness	Media modernity	Communication frequency	Multi-functional staff involvement	Knowledge of each other' requirements	Information quality	Communication willingness	Media modernity	Communication frequency	Multi-functional staff involvement	Knowledge of each other's requirements	Information quality
Knowledge of each other's requirements and expectations	+	n.s.	+	n.s.			+	n.s.	+	+		
Information quality	+	n.s.	n.s.	+	+		n.s.	n.s.	n.s.	+	n.s.	
Perceived communication benefits for companies	+	n.s.	n.s.	+	+	+	+	n.s.	+	+	+	+
Perceived communication benefits for customers	+	n.s.	+	+	+	+	n.a.	n.a.	n.a.	n.a.	n.a.	n.a.
Perceived communication benefits for suppliers	n.a.	n.a.	n.a.	n.a.	n.a.	n.a.	+	n.s.	+	+	+	+

+: the relationship is supported at 5% level.

n.s.: the relationship is not supported at 5% level.

n.a.: not applicable.

(e-mail) only; more advanced media (such as Electronic Data Interchange) are not yet widely used in the Chinese poultry chain. Nevertheless, companies still reported that they had perceived (realized) major benefits from the communication. This is in line with the statement of Media Richness Theory that traditional media, such as face-to-face communication, is the richest medium in terms of resolving ambiguity, negotiating varying interpretations, and facilitating understanding. On the one hand, these findings might imply that the companies should invest in more advanced information facilities, if they intend to obtain the benefits of modern media. On the other hand, companies should build a diverse communication system, which combines both traditional tools and modern media, and should try to realize the potential utility of these traditional and modern tools together, if they intend to approach optimal communication value.

Interestingly, 'communication frequency' was found to be associated with 'knowledge of each other's requirements and expectations', but not with 'information quality'. This might imply that although more frequent communication does not necessarily lead to a higher level of (regular) information quality, it is still valuable for companies to keep in frequent contact with each other, in order to gain a better understanding of the changing requirements and expectations of each other in this dynamic business world. In addition, communication frequency was also found to be helpful for a company and its main customers, and its main suppliers, to realize more benefits from the mutual communication, due to their improved knowledge of each other.

It was shown that by making use of senior managers and staff from different functions to communicate with their main customers and suppliers, the companies are likely to improve their communication quality, especially (regular) information quality. This finding is in conflict with that of Li and Lin (2006). They surveyed 196 organizations in industries in the USA, and found that top management had shown a positive impact on information sharing but not on information quality. This might imply that the use of senior managers solely in communication is not a valid strategy for improving information quality. Instead, arranging both senior managers and staff from different functions to communicate with business partners could jointly contribute to a higher level of (regular) information quality, a higher level of total communication quality, and furthermore a higher level of perceived communication benefits.

Of particular interest is that both 'knowledge of each other's requirements and expectations' and 'information quality' appeared to (similarly) significantly contribute to a higher level of 'perceived communication benefits' for a company and its main customers, and its main suppliers. According to Raghunathan (2001), information sharing might have zero benefit if the supplier is intelligent enough to retrieve all the demand information from the order history; and only sharing information on unexpected events is beneficial. Thus, we assume that knowledge of business partners' requirements and expectations might be valuable as a potential enabler for a company to capitalize on unexpected events and create joint knowledge in this dynamic business world. Moreover, it might be especially valuable for companies in non-highly integrated chains such as the Chinese poultry chain, but less valuable for companies in highly integrated chains such as the poultry chains in the West. This is an area worth further examination in future research, as we discussed in Section 7.4. In the literature, the quality of information exchange has been typically conceptualized and measured by information quality. However, the results of this research supported that communication quality is likely to be a multi-dimensional concept, rather than a one-dimensional concept. We would therefore like to call for attention to be paid to examining communication quality from various angles, including 'knowledge of each other's changing events' and regular 'information quality'.

Another very important finding was that, according to the relevant results of (high) means and (low) standard deviation (see Section 5.1), companies tended to believe that their communication with main customers, and with main suppliers, had provided high and almost equal benefits for a company and its main customers, and for a company and its main suppliers. In line with these results is the high and positive correlation between 'perceived communication benefits for firm in relationships with suppliers' and 'perceived communication benefits for firms in relationships with customers'. In the literature and in the real business world, the question 'to what extent a company should invest in inter-organizational information exchange, compared to its customers, and its suppliers' has been puzzled over. This research provides empirical and valuable proof that it might be advantageous for a company and its *main* customers, and its *main* suppliers, to invest heavily, and more or less equally, in their mutual communication; furthermore, it is worthwhile for a company to invest (not only for itself, but also) for its main business partners, if it intends to approach optimal benefits of information exchange. Such help for important business partners is actually a kind of self-help.

Thus, in answer to Research Question B, we conclude that:

1. Communication willingness and communication behavior are likely to contribute jointly to a higher level of communication quality, and lead to a higher level of benefits for a company and its main customers, and its main suppliers.
2. To realize more potential benefits from communication with business partners, companies should endeavor to improve both regular information quality and enrich their knowledge of each other's changing events, thus, jointly improve the overall communication quality; in order to improve communication quality, companies should invest not only in physical information facilities but also in their own psychological communication willingness *and* that of their main business partners, build a diverse communication system with both traditional and modern information tools, make frequent contact, and make use of senior managers and staff from different functions in the communication with their main business partners.
3. It has been shown that a company and its main customers, and its main suppliers are likely to benefit greatly and more or less equally from the mutual communication. Thus, it is advantageous for a company and its main business partners to communicate openly with each other.

We also examined the relationships between a company's characteristics and its communication with its main customers, and with its main suppliers (see Table 5.9). In general, a company's characteristics are likely to influence the level (i.e. magnitude) of each aspects of its communication with its main customers, and with its main suppliers in one way or the other. However, company characteristics again do not appear to automatically influence the interrelationships between important aspects of communication. Thus, we conclude that the results of the hypothesized relationships on inter-organizational communication (see Table 7.2) and our answers to Research Question B are likely to be tenable for different companies with different characteristics. Therefore, to examine the interrelationships of communication elements, it does not appear to be necessary to check company characteristics at the same time. However, to evaluate the level (i.e. magnitude) of each aspect of a company's communication, it is necessary to check its company characteristics simultaneously. For instance, for a specific company, a certain level of communication willingness might appear to be high and satisfactory if compared to companies with other characteristics, but might turn out to be low and unsatisfactory if compared with its main counterparts or main competitors with similar characteristics.

> *Research Question C: what is the relationship between inter-organizational communication and company performance? And how can inter-organizational communication to be used to improve company performance?*

To answer this research question, we took the perspective of Supply Chain Management and examined the relationships between 'perceived communication benefits' and 'company performance', with the mediating role of 'supply chain compliance' in Chapter 6. The research model (the Communication -Performance Model) and the proposed relationships are presented in Figure 7.3.

Of particular interest are, the results of mean and correlation (see Table 6.1, 6.2) indicate that the communication between a company and its main customers, and its main suppliers, produces significant and almost equal benefits not only for the companies, but also for its main customers and its main suppliers.

In general, the empirical results supported the significant and positive associations between 'perceived communication benefits for firms in relationships with customers' and 'supply chain compliance', and

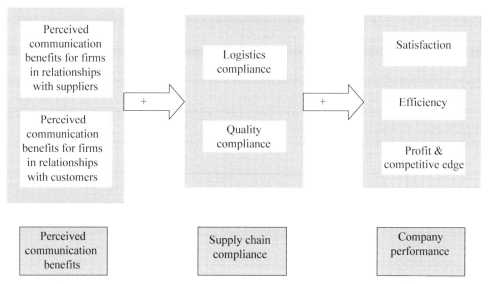

Figure 7.3. Proposed relationships between perceived communication benefits, supply chain compliance, and company performance (the Communication-Chain compliance-Performance Model).

between 'quality compliance' and each aspect of company performance. In addition, the positive and significant association between 'perceived communication benefits for firms in relationships with suppliers' and 'quality compliance' was not found with the sample of companies in relationships with their suppliers, but was found with the sample of companies in relationships with their main customers. Meanwhile, the expected positive relationship between 'logistics compliance' and 'company performance' was not supported here. Table 7.3 summarizes these relationships between perceived communication benefits, supply chain compliance, and company performance, based on the empirical results of this research.

The results in Table 7.3 indicate that when a company communicates with its main *suppliers*, it appears to be the communication benefits obtained by its main suppliers, rather than those obtained by itself, that help to improve the suppliers' supply chain compliance. In addition, when a company communicates with its main *customers*, it appears that both communication benefits obtained by itself and by its main customers helps to improve its supply chain compliance. Thus, a noteworthy finding is that the communication benefits obtained by a company and its main customers help to improve the company's compliance with its customers' requirements; meanwhile, it is the communication benefits obtained by a company and its main suppliers that help to improve its suppliers' compliance with its own requirements.

The results also indicate that when a company communicates with its main *suppliers*, it appears to be the communication benefits obtained by its main suppliers, rather than those obtained by itself, that make the company stand out in each aspect of company performance, compared to its main competitors. In addition, when a company communicates with its main *customers*, it appears to be the communication benefits obtained by the company that make it outstanding, compared to its main competitors. These results lead to another important finding: it is not only the communication benefits obtained by a

Table 7.3. Relationships between perceived communication benefits, supply chain compliance, and company performance.

	Companies with their suppliers				Companies with their customers			
	Communication benefits for the companies	Communication benefits for suppliers	Logistics compliance	Quality compliance	Communication benefits for the companies	Communication benefits for customers	Logistics compliance	Quality compliance
Logistics compliance	n.s.	+			+	n.s.		
Quality compliance	n.s.	+			+	+		
Satisfaction	n.s.	+	n.s.	+	+	n.s.	n.s.	+
Efficiency	n.s.	+	n.s.	+	n.s.	n.s.	n.s.	+
Profit & competitive edge	n.s.	+	n.s.	+	n.s.	n.s.	n.s.	+

+: the relationship is supported at 5% level.
n.s.: the relationship is not supported at 5% level.

company itself, but also those obtained by its main suppliers, which jointly make a company stand out, compared to its main competitors.

When looking at the relationships between supply chain compliance and company performance, we see that *logistics* compliance was not associated with company performance. This might reflect that there is still limited implementation of logistics compliance, and supply chain management is still at an early stage in the Chinese poultry chain, as was found in other meat products chain in the Mainland China (Chen and Luo, 2003; Han, 2009). Meanwhile, we can also see that when a company complies better with customers' *quality* requirements, it is likely to achieve better company performance, compared to its main competitors.

Thus, in answer to Research Question C, we hereby combine the above findings and further conclude that:
1. It is valuable for a company to help not only itself, but also its main suppliers, to truly realize the potential benefits of information exchange. Moreover, it is also important for a company to comply well with its main customers' quality requirements.
2. The communication benefits obtained by a company, by its main customers and its main suppliers are likely to jointly improve compliance, especially quality compliance, in the chain. Moreover, communication benefits obtained by a company and its main suppliers, together with the improved quality compliance, would jointly make the company outstanding in performance, compared to its main competitors. Regarding information exchange with main business partners, helping others acts as a kind of self-help.

We also examined the potential influence of a company's characteristics on supply chain compliance, and on company performance (see Table 6.9). In general, we found:

1. The characteristics of a company are likely to influence the level (namely, magnitude) of supply chain compliance and the company's performance in one way or another.

2. A company's characteristics (size, age, and type) are likely to influence how well it might comply with the requirements of its main customers, but do not necessarily affect how well its main suppliers are likely to comply with its own requirements;

3. A company's characteristics (type and administrative level of a location) are likely to influence the company's performance in a similar way, regardless of whether it is at the beginning (such as farms) or at the end (such as supermarkets and restaurants) of the poultry chain;

4. A higher quality standard adopted by a company appears to have no impact on the performance of a company that is closer to end consumers (such as supermarkets and restaurants), but does appear to have a *negative* impact on the performance of a company that is less close to end customers (such as a commercial farm); this finding might imply that for implementing a higher food quality standard, there is almost zero motivation for companies at the end stage of the poultry chain, whilst there is negative motivation for companies at the beginning stage of the chain. Based on this important finding, we further discuss the policy implementations in Section 7.2.

However, it has been shown that company characteristics do not necessarily influence the interrelationships between perceived communication benefits, supply chain compliance, and company performance. Thus, we conclude that the results of the hypothesized relationships on communication and company performance, and our answers to Research Question C, are likely to be tenable for different companies with different characteristics. Therefore, to examine the interrelationships between communication and company performance, it is not necessary to check company characteristics at the same time. However, to evaluate the level (magnitude) of supply chain compliance and company performance, it is necessarily to check company characteristics simultaneously. For instance, for a specific company, its quality compliance might appear to be high and satisfactory if compared to companies with other characteristics, but might turn out to be low and unsatisfactory if compared to its main counterparts or main competitors with similar characteristics.

7.2 Theoretical contributions and methodological applications

7.2.1 Theoretical contributions

This research is among the first to focus on inter-organizational communication in the Chinese poultry chain. It has made several important contributions to the literature, which is worthy to remark.

First, in answer to the central research question, this research has integrated different schools of thought, including transaction cost economics, the literature on inter-organizational communication (IOC), and supply chain management. Specifically, transaction cost economics was applied to reveal the potential antecedents of IOC. Then, insights obtained from the literature on IOC were adopted to discuss the interrelationship of IOC elements, and to find out how IOC could be used to provide more benefits for companies. Moreover, the perspective of Supply Chain Management was taken to reveal the influence of IOC on company performance. These theories have their own focus, assumptions, and framework for studying the relationships between companies. Nevertheless, they provide a complementary theoretical foundation on which to reveal the relationships between transaction attributes, governance structure,

IOC, and company performance. In addition, most of these theories are based on the contexts in the West. This research extended the adoption of these theories in a new context: China, a vast transitional country.

Second, this research is the extension of existing research on the relationships between contractual governance and communication, and between contractual governance and trust. To our knowledge, no other *empirical* research has been done to test the relationship between contractual governance and communication (willingness and behavior), though it was argued in the theories. The results of this present research indicated that suppliers paid greater attention to contractual customers than to non-contractual customers, and contractual governance assumed an important role in improving suppliers' willingness and actions in communicating with their main customers. Thus, for companies intending to improve the communication willingness and behavior of their most important suppliers, making use of contracts appears to be a valid and efficient strategy.

In addition, to our knowledge, this research for the first time empirically reveals the complementary roles between contractual governance and trust in the process of improving communication willingness. Thus, contractual governance and trust should be used jointly, especially for managers intending to improve the communication willingness of its main suppliers. However, for managers intending to improve the communication willingness of its main customers, a commitment to enhancing their customers' trust in them appears to be one of the most valid and efficient strategy.

Third, another theoretical contribution of this research is the extension of existing research that has typically limited communication quality to information quality. The results of this research strongly support the fact that communication quality should be measured with diverse dimensions. Besides 'information quality', the dimension of 'knowledge of each other's (changing) requirements and expectations' appears to be a valid and complementary indicator to reveal the total quality of the communication between companies. In addition, being well aware of each other's changing requirements and expectations might be especially important for companies in a developing or transitional country. The main reasons are: (1) the poultry chains in these countries are normally less integrated than the poultry chains in the West. Many transactions in developing and transitional countries are often short-term or medium-term cooperation, and are often based on oral agreements or acquiescence. In contrast, official contracts and long-term collaboration are dominant in the West; (2) companies in a developing or transitional country may often have business partners with larger characteristics variations, and they may change their main business partners more often than their counterparts in the West; and (3) the population requirements and concepts regarding food quality and food safety in developing and transitional countries might fluctuate largely based on the changing economic situation and the more frequent occurrence of food safety incidents, compared to those in the West.

Fourth, this research has confirmed and extended existing scientific findings regarding communication benefits and company performance. The literature has often take communication benefits to mean improved company performance, and often measures them by making use of the constructs of company performance. Using a different approach, the present research proposed that communication benefits should be operationalized in a way that measures the direct benefits that a company obtains from the communication, whist company performance might partly be an indirect result of communication. Furthermore, the empirical results of this research have supported the fact that perceived communication benefits and company performance are different constructs. Moreover, the results have shown that when companies obtain benefits from IOC, they could make use of such benefits to improve the quality compliance with chain partners, which would in turn lead to outstanding performance, compared to their main competitors.

Here, we found that communication between a company and its most important customers, and its main suppliers, is likely to provide significant and more or less equal (!) benefits to the company and its main customers, and its main suppliers. Moreover, we found that it is the communication benefits obtained by a company and its main suppliers that jointly improve chain compliance, and furthermore, make the company stand out in company performance, compared to its main competitors. Thus, we argued that it might be advantageous for both sides of a transaction to try their best to invest and to help not only its own companies, but also its main business partners, in order to realize the potential benefits of communication and to approach optimal performance. In this way, this empirical research goes some way to providing a valuable answer to the important discussion 'to what extent a company should invest in its communication with business partners?'

Fifth, this research took the perspective of Supply Chain Management in the research design and data collection. In the literature, most extant studies are limited in collecting data on focal companies or only take into account the customer or the supplier sides of the focal companies. The present research is distinctive in that it has collected data from both the customer and the supplier sides of focal companies, and asked their opinion about their relationships with main customers and main suppliers, respectively. Our research results have provided empirical proof that some differences exist between a company's relationships with its main customers, and with its main suppliers. As such, this research has contributed to the adoption of such innovative method, which focuses on both the customer and supplier sides of multiple companies.

7.2.2 Methodological implications

It is also worth mentioning the following methodological implications of this research.

First, the 'mixed-methodology' approach was applied in this research and turned out to be useful. As introduced in Section 3.1.1, we first started with extensive, then, intensive literature study, which helped to identify the research topic, design the research, and draft a questionnaire. Then, the researcher visited practitioners, administrative officers, and academics associated with the Chinese poultry chain. They provided insights into the Chinese poultry sector and the distribution status of poultry companies in the sampling area. Moreover, they also gave their comments on the draft questionnaire. These comments were valuable, because no validated constructs of governance, inter-organizational communication and supply chain practices in the Chinese poultry chain were available. The insights obtained from the interviews and site visits, together with those from the literature, jointly contributed to a structured questionnaire. Using this questionnaire, a pre-test with 2-5 selected companies from each stage of the poultry chain was then performed. Based on the pre-test, the questionnaire was further revised, and resulted in the final structured questionnaire for the survey. The three-step procedure of the field research, which combined face-to-face interview and site visits, the pre-test, and the survey, has proved to be beneficial by providing: (1) validated constructs and items for the questionnaire, and (2) valuable insights for the analysis and interpretation of the data results.

Second, partial least squares (PLS) modeling was used in this research, and proved to be successful in examining the proposed relationships between the major constructs. PLS modeling belongs to one of the family of structural equation modeling (SEM) techniques. There are two distinct families of SEM techniques (Chin, 1998b; Henseler *et al.*, 2009): (1) the covariance-based SEM techniques developed by (Jöreskog, 1969) and represented by LISREL and AMOS; and (2) the component-based (namely, variance-based) SEM techniques designed by (Wold, 1974, 1982, 1985){Wold, 1974 #808;Jöreskog, 1982 #822} and represented by PLS modeling. Comparatively, PLS path modeling obtained its initiation and implementation later than the more popularly employed LISREL and AMOS. However, it is increasingly apparent that applying PLS modeling has some advantages over covariance-based SEM tools (Chin, 1998b; Brown and Chin, 2004; Henseler *et al.*, 2009). These advantages have been discussed in Section 3.4.1. Owing to these advantages, PLS modeling has gradually increased its popularity. To our knowledge, no study has made use of SEM techniques to examine inter-organizational communication in the Chinese poultry chain. As such, we have contributed to the adoption of SEM techniques, especially the adoption of PLS modeling, in social science research and in a new socio-economic context.

7.3 Managerial and policy implications

This section contains a translation of the empirical results of this research into practical implications for managers and policy makers. Several important implications are formulated to answer the central research question of this research: *how to improve companies' practices in inter-organizational communication, in order to enhance companies' performance at the end?*

Based on the results of this research, approaches to communication and performance were identified for a company in relationships with its most important suppliers, and with its most important customers, respectively (Figure 7.4 and 7.5). In relationships with its main suppliers a company should look not only at its own approach, but also that of its suppliers. Correspondently, in relationships with its main customers a company should look not only at its own approach, but also that of its customers.

Implications for companies in relationships with their most important suppliers

First, regarding governance structure, trust appears to be a key to improve communication willingness. In order to improve the communication with its most important suppliers, a company should focus on building mutual trust.

For a company in relationships with their main suppliers, contractual governance does not take a critical role in improving communication and achieving performance. A likely explanation is that, in a market-oriented economy, the company holds such high negotiating power than their suppliers, that it is not necessary to use contractual governance to facilitate its business or to find new suppliers. Although a company in relationships with its main suppliers tends to ignore the need for contracts and prefer flexibility in purchasing sources, it should bear in mind that a contract does make sense for its suppliers. For its suppliers, a contract is a sign of a guaranteed market. Thus, in relationships with its main suppliers a company could consider adopting certain types of contracts (e.g. short-term contracts at least), if it intends to improve the communication willingness and behavior of its most important suppliers.

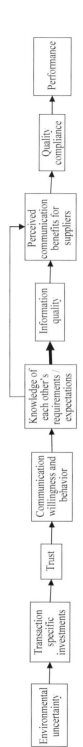

Figure 7.4. Paths to achieve performance for the company-supplier sample[1].
[1] Thin arrows show path coefficients significant at 5% for both samples; thick arrows show path coefficients only significant at 5% for one sample.

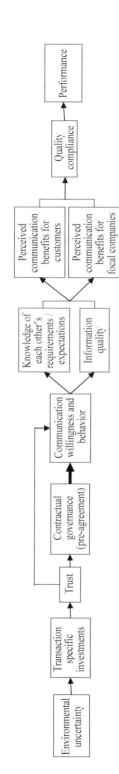

Figure 7.5. Paths to achieve performance for the company-customer sample[1].
[1] Thin arrows show path coefficients significant at 5% for both samples; thick arrows show path coefficients only significant at 5% for one sample.

Second, in order to realize more potential benefits of communication with its main suppliers, a company should invest to improve the communication willingness of its own and its suppliers' staff. In addition, special attention should be paid to understand the suppliers' changing requirements and expectations. This will substantially enhance its knowledge of its suppliers and information quality, and thus help to realize more of the potential communication benefits.

Third, in order to advance from realizing potential communication benefits to making itself stand out from its main competitors, a company should not only commit to realizing the potential communication benefits for itself, but also commit to making sure that its main suppliers realize the potential benefits as well. A company is often in a more powerful position than its suppliers. However, it should always bear in mind that comparatively, it is the communication benefits obtained by its main suppliers, rather than those by the company itself, that make it stand out from its main competitors. When the suppliers obtained such benefits, they will then comply better with the company's logistics and quality requirements, thus, significantly contribute to the company's 'comparative performance' ultimately.

Implications for companies in relationships with their most important customers

First, regarding governance structure, in order to improve the communication with its main customers, a company should also focus on building mutual trust. A company should bear in mind that trust is the most important way of improving communication willingness among its main customers, while it also helps to improve its own communication willingness. As discussed above, a customer is often in a more powerful position than its suppliers. Only when it trusts greater in its main suppliers, will it have greater willingness to communicate with the suppliers.

Being different from their customers, a company in relationships with their main customers tends to pay more attention to contractual governance. With its relatively weaker negotiating power than its main customers in the market-oriented economy, it might take contractual governance as a way to safeguard its specific investments, and make use of trust and contractual governance to jointly improve communication willingness and behavior with its main customers. Although a company might like to promote contractual relationships with its main customers, it should be aware that this is not the main interests of the customers. A contract is only a market promise provided by a customer for a limited period. However, it is the mutual trust that a company builds with its customers, jointly with contracts, that lead to long-term market opportunities for a company. Therefore, the company should pay attention to both trust and contractual governance, and make use of them to jointly facilitate its business, and thus safeguard its specific investments and markets.

Second, in order to realize more potential benefits of the communication with its main customers, a company should make use of senior managers and staff from different functions to communicate with the customers. In this way, the company would obtain a greater understanding of the customer's changing requirements and expectations, and could ensure such knowledge is used by staff in the different functions, thereby grasp markets demands better and facilitate its operations and pricing decision.

Third, in order to advance from realizing potential communication benefits to making itself stand out from its main competitors, a company should not only commit to realizing the potential communication benefits for itself, but also commit to making sure that its main customers realize the potential benefits as well. It should always bear in mind that it is not only the communication benefits obtained by itself, but also those by its main customers, that make it stand out from its main competitors. When a company's main customers obtain such benefits, they will help the company comply better with their quality requirements, thus, significantly contribute to the company's performance.

Implications for both customers and suppliers

First, a company should make good use of some of the opportunities provided by higher environmental uncertainty, in order to stimulate its main business partners to invest specifically in it. In this way, a company could transform the negative effect of higher environment uncertainty into a more positive opportunity. When environmental uncertainty is lower for a company, it might be higher for its main customers or suppliers. In such business environment, if the company cooperates well with the requirements of its most important customers or suppliers, provides them with materials or markets in need, and reduces their uncertainty and risks, it would be less difficult to persuade and facilitate the customers or suppliers to invest specifically in it, and also help to build up mutual trust. Moreover, it can also make use of such an opportunity of higher certainty among its customers to promote its contractual relationships with the customers.

Second, a company should truly invest to improve its own communication willingness and that of its main customers, and its main suppliers; it should make frequent contact and make use of senior managers and staff from different functions to communicate with its main customers, and suppliers. In this way, it can substantially enhance communication quality.

Third, a company should not only focus on regular information quality, but also commit to understand the changing requirements and expectations of its main customers, and suppliers, while helping its main customers and suppliers to obtain a good understanding of its own requirements and expectations. These will jointly lead to improved communication quality, and further help the company and its main customers, and its main suppliers to realize the potential communication benefits.

Fourth, a company should pay great attention to quality management in its supply chain. It should commit to ensure that its main suppliers comply well with its own quality requirements, and also make sure that it complies well with its customers' quality requirements. These will jointly make it stand out in performance, compared to its main competitors.

Fifth, there seem to be huge potential opportunities for improving performance with modern media and logistics compliance. In this research, these two aspects do not yet reveal their contribution to communication values and company performance, though the literature argued that they should have. A company should build a diverse communication system with both traditional and modern information media, and improve their knowledge and capability in the area of logistics management. These might lead to unexpected achievements for companies, especially for those in developing and transitional countries.

Sixth, by examining the influence of company characteristics, we find that the level of communication and supply chain compliance, as well as the level of performance of a company, should be evaluated on the basis of company characteristics. By cross-checking with their main counterparts and competitors with similar characteristics, a company could have a clearer understanding of how well it has performed in the area of inter-organizational communication, supply chain compliance, and company performance.

Implications for policy makers

Explicit attention should be paid to how to motivate food companies to implement quality standards. The results of this research indicated that companies adopting higher quality standards were likely to suffer from lower customer satisfaction and lower external efficiency. This might imply that there is no much motivation in the Chinese poultry to adopt a higher level of quality standard. And this lack of motivation might be the main reason why food quality incidents happen more frequently in developing and transitional countries than in the West. Thus, an important means of solving the food quality problem in developing and transitional country might be to facilitate companies' self-motivation to adopt quality standards, by adjusting the trade-off that is brought by the quality standards. In addition, it might be valuable to draft relevant food policy that encourages retailers to adopt high food quality standards. In the face of very powerful retailers, food production companies and food logistics companies are likely to comply with the increased quality requirements of the retailers.

Overall implications

All in all, we draw attention to the following:
1. The performance of a company is a broad issue covering diverse aspects. Each of these aspects tends to be affected by distinct factors. Managers should vet each aspect of company performance, such as customer satisfaction, internal and external efficiency, profitability, as well as competitive edge, and focus primarily on those performance aspects that are most problematic.
2. For managers who aim to approach optimal performance, inter-organizational communication with its main customers, and with its main suppliers, could be used as a powerful enabler. Such communication is also a broad issue covering diverse aspects; each of these aspects also tends to be affected by distinct factors. An efficient way to improve the communication of a company with its main customers, and its main suppliers, is to vet each aspect of its communication (with its main customers and suppliers, respectively), to target the major problem areas, and further improve these aspects jointly through their specific antecedents.
3. Based on the limited adoption of modern media and limited implementation of logistics compliance, there are huge potential opportunities for managers to improve their company performance.

7.4 Limitations and future research

As discussed in the above chapters, this research has its limitations. When learning something from this research, it would be wise to bear in mind the following limitations, which also point out directions for future research.

First, the main findings and conclusions of this research are based mainly on the Chinese poultry chain. In general, they are valuable for other non-highly integrated food chains in China or in other developing or transitional countries. However, some of these findings and conclusions should be carefully examined, if they are to be generalized to non-meat chains or highly integrated chains in the West. For instance, modern communication media are widely adopted in poultry chains in the West, and they might have been made good use. Therefore, we expect that modern media might be positively and significantly linked to communication quality, and furthermore with perceived communication benefits in the West. Another example concerns the knowledge of each other's requirements and expectations. Such knowledge might be more valuable in a developing or a transitional country than in the West. Normally, food markets and food quality are less stable in developing and transitional countries than in the West. The third example is that communication formality has been omitted in this research, due to the frequent absence of formal communication in the study domain, as the researcher noticed in the field research. However, it might be a critical communication element in the West. The fourth example is that the expected positive association between logistics compliance and company performance was neither supported in the Chinese poultry chain in this research, nor in the Chinese pork chain (Han, 2009), but was found in the Chinese vegetable chain (Lu, 2007). Therefore, we expect that the positive association between logistics compliance and company performance might not exist in other Chinese meat chains, but might exist in the Chinese fruit chain, which has similar logistic requirements to the vegetable chain. Based on these differences above, we also assume that it would be valuable to conduct a comparative study in the future between the non-highly integrated poultry chain in China and a highly integrated poultry chain in the West; such a study might provide valuable insights into the unexpected disadvantages of integrated supply chain management, or unexpected advantages of non-integrated supply chain.

Second, this research focused on the communication of companies with their *most important* customers, and with their *most important* suppliers. Its empirical results have provided valuable insights for us to understand and design managerial strategy, regarding the communication with the most important business partners. However, we assume that the communication of companies with *less important* business partners might reveal a different picture. Moreover, based on the polarization of power and benefits, we can expect that (1) there might be more game and bargaining than collaboration in the process of communication with less important partners; and (2) managers have to consider more carefully the trade-off between communication benefits and communication costs, and adjust their communication strategy based on the trade-off. We hereby call for attention to be paid to research on the communication of companies with their less important customers, and with their less important suppliers, which is absent from the literature.

Third, the development of a relationship contains loops and is not always a sequential process (Claro, 2004). The formulation of the hypotheses in Chapter 2 tried to build up certain sequence and causality based on the literature. However, it is noteworthy that some constructs might influence each other. For instance, greater trust might lead to more specific investments, and turn out to induce even greater trust; improved communication willingness and behavior might induce greater trust, thus, turn out to motivate even greater willingness and closer contacts between the companies; more perceived communication benefits might motivate further improvement of communication willingness and behavior; and improved logistics compliance might lead to improved quality compliance. Thus, we should be aware of the potential mutual influence behind the current findings and conclusions. Finally, it would be useful to examine such influence in future research.

References

Al-Tameem, A.A. (2004) "An inhibiting context hampering role of information technology as an enabler in organizational learning," *Journal of Computer Information Systems* (44:4)34-40.

Alvarado, U.Y., and Kotzab, H. (2001) "Supply chain management: the integration of logistics in marketing," *Industrial Marketing Management* (30:2)183-198.

Amanor-Boadu, V., Trienekens, J.H., and Willems, S. (2002) "Informaiton and communication technologies, strategic power and inter-organisational relationships," In: *Agribusiness and Food Industry: Paradoxes in Food Chains and Networks*, Wageningen Academic Publishers, Wageningen, the Netherlands, pp. 908-918.

Ambrose, E., Marshall, D., Fynes, B., and Lynch, D. (2008) "Communication media selection in buyer-supplier relationships," *International Journal of Operations & Production Management* (28:4)360-379.

Anderson, E., Lodish, L., and Weitz, B. (1987) "Resource allocation behavior in covnential channels," *Journal of Marketing Research* (24:1 Februry)85-97.

Anderson, J.C., and Gerbing, D.W. (1988) "Structural equation modeling in practice: a review and recommended two-step approach," *Psychological Bulletin* (103:3)411-423.

Anderson, J.C., and Narus, J.A. (1990) "A model of distributor firm and manufacturer firm working partnerships," *Journal of Marketing* (54:1)42-58.

Aramyan, L.H. (2007) "Measuring supply chain performance in the agri-food sector", Wageningen University, Wageningen, the Netherlands.

Arana, J.J.C. (2010) "Supply chain practices, performance and organizational configuration in the Mexican avocado industry," Wageningen University, Wageningen, The Netherlands, p. 151.

Bagozzi (1994) "*Principles of marketing research*", Blackwell, Oxford, UK.

Bakos, J.Y., and Kemerer, C.F. (1992) "Recent Applications of Economic Theory in Information Technology Research," *Decision Support Systems* (8:5)365-386.

Bandyopadhyay, S., Robicheaux, R.A., and Hill, J.S. (1994) "Cross-cultural differences in intrachannel communications: the United States and India," *Jounal of International Marketing* (2:3)83-100.

Barney, J.B., and Hesterly, W. (1999) "Organizational economics: understanding the relationship between organizations and economic analysis," in: *Studying organization,* R.C. Steward and H. C. (eds.), Sage Publications, Thousand Oaks, USA, pp. 109-141.

Barratt, M. (2004) "Understanding the meaning of collaboration in the supply chain," *Supply Chain Management-an International Journal* (9:1)30-42.

Barrett, S., and Konsynski, B. (1982) "Inter-organization ifnromation sharing systems," *MIS Quarterly* (6:Special Issue)93-105.

Barthélemy, J., and Quélin, B.V. (2006) "Complexity of outsourcing contracts and ex post transaction costs: an empirical investigation," *Journal of Management Studies* (43:8)1775-1797.

Beath, C.M. (1987) "Managing the user relationship in IS development projects: a transaction governance approach," The 8th International Conference on Information Systems, Pittsburgh, PA, USA, pp. 415-427.

Bechtel, C., and Jayaram, J. (1997) "Supply Chain Management: a strategic perspective," *International Journal of Logistics Management* (8:1)15-33.

Bensaou, M. (1995) "Configurations of inter-organizational relationships: a comparision between U.S. and Japanese Auto-makers," *Management Science* (41:9)1471-1492.

References

Bensaou, M. (1999) "Portfolios of buyer-supplier relationships," *MIT Sloan Management Review* (40:4)35-44.

Bigley, G.A., and Pearce, J.L. (1998) "Straining for shared meaning in organization science: Problems of trust and distrust," *Academy of Management Review* (23:3)405-421.

Bijman, W.J.J. (2002) "Essays on agricultural co-operatives: governance structures in fruit and vegetable chains," Erasmus University Rotterdam, Rotterdam, The Netherlands.

Blalock, H.M. (1964) "*Causal inferences in nonexperimental research*", University of North Carolina Press, Chapel Hill, NC, USA.

Boger, S. (2001a) "Agricultural markets in transition, an empirical study on contracts and transaction cost in the Polish hog sector," Shaker Verlag, Aachen, Germany.

Boger, S. (2001b) "Quality and contractual choice: a transaction cost approach to the Polish pork market," *European Review of Agricultural Economics* (28:3)241-261.

Bogetoft, P., and Olesen, H.b. (2004) "Design of production contracts: lessons from theory and agriculture," Copenhagen Business School Press, Copenhagen, Denmark.

Bollen, K., and Lennox, R. (1991) "Conventional wisdom on measurement: a structural equation perspective," *Psychological Bulletin* (110:2)305-314.

Bowersox, D.J., and Closs, D.J. (1996) "Logistical management: the integrated supply chain process", McGraw-Hill, New York, NY, USA.

Bowersox, D.J., Closs, D.J., and Stank, T. (2003) "How to master cross-enterprise collaboration," *Supply Chain Management Review* (7:4)18-27.

Brown, J. (1981) "A cross-channel comparison of supplier-retailer relationship," *Journal of Retailing* (57:Winter)3-18.

Brown, S.P., and Chin, W.W. (2004) "Satisfying and retaining customers through independent service representatives," *Decision Sciences* (35:3)527-550.

Brynjolfsson, E., Malone, T.W., and Gurbaxani, V. (1988) "Hierarchiese and the impact of information technology," in: *MIT Sloan School of Management Working Paper*, pp. 2113-2188.

Brynjolfsson, E., Malone, T.W., Gurbaxani, V., and Kambil, A. (1994) "Does information technology lead to smaller firms?," *Management Science* (40:12)1628-1644.

Butler, J. and John, K. (1999) "Trust expectations, information sharing, climate of trust, and negotiation effectiveness and efficiency," *Group & Organization Management* (24:2)217.

Cai, S., Jun, M., and Yang, Z. (2010) "Implementing supply chain information integration in China: The role of institutional forces and trust," *Journal of Operations Management* (28:3)257-268.

Camps, T., Diederen, P., Hofstede, G.J., and Vos, G.C.J.M. (2004) "The emerging world of chains and networks: bridging theory and practice", Reed Business Informaiton, The Hague, the Netherlands.

Cao, M. (2007) "Achieving collaborative advantage through IOS-enabled supply chain collaboration: An empirical examination," The University of Toledo, Ohio, USA, p. 212.

Cao, M., Vonderembse, M.A., Zhang, Q.Y., and Ragu-Nathan, T.S. (2010) "Supply chain collaboration: conceptualisation and instrument development," *International Journal of Production Research* (48:22)6613-6635.

Carr, A.S., and Smeltzer, L.R. (2002) "The relationship between information technology use and buyer – supplier relationships: an exploratory analysis of the buying firm's perspective"," *IEEE Transactions on Engineering Management* (49:3)293-304.

Carr, S.A., and Kaynak, H. (2007) "Communication methods, information sharing, supplier development and performance," *International Journal of Operations & Production Management* (27:4)346.

Carson, S.J., Madhok, A., and Wu, T. (2006) "Uncertainty, opportunism, and governance: the effects of volatility and ambiguity on formal and relational contracting," *Academy of Management Journal* (49:5)1058-1077.

Case, B.M. (2007) "How well do you know your business partner?," *Dallasnews*, 17 March, 2010. Available at http://www.dallasnews.com/sharedcontent/dws/bus/stories/DN-TUINEI_18bus. ART0.State.Edition1.365b19e.html.

Chen, C., and Luo, Y.Z. (2003) "Establishment of supply chain model of the processed meat products in China," *Journal of Nanjing Agricultural University* (1)89-92 (in Chinese).

Chen, I.J., and Paulraj, A. (2004) "Towards a theory of supply chain management: the constructs and measurements," *Journal of Operations Management* (22:2)119-150.

Chin, W.W. (1998a) "Issues and opinion on structural equation modeling," *MIS Quarterly* (22:1)VII-XVI.

Chin, W.W. (1998b) "The partial least squares approach to structural equation modeling," in: *Modern Methods for Business Research,* G.A. Marcoulides (ed.), Lawrence Erlbaum Associates, Mahwah, NJ, USA, pp. 295-358.

Chin, W.W., and Newsted, P.R. (1999) "Structural equation modeling analysis with small samples using partial least squares," in: *Statistical strategies for small sample research,* R.H. Hoyle (ed.), Sage, Thousand Oaks, CA, USA, pp. 307-342.

Chopra, S., and Meindl, P. (2007) "Supply chain management: strategy, planning and operations", (3 ed.) Prentice Hall, Upper Saddle River, NJ, USA.

Churchill, G.A. (1979) "Paradigm for Developing Better Measures of Marketing Constructs," *Journal of Marketing Research* (16:1)64-73.

Churchill, G.A. (1999) "Marketing research: methodological foundations", Dryden Press, Orlando, FL, USA, 1017p.

Ciborra, C.U. (1985) "Reframing the role of computers in organizations: the transaction costs approach. In: Proceedings of the sixth international Conference on Information Systems," Indianapolis, IN, USA, pp. 57-69.

Clare, B., Shadbolt, N., and Reid, J. (2002) "Supply base relationships in the New Zealand red meat industry: a case study," In: *Paradoxes in Food Chains and Networks*, Wageningen Academic Publishers, Wageningen, the Netherlands, pp. 805-816.

Claro, D.P. (2004) "Managing business networks and buyer-supplier relationships," Wageningen University, Wageningen, the Netherlands, p. 196.

Clemons, E.K., and Row, M. (1989) "Information technology and economics reorganization," In: The 10th International Conference on Information Systems, Boston, MA, USA, pp. 341-352.

Collins, A. (2002) "The organisation of retailer-manufacturere relaionships," In: *Paradoxes in Food Chains and Networks*, Wageningen Academic Publishers, Wageningen, the Netherlands, pp. 593-605.

Constant, D., Kiesler, S., and Sproull, L. (1994) "What mine is ours, or is it – a study of attitudes about information sharing," *Information Systems Research* (5:4)400-421.

Cook, K.S., and Emerson, R.M. (1978) "Power, equity and commitment in exchagne networks," *American Sociological Review* (43:October)721-739.

Cool, K., Dierickx, I., and Jemison, D. (1989) "Business strategy, market structure and risk-return relationships: a structural approach," *Strategic Management Journal* (10:6)507-522.

Cooper, M.C., and Ellram, L.M. (1993) "Characteristics of supply chain management and the implications for purchasing and logistics strategy," *International Journal of Logistics Management* (4:2)13-24.

References

Cooper, M.C., Lambert, D.M., and Pagh, J.D. (1997) "Supply chain management: more than a new name for logistics," *International Journal of Logistics Management* (8:1)1-13.

Corsten, D., and Kumar, N. (2005) "Do suppliers benefit from collaborative relationships with large retailers? An empirical investigation of efficient consumer response adoption," *Jounal of Marketing* (69:3)80-94.

Croom, S., Romano, P., and Giaanakis, M. (2000) "Supply chain management: an analytical framework for critical literature review," *European Journal of Purchasing & Supply Management* (6:1)67-83.

Cunningham, C., and Tynan, C. (1993) "Electronic trading, inter-organizational systems and the nature of buyer-seller relationships: the need for a network perspective," *International Journal of Information Management* (13:1)3-28.

Daft, R.L., and Lengel, R.H. (1984) *"Information richness: A new approach to managerial information processing and organizational design"*, JAI Press, Greenwich, UK.

Daugherty, P.J., Ellinger, A.E., and Gustin, C.M. (1996) "Integrated logistics: achieving logistics performance improvements," *Supply Chain Management Review* (1:3)25-33.

Deutsch, M. (1958) "Trust and suspicion," *Journal of Conflict Resolution* (2)265-279.

De Vries, E. (2009) "Creating value in organizations – ICT governance." manuscript, Wageningen University, Wageningen, the Netherlands.

Diamantopoulos, A., and Winklhofer, H.M. (2001) "Index construction with formative indicators: an alternative to scale development," *Journal of Marketing Research* (38:2)269-277.

Dibbern, J., Goles, T., Hirschheim, R.A., and Jayatilaka, B. (2004) "Information systems outsourcing: a survey and analysis of the literature," *The Data Base for Advances in Information Systems* (35:4)6-102.

Dillman, D.A. (1978) *"Mail and telephone surveys: the tailored design method"*, Wiley, New York, NY, USA.

Dillman, D.A. (2000) *"Mail and internet surveys: the tailored design method"*, Wiley, New York, NY, USA.

Dixit, A. (2009) "Governance institutions and economic activity," *American Economic Review* (99)5-24.

Doll, W.J., and Torkzadeh, G. (1988) "The measurement of end-user computing satisfaction," *MIS Quarterly* (12:2)259-274.

Dyer, J., and Singh, H. (1998) "The relational view: cooperative strategy and sources of interorganizational competitive advantage," *Academy of Management Review* (23:4)660-679.

Dyer, J.H. (1996) "Does governance matter? Keiretsu alliances and asset specificity as sources of Japaneses competitive advantage," *Organization Science* (7:6)649-666.

Edwards, J.R., and Bagozzi, R.P. (2000) "On the nature and direction of relationships between constructs and measures," *Psychological Methods* (5:2)155-174.

Eisenberg, E., and Witten, M.G. (1987) "Reconsidering openness in organizational communication," *Academy of Management Review* (12:3)418-426.

Ellram, L.M., and Cooper, M.C. (1990) "Supply chain management, partnership and the supplier-third party relationship," *International Journal of Logistics Management* (1:2)1-10.

Fawcett, S., E., Osterhaus, P., Magnan, G., M., Brau, J., C., and McCarter, M., W. (2007) "Information sharing and supply chain performance: the role of connectivity and willingness," *Supply Chain Management* (12:5)358-368.

Fawcett, S.E., Magnan, G.M., and McCarter, M.W. (2008) "Benefits, barriers, and bridges to effective supply chain management," *Supply Chain Management-an International Journal* (13:1)35-48.

Fornell, C. (1982) "A second generation of multivariate analysis: an overview," in: *A second generation of multivariate analysis,* C. Fornell (ed.), Praeger, New York, NY, USA, pp. 1-21.

Fornell, C. (1987) "A second generation of multivariate analysis: classification of methods and implications for marketing research," in: *Review of Marketing,* M.J. Houston (ed.), American Marketing Association, Chicago, IL, USA, pp. 407-450.

Fornell, C., and Robinson, W.T. (1983) "Industrial organization and consumer satisfaction / dissatisfaction," *Journal of Consumer Research* (9:4)403-412.

Forrester, J.W. (1958) "Industrial dynamics – a major breakthrough for decision makers," *Harvard Business Review* (36:4)37-66.

Forrester, J.W. (1961) "Industrial dynamics", MIT Press, Cambridge, MA, USA.

Frazier, G., and Summers, J. (1984) "Interfirm influence strategies and their application within distribution channels," *Journal of Marketing* (48:Summer)43-55.

Ganesan, S. (1994) "Determinants of long-term orientation in buyer-seller relationships," *Journal of Marketing* (58:2)1-19.

Ganeshan, R., Jack, E., Magazine, M.J., and Stephens, P. (1999) " A taxonomic review of Supply Chain Management research," in: *Quantitative models for Supply Chain Management,,* S. Tayur, R. Ganeshan and M. Magazine (eds.), Kluwer, Dordrecht, the Netherlands.

Gang, L., Yi, L., Shouyang, W., and Hong, Y. (2006) "Enhancing agility by timely sharing of supply information," *Supply Chain Management* (11:5)425.

Gaski, J. (1984) "The theory of power and conflict in channels of distribution," *Journal of Marketing* (48 (Summer):9-29).

Gefen, D., and Straub, D. (2005) "A practical guide to factorial validity using PLS-graph: tutorial and annotated example," *Communications fo the Association for Information Systems* (16)91-109.

Gefen, D., and Straub, D.W. (1989) "Validating Instruments in MIS Research," *MIS Quarterly* (13:2, June)147-169.

Ghoshal, S., and Moran, P. (1996) "Bad for practice: a critique of the transaction cost theory," *Academy of Management Review* (21:1)13-47.

Gibbons, R. (2010) "Transaction-Cost Economics: Past, Present, and Future?," *Scandinavian Journal of Economics* (112:2)263-288.

Gopal, A., and Koka, B.R. (2009) "When do vendors benefit from relational governance? Contracts, relational governance and vendor profitability in software development outsourcing," Thirtieth International Conference on Information Systems, Phoenix, USA, pp. 1-15.

Grievink, J.W., Josten, L., and Valk, C. (2002) "State of the art in food: th changing face of the worldwide food industry", Elsevier Business Information, Meppel, the Netherlands.

Gu, H., and Wang, X. (2007) "On the current status and development of Chinese chicken industry," *China Poultry* (29:14)45-50. (In Chinese).

Guiltinan, J., Rejab, I., and Rodgers, W. (1980) "Factors influencing coordination in a franchise channel," *Journal of Retailing* (56 (Fall))41-58.

Gulati, R. (1995) "Does familiarity breed trust? The implications of repeated ties for contractual choice in alliances," *Academy of Management Journal* (38:1)85-112.

Hair, J.F., Anderson, R.E., Tatham, R.L., and Black, W.C. (1998) "Multivariate data analysis with readings", (5th ed.) Prentice Hall, Englewood Cliffs, NJ, USA.

Han, J. (2009) *"Supply chain integration, quality management and firm performance: in the pork processing industry in China"*, Wageningen Academic Publishers, Wageningen, the Netherlands.

Han, J., Trienekens, J.H., and Omta, S.W.F. (2009) "Integrated information and logistics management, quality management and firm performance of pork processing industry in China," *British Food Journal* (111:1)9-25.

References

Hansmann, H. (1996) *"The ownership of enterprise"*, The belknap Press of Harvard University Press, Boston, MA, USA.

Hardman, P.A., Darroch, M.A.G., and Ortmann, G.G. (2002) "Improving cooperation to make the South African fresh apple export value chain more competitive," In: *Paradoxes in Food Chains and Networks*, Wageningen Academic Publishers, Wageningen, the Netherlands, pp. 434-443.

Harland, C. (1999) "Supply network strategy and social capital," in: *Corporate social capital*, R.T.A.J. Leenders and S. Gabbay (eds.), Kluwer Academic Publishers, MA, USA, pp. 409-431.

Hart, P., and Saunders, C. (1997) "Power and trust: Critical factors in the adoption and use of electronic data interchange," *Organization Science* (8:1)23-42.

Hart, P., and Saunders, C. (1998) "Emerging electronic partnerships: antecedents and dimensions of EDI use from the supplier's perspective," *Journal of management information systems* (14:4)87-111.

Heide, J.B., and John, G. (1988) "The role of dependence balancing in safeguarding transaction specific assets in conventional channels," *Journal of Marketing*:(52:1)20-35.

Heide, J.B., and John, G. (1992) "Do norms matter in marketing relationships?," *Journal of Marketing* (56:April)32-44.

Hendriks-Gusc, J.S. (2007) "Headquarters-subsidiary relationship governance in emerging markets of central eastern Europe. A study in Poland", Wageningen Academic Publishers, Wageningen, the Netherlands.

Henseler, J., Ringle, C.M., and Sinkovics, R.R. (2009) "The use of partial least squares path modeling in international marketing," in: *Advances in International Marketing*, Emerald Group Publishing Limited, Bingley, UK, pp. 277-319.

Higgins, C.A., Duxbury, L.E., and Irving, R.H. (1992) "Work-family conflict in the dual-career family," *Organizational Behavior and Human Decision Processes* (51:1)51-75.

Hobbs, J.E. (1997) "Measuring the importance of transaction costs in cattle marketing," *American Journal of Agricultural Economics* (79:4)1083-1095.

Hoetker, G., and Mellewigt, T. (2009) "Choice and performance of governance mechanisms: matching alliance governance to asset type," *Strategic Management Journal* (30:10)1025-1044.

Hoogewegen, M.R. (1997) "Modular Network Design: assessing the impact of EDI," Erasmus Universiteit, Rotterdam, the Netherlands.

Hoskisson, R.E., Eden, L., Lau, C.M., and Wright, M. (2000) "Strategy in emerging economics," *Academy of Management Journal* (43:3)249-267.

Hsu, L.L., Chiu, C.M., Chen, J.C.H., and Liu, C.C. (2009) "The impact of supply chain management systems on information sharing and integrated-performance," *Human Systems Management* (28:3)101-121.

Hu, D. (2003) "An overview on integrated business models of foreign poultry industries," *China Poultry* (25:5)35-38. (In Chinese).

Hu, D., Yu, H., and Reardon, T. (2003) "The operation of fresh and live non-staple foodstuff food in Chinese supermarkets and the consumer buying behaviour," *Chinese Rural Economy* (8:12-17).

Hu, H., and Liu, C. (2007) "Analysis on restrictive factors for China broiler products export based on international markets and characteristics of products," *China Poultry* (29:24)9-15 (In Chinese).

Huan, S.H., Sheoran, S.K., and Wang, G. (2004) "A review and analysis of supply chain operations reference (SCOR) model," *Supply Chain Management* (9:1)23-29.

Hulland, J. (1999) "Use of partial least squares (PLS) in strategic management research: A review of four recent studies " *Strategic Management Journal* (20:2)159.

Hult, G.T.M., Ketchen, D.J., and Slater, S.F. (2004) "Information processing, knowledge development, and strategic supply chain performance," *Academy of Management Journal* (47:2)241-253.

Humphreys, P.K., Li, W.L., and Chan, L.Y. (2004) "The impact of supplier development on buyer–supplier performance," *Omega: The International Journal of Management Science* (32)131-143.

Issar, G.S., Cowan, R.T., Woods, E.J., and Wegener, M. (2004) "Dynamics of Australian dairy-food supply chain: strategic options for participants in a deregulated environment," In: *Dynamics in Chains and Networks*, Wageningen Academic Publishers, Wageningen, the Netherlands, pp. 458-464.

Jarvis, C.B., and MacKenzie, S.B. (2003) "A critical review of construct indicators and measurement model misspecification in marketing and consumer research " *Journal of Consumer Research* (30:2)199-218.

Jonsson, P., and Zineldin, M. (2003) "Achieving high satisfaction in supplier-dealer working relationships," *Supply Chain Management* (8:3)224-240.

Jöreskog, K.G. (1969) "A general approach to confirmatory maximum likelihood factor analysis," *Psychometrika* (34)183-202.

Jöreskog, K.G., and Goldberger (1975) "Estimation of a model with multiple indicators and multiple causes of a single latent variable," *Journal of the American Statistical Association* (70:351)631-639.

Jöreskog, K.G., and Sörbom, D. (1996) "LISREL 8: structural equation modeling with the SIMPLIS command language", Scientific Software International, Chicago, IL, USA.

Joskow, P.L. (1987) "Contract duration and relationship-specific investments: empirical evidence from coal markets," *The American Economic Review* (77:1)168-185.

Kalwani, M., and Narayandas, N. (1995) "Long-term manufacturer-supplier relationships: do they pay?," *Journal of Marketing* (59:1)1-15.

Katsikeas, C.S., Skarmeas, D., and Bello, D.C. (2009) "Developing successful trust-based international exchange relationships," *Journal of International Business Studies* (40:1)132-155.

Kim, K., and Umanath, N. (2005) "Information transfer in B2B procurement: an empirical analysis and measurement," *Information & Management* (42:6)813-828.

Kim, S.W. (2006) "Effects of supply chain management practices, integration and competition capability on performance," *Supply Chain Management: an International journal* (11:3)241-248.

King, R.P., Hand, M.S., DiGiacomo, G., Clancy, K., Gómez, Miguel L., Hardesty, S.D., Lev, L., and McLaughlin, E.W. (2010) "Comparing the structure, size, and performance of local and mainstream food supply chains," United States Department of Agriculture, pp. 1-73.

Klein, R., Rai, A., and Straub, D.W. (2007) "Competitive and cooperative positioning in supply chain logistics," *Decision Sciences* (38:4)611-646.

Kogut, B. (1988) "Joint ventures: theoretical and empirical perspectives," *Strategic Management Journal* (9:4)319-332.

Kottila, M.-R., and Rönni, P. (2008) "Collaboration and trust in two organic food chains," *British Food Journal* (110:4/5)376-394.

Krause, D.R., and Ellram, L.M. (1997) "Success factors in supplier development," *International Journal of Physical Distribution & Logistics Management* (27:1)39-52.

Krijnen, W.P., Dijkstra, T.K., and Gill, R.D. (1998) "Conditions for factor (in) determinacy in factor analysis," *Psychometrika* (63:4)359-367.

Lambert, D.M., Cooper, M.C., and Pagh, J.D. (1998) "Supply chain management: implementation issues and research opportunities," *The International Journal of Logistics Management* (9:2)1-19.

Lamming, R. (1996) "Squaring lean supply with supply chain management," *International Journal of Operations & Production Management* (10:2)183-196.

References

Lazzarini, S.G., Miller, G.J., and Zenger, T.R. (2004) "Order with some law: complementary versus substitution of formal and informal arrangement," *Journal of Law, Economics and Organisation* (20:2)261-298.

Lee, B.C., Kim, P.S., Hong, K.S., and Lee, I. (2010) "Evaluating antecedents and consequences of supply chain activities: an integrative perspective," *International Journal of Production Research* (48:3)657-682.

Lee, H., and Whang, S. (2001) "E-Business and supply chain itegration." in Harrison, T.P., Lee, H.L., Neale, J.J., Whang, S. (eds.) The Practice of Supply Chain Management: Where Theory and Application Converge. Springer, New York, NY, USA. pp.123-138.

Lee, H.L. (2000) "Creating value through supply chain integration," *Supply Chain Management Review* (4:4)30-36.

Lee, H.L., and Billington, C. (1992) "Managing supply chain: pitfalls and opportunities," *Sloan Management Review* (33:3)65-73.

Lee, H.L., Padmanabhan, V., and Whang, S. (1997a) "The bullwhip effect in supply chains," *Sloan Management Review* (38:3)93-102.

Lee, H.L., Padmanabhan, V., and Whang, S.J. (1997b) "Information distortion in a supply chain: the bullwhip effect," *Management Science* (43:4)546-558.

Lee, H.L., So, K.C., and Tang, C.S. (2000) "The value of information sharing in a two-level supply chain," *Management Science* (46:5)626-643.

Lee, L.H., and Whang, S. (2000) "Information sharing in a supply chain," *International Journal of Manufacturing Technology and Management* (1:1)79.

Lefebvre, E., Cassivi, L., Lefebvre, L., Léger, P.-M., and Hadaya, P. (2003) "Supply chain management, electronic collaboration tools and organizational innovativeness," *Chain and Network Science* (3:2)81-94.

Leiblein, M.J. (2003) "the choice of organizational governance form and performance: predictions from transaction cost, resource-based and real options theories," *Journal of Management* (29:6)937-961.

Lemke, F., Goffin, K., and Szwejczewski, M. (2003) "Investigating the meaning of supplier-manufacturer partnerships: an exploratory study," *International Journal of Physical Distribution & Logistics Management* (33:3)209-228.

Li, J., Sikora, R., Shaw, M.J., and Tan, G.W. (2006) "A strategic analysis of inter organizational information sharing " *Decision Support Systems* (42:1)251-266.

Li, L. (2002) "Information sharing in a supply chain with horizontal competition " *Management Science* (48:9)1196-1212.

Li, S.H., and Lin, B.S. (2006) "Accessing information sharing and information quality in supply chain management," *Decision Support Systems* (42:3)1641-1656.

Lindgreen, A., Palmer, R., and Trienekens, J. (2005) "Relationships within the supply chains: a case study," *Journal on Chain and Network Science* (5:2)85-99.

Lindgreen, A., Trienekens, J.H., and Velinga, K. (2004) "Contemporary marketing practice: a case study of the Dutch pork supply chain," In: Dynamics in Chains and Networks, Wageningen Academic Publishers, Wageningen, The Netherlands, pp. 273-279.

Little, R.J.A., and Rubin, D.B. (1987) "Statistical analysis with missing data", Wiley, New York, NY, USA.

Liu, D., Zhou, G., and Xu, X. (2005) "Current situation and development trend of Chick processing industry in China," *Food Sciences* (26:11)266-269. (In Chinese).

Lohmöller, J.-B. (1989) "*Latent variable path modeling with partial least squares*", Physica, Heidelberg.

Lu, H. (2007) "The role of guanxi in buyer-seller relationships in China: a survey of vegetable supply chains in Jiangsu province", Wageningen Academic Publishers, Wageningen, the Nteherlands, 239p.

Lu, H., Trienekens, J., Omta, O., and Feng, S. (2007) "The role of guanxi networks and contracts in Chinese vegetable supply chains," *Journal on Chain and Network Science* (7:2)121-131.

Luo, Y.D., and Park, S.H. (2001) "Strategic alignment and performance of market-seeking MNCs in China," *Strategic Management Journal* (22:2)141-155.

Lusch, R.F., and Brown, J.R. (1996) "Interdependency, contracting, and relational behavior in market channels," *Journal of Marketing* (60:October)19-38.

MacCallum, R.C., and Browne, M.W. (1993) "The use of causal indicators in covariance structure models: some practical issues," *Psychological Bulletin* (114:3)533-541.

Mahmoudi, J., Lamothe, J., and Thierry, C. (2007) "A simulation model for customer-supplier cooperation in the telecom supply chain," *International Journal of Business Performance Management* (9:2)188-205.

Malhortra, N.K., Peterson, M., and Kleiser, S.B. (1999) "Marketing research: a state-of-the-art review and directions for the twenty-first century," *Journal of the Academy of Marketing Science* (27:2)160-183.

Malhotra, N.K., Peterson, M., and Kleiser, S.B. (1999) "Marketing research: a state-of-the-art review and directions for the twenty-first century," *Journal of the Academy of Marketing Science* (27:2)160-183.

Malone, T.W., Yates, J., and Benjamin, R.I. (1987) "Electronic markets and electronic hierarchies," *Communications of the ACM* (30:6)484-497.

Martinez, S., Hand, M., Pra, M.D., Pollack, S., Ralston, K., Smith, T., Vogel, S., Clark, S., Lohr, L., Low, S., and Newman, C. (2010) "Local food systems: concepts, impacts, and issues," USDA, ERS, Economic Research Report Number 97. Available at: http://www.ers.usda.gov/Publications/ERR97/ERR97.pdf.

Masten, S.E. (1993) "Transaction costs, mistakes, and performance: assessing the importance of governance," *Managerial and Decision Economics* (14:2)119-129.

Masten, S.E. (2000) "Transaction-cost economics and the organization of agricultural transaction," in: *Advances in applied microeconomics – industrial organization,* M.R. Baye (ed.), Elsevier Science, New York, NY, USA, pp. 173-195.

Mayer, K.L., and Argyres, N. (2004) "Learning to contract: evidence from the personal computer industry," *Organization Science* (15:4)394-410.

Mayer, R.C., Davis, J.H., and Schoorman, F.D. (1995) "An integrative model of organizational trust," *Academy of Management Review* (20:3)709-734.

McKinnon, J.L., Harrison, G.L., Chow, C.W., and Wu, A. (2003) "Organizational culture: association with commitment, job satisfaction, propensity to remain, and information sharing in Taiwan," *International Journal of Business Studies* (11:1)25-44.

Mendelson, H. (2000) "Organizational architecture and success in the information technology industry," *Management Science* (46:4)513-529.

Mentzer, J.T., Foggin, J., and Golicic, S. (2000) "Collaboration: the enablers, impediments, and benefits," *Supply Chain Management Review* (5:6)52-58.

Milgrom, P., and Roberts, J. (1990) "Bargaining cost, influence cost, and the organization of economic activity," in: *Perspectives on positive political economy,* J. Alt and K. Shepsle (eds.), Cambridge University Press, Cambridge, UK.

Milgrom, P., and Roberts, J. (1992) "Economics, organization and management", Prentice Hall, NJ, USA, 600p.

References

Milliken, F.J. (1987) "Three types of perceived uncertainty about the environment: state, effect, and response uncertainty," *Academy of Management Review* (12:1)133-143.

Min, S., Roath, A.S., Daugherty, P.J., Genchev, S.E., Chen, H., Arndt, A.D., and Richey, R.G. (2005) "Supply chain collaboration: what's happening?," *International Journal of Logistics Management* (16:2)237-256.

Mohr, J., and Nevin, J.R. (1990) "Communication strategies in marketing channels: a theoretical perspective," *Journal of Marketing* (54:4)36.

Mohr, J.J., Fisher, R.J., and Nevin, J.R. (1996) "Collaborative communication in interfirm relationships: moderating effects of integration and control," *Journal of Marketing* (60:3)103-115.

Mohr, J.J., and Sohi, R.S. (1995) "Communication flows in distribution channels: impact on assessments of communication quality and satisfaction," *Journal of Retailing* (71:4)393-415.

Morgan, R.M., and Hunt, S.D. (1994) "The commitment-trust theory of relationship marketing," *Journal of Marketing* (58:3)20-38.

Narasimhan, R., and Kim, S.W. (2001) "Information system utilization strategy for supply chain integration," *Journal of Business Logistics* (22:2)51.

Neely, A., Gregory, M., and KenPlatts (1995) "Performance measurement system design: a literature review and research agenda," *International Journal of Operations & Production Management* (15:4)80-116.

Noordewier, T.G., John, G., and Nevin, J.R. (1990) "Performance outcomes of purchasing arrangements in industrial buyer-vendor relationships," *Journal of Marketing* (54:4)80.

Nooteboom, B., Berger, H., and Noorderhaven, N.G. (1997) "Effects of trust and governance on relational risk," *Academy of Management Journal* (36)794-829.

Nunnally, J.C. (1978) "Psychometric theory", (2 ed.) McGraw-Hill, New York, NY, USA.

Nyaga, G.N., Whipple, J.M., and Lynch, D.F. (2010) "Examining supply chain relationships: Do buyer and supplier perspectives on collaborative relationships differ?," *Journal of Operations Management* (28:2)101-114.

O'Reilly, C. (1982) "Variations in decision markers' use of information sources: the impact of quality and accessibility of information," *Academy of Management Journal* (25:4)756-771.

Oliver, R.K., and Webber, M.D. (1982) " Supply Chain Management: Logistics catches up with strategy," Outlook, Booz, Allen and Hamilton Inc. Reprinted 1992, in Logistics: The Strategic Issues, ed. M Christopher, Chapman Hall, London, UK, pp. 63-75.

Omta, S.W.F., Trienekens, J.H., and Beers, G. (2001) "Chain and network science: a research framework," *Journal on Chain and Network Science* (1:1)1-6.

Park, N., Mezias, J., and Song, J. (2004) "A resource-based view of strategic alliances and firm value in the electronic marketplace," *Journal of Management* (30:1)7-27.

Paulraj, A., Lado, A.A., and Chen, I.J. (2008) "Inter-organizational communication as a relational competency: antecedents and performance outcomes in collaborative buyer-supplier relationships," *Journal of Operations Management* (26:1)45-64.

Pavlou, P.A., and Chai, L. (2002) "What drives electronic commerce across cultures? A cross cultural empirical investigation of the theory of planned behaviour," *Journal of Electronic Commerce Research* (3:4)240-253.

Pfohl, H.-C., and Buse, H.P. (2000) "Inter-organizational logistics systems in flexible production networks," *International Journal of Physical Distribution & Logistics Management* (30:5)338-408.

Poppo, L., and Zenger, T. (2002) "Do formal contracts and relational governance function as substitutes or complements?," *Strategic Management Journal* (23:8), Aug, pp 707-725.

Poppo, L., Zhou, K.Z., and Ryu, S. (2008) "Alternative origins to interorganizational trust: an itnerdependence perspective on the shadow of the past and the shadow of the future," *Organization Science* (19:1)39-55.

Powell, W., Kogut, K., and Smith-Doerr, L. (1996) "Interorganizational collaboration and the locus of innovation: networks of learning in biotechnology," *Administrative Science Quarterly* (41:1)116-145.

Powell, W.W. (1990) "Neither market nor hierarchy: network forms of organization," *Research in Organization Behavior* (12)295-336.

Raghunathan, S. (2001) "Information sharing in a supply chain: a note on its value when demand is nonstationary," *Management Science* (47:4)605-610.

Rindfleisch, A., and Heide, J.B. (1997) "Transaction cost analysis: past, present and future applications," *Journal of Marketing* (61:4)30-54.

Ring, P.S., and Van de Ven, A.H. (1992) "Structuring cooperative relationships between organizations," *Strategic Management Journal* (13)483-498.

Ruben, R., Lu, H., and Kuiper, E. (2007) "Marketing chains, transaction costs and resource management: efficiency and trust within tomato supply chains in Nanjing City," in: *Dragons with Clay Feet? Transition, sustainable land use and rural environment in China and Vietnam,* M. Spoor, N. Heerink and F. Qu (eds.), Rowman & Littlefield Publishers, Inc., Lanham, MD, USA.

Sachan, A. (2005) "Review of supply chain management and logistics research," *International Journal of Physical Distribution & Logistics Management* (35:9)664-705.

Sahin, F., and Robinson, E.P. (2002) "Flow coordination and information sharing in supply chains: Review, implications, and directions for future research," *Decision Sciences* (33:4)505-536.

Schiefer, G. (2004) "New technologies and their impact on the agri-food sector: an economists view " *Computers and Electronics in Agriculture* (43:2)163.

Scholten, V.E. (2006) "The early growth of academic spin-offs : factors influencing the early growth of Dutch spin-offs in the life sciences, ICT and consulting", Wageningen University, Wageningen, the Netherlands, p. 200.

Shepherd, C., and Günter, H. (2005) "Measuring supply chain performance: current research and future directions," *International Journal of Productivity and Performance Managment* (55:3/4)242-258.

Sheu, C., Yen, H., and Chae, D. (2006) "Determinants of supplier-retailer collaboration: evidence from an international study," *International Journal of Operations & Production Management* (26:1)24-49.

Siemieniuch, C.E., Waddell, F.N., and Sinclair, M.A. (1999) "The role of "partnership" in supply chain management for fast-moving consumer goods: a case study," *International Journal of Logistics: Research Applications* (2:1)87-101.

Silver, E.A., Pyke, D.F., and Peterson, R. (1998) "Inventory Management and Production Planning and Scheduling", (3rd ed.), John Wiley & Sons, London, UK.

Simatupang, T.M., and Sridharan, R. (2005) "An integrative framework for supply chain collaboration," *International Journal of Logistics Management* (16:2)257-274.

Simons, D., Francis, M., Bourlakis, M., and Fearne, A.P. (2003) "Identifying the determinants of value in the U.K. red meat industry: a value chain analysis approach," *Chain and Network Science* (3:2)109-121.

Skinner, W. (1985) "The taming of lions: how manufacturing leadership evolved," in: *The uneasy alliance: managing the productivity-technology dilemma,* K. Clark and e. al. (eds.), Harvard Business School Press, Boston, MA, USA, pp. 63-114.

Slack, N., Chambers, S., Harland, C., Harrison, A., and Johnston, R. (1998) *"Opertions management"*, Pitman Publishing, London, UK.

References

Son, J.Y., Kim, S.S., and Riggins, F.J. (2006) "Consumer adoption of net-enabled informediaries: Theoretical explanations and an empirical test," *Journal of the Association for Information Systems* (7:7)473-508.

Son, J.Y., Narasimhan, S., and Riggins, F.J. (2005) "Effects of relational factors and channel climate on EDI usage in the customer-supplier relationship," *Journal of Management Information Systems* (22:1)321-353.

Spekman, R. E., Kamauff, J. W. J. and Myhr, N. (1998) "An empirical investigation into supply chain management: a perspective on partnerships," *International Journal of Physical Distribution & Logistics Management* (28:8)630-650.

Stanford, L. (1998) "Mexico's empresario in export agriculture: examining the avocado industry of Michoacan," Meeting of the Latin American Studies Association, Chicago, IL, USA. Available at: http://168.96.200.17/ar/libros/lasa98/Standfor.pdf. Accessed 20 Jan. 2008.

Stank, T.P., Keller, S., and Daugherty, P. (2001) "Supply chain collaboration and logistical service performance," *Journal of Business Logistics* (22:1)29-48.

Steenkamp, J.-B.E.M., and Baumgartner, H. (2000) "On the use of structural equation models in marketing modeling," *International Journal of Research Iin Marketing* (17:Jun.-Sept.)195-202.

Steenkamp, J.-B.E.M., and Trijp, H.C.M.v. (1991) "The use of LISREL in validating marketing constructs," *International Journal of Research in Marketing* (8:283-299).

Stock, J.R. (1988/1989) "A compendium of doctoral research in logistics: 1970-1986," *Journal of Business Logistics.* (8:2) 123-202 and (9:1)125-233.

Stock, J.R. (1997) "Applying theories from other disciplines to logistics," *International Journal of Physical Distribution & Logistics Management* (27:9/10)515-539.

Stock, J.R. (2001) "Doctoral research in logistics and logistics-related areas: 1992-1998," *Journal of Business Logistics* (22:1)125-256.

Stock, j.R., and A., L.D. (1993) "Doctoral research in logistics-related areas: 1987-1991," *Journal of Business Logistics* (14:2)197-373.

Stock, J.R., and C.J., B. (2006) "Doctoral research in supply chain management and/or logistics-related areas: 1999-2004," *Journal of Business Logistics* (27:1)139-115.

Stohl, C., and Redding, W.C. (1987) "Messages and message exchange processes," in: *handbook of organization communication,* Sage, Newbury Park, CA, USA, pp. 451-502.

Storer, C. (2006) "Information communication tools used to coordinate food chains," *Australsian Agribusiness Review* (14)1-23.

Storer, C.E. (2005) "Inter-organizational information management systems and relationships in agribusiness food chains of organizations," in: *Graduate School of Business,* Curtin University of Technology, Perth, Australia, p. 357.

Storer, C.E., Trienekens, J.H., Beulens, A.J.M., and Quaddus, M.A. (2006) "Review of Published Chain Information System Research," the 7th International Conference on Management in AgriFood Chains and Networks, Ede, The Netherlands.

Straub, D., Boudreau, M.-C., and Gefen, D. (2004) "Validation guidelines for IS positivist," *Communications of the Association for Information systems* (13)380-427.

Stuart, F., and McCutcheon, D. (1996) "Sustaining strategic supplier alliances," *International Journal of Operations & Production Management* (16:10)5-22.

Subramani, M. (2004) "How do suppliers benefit from information technology use in supply chain relationships?," *MIS quarterly* (28:1)45-73.

Suh, T., and Kwon, I.W.G. (2006) "Matter over mind: When specific asset investment affects calculative trust in supply chain partnership," *Industrial Marketing Management* (35:2), Feb, pp 191-201.

Tenenhaus, M., Vinzi, V.E., Chatelin, Y.M., and Lauro, C. (2005) "PLS path modeling" *Computational Statistics and Data Analysis* (48:1)159-205.

Thompson, J.D. (1967) *"Organizations in action"*, McGraw-Hill, New York.

Trienekens, J.H. (1999) "Management of processes in chains: a research framework," Wageningen University, Wageningen, the Netherlands.

Tyndall, G.R., Gopal, C., Partsch, W., and Kamauf, J. (1998) *"Supercharging Supply Chains: new ways to increase value through global operational excellence"*, John Wiley & Sons, Inc., New York, NY, USA.

Uzzi, B. (1997) "Social structure and competition in interfirm networks: the paradox of embeddedness," *Administrative Science Quarterly* (42)35-67.

Van der Vorst, J.G.A.J. (2000) "Effective food supply chains: generating, modelling and evaluating supply chain scenarios," Wageningen University, Wageningen, the Netherlands.

Van der Vorst, J.G.A.J. (2004) "Supply chain management: theory and practices", Reed Business Information, Doetinchem, the Netherlands.

Van der Vorst, J.G.A.J., Beulens, A.J.M., and Van Beek, P. (2005) "Innovations in logistics and ICT in food supply chain networks," in: *Innovation in agri-food systems, product quality and consumer acceptance*, W.M.F. Jongen and M.T.G. Meulenberg (eds.), Wageningen Academic Publishers, the Netherlands.

Van Dorp, C.A. (2004) "Reference-data modeling for tracking and tracing," Wageningen University, Wageningen, the Netherlands.

Van Plaggenhoef, W. (2007) "Integration and self regulation of quality management in Dutch agri-food supply chains: a cross-chain analysis of the poultry meat, the fruit and vegetable and the flower and potted plant chains," Management Studies Group, Wageningen University and Research Center, Wageningen, the Netherlands, p. 295.

Verwaal, E., and Hesselmans, M. (2004) "Drivers of supply network governance: an explorative study of the Dutch chemical industry," *European Management Journal* (22:4)442-451.

Vlosky, R.P., Smith, P.M., and Wilson, D.T. (1994) "Electronic data interchange implementation strategies: a case study," *Journal of Business and Industrial marketing* (9:4)5-18.

Wang, H.W. (1999) "The method of partial least squares regression and its application". National Defence Industry Press, Beijing, China (in Chinese).

Weitz, B.A., and Sjap, S.D. (1995) "Relationship marketing and distribution channels," *Academy of Marketing Science* (23:4)305-320.

Williamson, O.E. (1979) "Transaction cost economics: the governance of contractual relations," *The Journal of Law and Economics* (22:2)233-261.

Williamson, O.E. (1985) "The economic institutions of capitalism: firms, markets and relational contracting", The Free Press, New York, NY, USA, p. 450.

Williamson, O.E. (1991) "Comparative economic organization: the analysis of discrete structural alternatives," *Administrative Quarterly* (36)269-296.

Williamson, O.E. (1996) "The mechanism of governance", Oxford University Press, New York, NY, USA.

Wilson, D.T., and Vlosky, R.P. (1998) "Interorganizational information system technology and buyer-seller relationships," *Journal of Business and Industrial marketing* (13:3)215-228.

Wold, H. (1974) "Causal flows with latent variables: partings of the ways in the light of NIPALS modeling," *European Economic Review* (5:1)67-86.

Wold, H. (1982) "Soft modeling: the basic design and some extensions," in: *Systems under indirect observations: causality, structure, prediction (Part II)*, K.G. Jöreskog and H. Wold (eds.), Elsevier, Amsterdam, the Netherlands, pp. 1-54.

References

Wold, H. (1985) "Partial least squares," in: *Encyclopedia of Statistical Sciences*, S. Kotz and N.L. Hohnson (eds.), Wiley, New York, NY, USA, pp. 581-591.

Wollni, M., and Zeller, M. (2007) "Do farmers benefit from participating in specialty markets and cooperatives? The case of coffee marketing in Costa Rica," *Agricultural Economics* (37)243-248.

Womack, J., Jones, D., and Roos, D. (1990) "The machine that changed the world", Harper Perennial, New York, NY, USA.

Woolthuis, R.K., Hillebrand, B., and Nooteboom, B. (2005) "Trust, contract and relationship development," *Organization Studies* (26:6)813-840.

Yang, G., and Jarvenpaa, S.L. (2005) "Trust and radio frequency identification (RFID) adoption within an alliance," the 38th Hawaii international conference on system sciences, pp. 1-10.

Yin, R.K. (2003) "Case study research: design and methods", (3rd ed.) Sage Publications, Thousand Oaks, CA, USA, p. 174.

Zaheer, A., McEvily, B., and Perrone, V. (1998) "Does trust matter? Exploring the effects of interorganizational and interpersonal trust on performance," *Organization Science* (9:2)141-159.

Zaheer, A., and Venkatraman, N. (1995) "Relational governance as an interorganizational strategy – an empirical test of the role of trust in economic exchange," *Strategic Management Journal* (16:5)373-392.

Zhou, K.Z., and Poppo, L. (2010) "Exchange hazards, relational reliability, and contracts in China: The contingent role of legal enforceability," *Journal of International Business Studies* (41:5)861-881.

Zhou, K.Z., Poppo, L., and Yang, Z. (2008) "Relational ties or customized contracts? An examination of alternative governance choice in China," *Journal of International Business Studies* (39:526-534).

Zinkhan, G., Joachimsthaler, E., and Kinnear, T. (1987) "Individual difference and marketing decision support system usage and satisfaction," *Journal of Marketing Research* (24)208-214.

Appendices

Appendix 3.1. The survey questionnaire

Note: Each company was asked the following questions related to its most important supplier and its most important customer.

Part I. Company profile

Question for all companies
1. Our firm started business since year _____. The amount of employees is: _____ persons.
2. The address of our company is: _____.
3. I have been involved in poultry business since year _____.
4. My job position is: _____.
5. Among poultry products that we sold in the last year, the percentages of the following products are:
   - a. chick: _____%;
   - b. duck: _____%;
   - c. poultry egg: _____%;
   - d. others: _____%.
6. The quality standard(s) that our company follows is/are:_____. (multi-choices allowed)
   - a. unknown or no specific standards;
   - b. "QS" systems;
   - c. non-environmental damage food;
   - d. green food A;
   - e. green food AA or organic food;
   - f. firm internal standard;
   - g. ISO9000;
   - h. ISO22000;
   - i. ISO14001;
   - j. 18000 system;
   - k. HACCP or GlobalGap;
   - l. Others: _____.

Questions for supermarkets and restaurants
1. The stores of our company are mainly located in: _____.
   - a. local city / county;
   - b. local province;
   - c. more than one province;
   - d. more than one country.
2. Our company has _____ stores in the mainland of China.
3. The amount of employees of my store is _____ persons. We can service at most _____ persons at the same time (for restaurants only).

Part II. Transaction attributes and governance structures

(5-point Likert scale, from '1 = totally disagree' to '5 = totally agree')

Environmental uncertainty (EUn)
EUn1: Currently, the market of poultry products is complex.
EUn2: Currently, the price of poultry products is volatile.
EUn3: Currently, the quality of poultry products is variable.

Transaction specific investments (TSI)

TSI1: We have made large investments for poultry sale to our most important customers / for poultry procurement from our most important supplier, in the last three years.

TSI2: We have made large investment to control poultry quality of ours / of major supplier in the last three years.

TSI3: If switching to other customers / suppliers, we would waste a lot of knowledge, regarding the operation methods of our most important customer / supplier (dropped for the company-supplier sample).

Trust (Trust)

Based on experience in the last 12 months, we believe that:

Trust1: Our most important customer / supplier is credible.

Trust2: Our major customer / supplier will keep promises made to us.

Trust3: The staff of our most important customer / supplier are credible.

Contractual governance (CG)

CG1: Price is pre-agreed with our most important customer / supplier.

CG2: Quality is pre-agreed with our most important customer / supplier.

CG3: Transaction volumes are pre-agreed with our most important customer / supplier.

CG4: Delivery time and places are pre-agreed with our most important customer / supplier.

Part III. Inter-organizational communication (IOC)

(For all questions except for 'media modernity' and 'communication frequency', 5-point Likert scale was used ranging from '1 = totally disagree' to '5 = totally agree'.)

Communication willingness (Willing)

(*Sources*: Fawcett *et al.*, 2007; Mohr *et al.*, 1995)

Willing1: We are willing to provide proprietary information to our most important customer / supplier if it is helpful for them.

Willing2: We (our most important customer/supplier) are expected to provide our most important customer/supplier (us) with proprietary information that may be of help.

Willing3: We have formal and official channel to communicate with our most important customer / supplier (Dropped for both the company-supplier and the company-customer samples).

Media modernity (Media)

(*Sources*: Ambrose *et al.*, 2008; Carr *et al.*, 2007; Daft *et al.*, 1984; Mohr *et al.*, 1995)

Media: *In the last 12 months, the most modern media used to communicate with our most important customer / supplier is:*

1: Face-to-face discussion or/and phone (traditional media).

2: E-mail (middle advanced media).

3: EDI / intranet (modern media).

Notes: EDI – Electronic Data Interchange. This is an one-item construct measured by 3-point Likert scale. The answer to this construct is the most modern media employed by the focal firms.

Communication frequency (Freq)

(*Sources*: Mohr *et al.*, 1995; Storer, 2006)

In the last 12 months, the frequency that we communicate on the following information with our most important customer / supplier was: 1 – never; 3 – per month; 5- per day.

Freq1: Problem resolution.
Freq2: Product quality control.
Freq3: Timely and precise delivery.
Freq4: Product price decision.

Multi-functional staff involvement (Staff)

(*Sources*: Lindgreen *et al.*, 2004; Siemieniuch *et al.*, 1999; Vlosky *et al.*, 1994)

Staff1: We use cross-functional teams to communicate with our most important customer / supplier.
Staff2: Senior level managers interact frequently with each other.

Information quality (IQuali)

(*Sources*: Mohr *et al.*, 1995; O'Reilly, 1982; Stohl *et al.*, 1987)

Information communicated between us and our most important customer / supplier is:

IQuali1: Timely.
IQuali2: Adequate.
IQuali3: Accurate and credible.

Knowledge on each other's requirements and expectations (KnowP).

(Designed for this study)

Know1: We are well aware of expectations and requirements of our most important customer / supplier.
Know2: Our most important customer / supplier is well aware of our expectations and requirements.

Perceived communication benefits for firms in relationships with suppliers (BenefitA)

(Designed for this study)

We (our customers) get information from our most important supplier (us), which supports us (it) **directly** *in:*

BenefitA1: Problem resolution.
BenefitA2: Product quality control.
BenefitA3: Timely and precise delivery.
BenefitA4: Product price decision.

Perceived communication benefits for firms in relationships with customers (BenefitB)

(Designed for this study)

We (our supplier) get information from our most important customers (us), which supports us (it) **directly** *in:*

BenefitB1: Problem resolution.
BenefitB2: Product quality control.
BenefitB3: Timely and precise delivery.
BenefitB4: Product price.

Part IV. Supply chain compliance and performance

Supply Chain Compliance
(5-point Likert scale, from '1 = totally disagree' to '5 = totally agree')

Logistics compliancec(LC)
LC1: Our most important supplier (We) delivers products timely and precisely to us (to our most important customer).
LC2: Our most important supplier (We) packages products according to requirements of us (our most important customer).

Quality compliance (QC)
QC1: Our most important supplier (We) will help us (our most important customer) if we (they) meet quality problems or troubles.
QC2: Our most important supplier (We) provides products which fit quality requirements of us (our most important customer).
QC3: Our most important supplier (We) provide products with better quality than its (our) major competitors.

Firm Performance
(7-point Likert scale, from '1 = totally disagree' to '7 = totally agree')

Satisfaction (Satis)
Satis1: We (Our most important customer) are satisfied with product quality of our most important supplier (us).
Satis2: We (Our most important customer) are happy with the price paid to our most important supplier (us).

Efficiency (Effi)
Effi1: It costs us less money when we purchase (sell) poultry from our most important supplier (to our most important customer).
Effi2: It costs us less time to finish an order with our most important supplier (customer) than with others.

Profit & Competitive edge (P&C)
Comparing to our main competitors in the last 12 months, we achieved better business of poultry products in term of:
P&C1: Profitability.
P&C2: Sale growth rate.
P&C3: Market share (dropped in both the company-supplier and the company-customer samples).[18]
P&C4: Overall competitive edge.

---

[18] The Pearson correlation coefficients between 'market share' and 'overall competitive edge' for the both samples are higher than the threshold of 0.80, which show problem of item multicollinearity and preclude their use in one model. Thus 'market share' was dropped.

Appendix 3.2. Category criteria of firm size used in this research

Regarding company size, we divided the surveyed firms into five categories, including mini, small, middle, large, and super & international firms, based on the "National Criteria to Divide Big-, Middle-, and Small-sized Enterprises" (National Committee of Trade and Economics of China [2003]143[19]). According to the original and official criteria, companies in each sector are divided into three categories, including: the big-, the middle-, and the small-sized firms. However, as many small/mini companies are involved in the poultry chain, and some international firms as well, thus we divided the surveyed firms into five categories instead of the three categories grounded on the national criteria. This appendix shows these five categories.

	Index	Mini	Small	Middle	Large	Super & International
Restaurant	Store number / locations	I store only	2-5 stores, only in local county/city	Stores in multi-counties/cities, only in local province	Stores in multiple provinces	Stores worldwide
Supermarket	Store number / locations	I store only	2-5 stores, only in local county/city	Stores in multi-counties/cities, only in local province	Stores in multiple provinces	Stores worldwide
Trader	Employee	<50	50-100	100-150	150-200	>200
Processor	Employee	<150	150-300	300-1,150	1,150-2,000	>2,000
Intermediary	Employee	<50	50-100	100-150	150-200	>200
Commercial farm	Employee	<150	150-300	300-1,150	1,150-2,000	>2,000

[19] The original government document was accessible on http://www.stats.gov.cn/tjbz/t20061018_402369829.htm in September 2011.

Appendix 4.1. Results of hypotheses testing of the Communication Antecedents Model for the company-supplier sample (N=165)

Relationships	Path coefficient	(S.E.)	t-value[1,2]	Total effect	(S.E.)	t-value[1,2]
Environmental uncertainty → Contractual governance	0.13	(0.09)	1.48	0.13	(0.08)	1.48
Environmental uncertainty → Communication willingness	-			0.02	(0.02)	0.55
Environmental uncertainty → Media modernity	-			-0.00	(0.01)	0.09
Environmental uncertainty → Communication frequency	-			0.00	(0.03)	0.33
Environmental uncertainty → Multi-function staff involvement	-			0.02	(0.02)	0.66
Transaction specific investments → Trust	0.26	(0.08)	3.10**	0.26	(0.08)	3.10**
Transaction specific investments → Contractual governance	0.06	(0.08)	0.72	0.20	(0.09)	2.25*
Transaction specific investments → Communication willingness	-			0.12	(0.06)	1.86
Transaction specific investments → Media modernity	-			0.03	(0.02)	0.95
Transaction specific investments → Communication frequency	-			0.03	(0.04)	0.66
Transaction specific investments → Multi-function staff involvement	-			0.06	(0.04)	1.28
Trust → Contractual governance	0.55	(0.10)	5.78**	0.55	(0.10)	5.78**
Trust → Communication willingness	0.36	(0.09)	3.67**	0.41	(0.08)	4.83**
Trust → Media modernity	0.11	(0.09)	1.13	0.10	(0.07)	1.42
Trust → Communication frequency	0.04	(0.17)	0.27	0.08	(0.13)	0.68
Trust → Multi-function staff involvement	0.11	(0.12)	0.94	0.19	(0.10)	0.86
Contractual governance → Communication willingness	0.10	(0.11)	0.86	0.10	(0.11)	0.86
Contractual governance → Media modernity	-0.02	(0.10)	0.19	-0.02	(0.10)	0.19
Contractual governance → Communication frequency	0.08	(0.17)	0.43	0.08	(0.17)	0.43
Contractual governance → multi-function staff involvement	0.14	(0.12)	1.04	0.14	(0.12)	1.04

[1] A relationship is significant at * P<0.05, or ** P<0.01.

[2] Average R^2 = 0.111.

Appendix 4.2. Results of hypotheses testing of the revised Communication Antecedents Model for the company-supplier sample (N=165)

Relationships	Path coefficient	(S.E.)	t-value[1,2]	Total effect	(S.E.)	t-value[1,2]
Environmental uncertainty → Contractual governance	0.12	(0.08)	1.36	0.18	(0.08)	2.11*
Environmental uncertainty → Transaction specific investments	0.30	(0.07)	4.26**	0.30	(0.07)	4.26**
Environmental uncertainty → Trust	-			0.08	(0.03)	2.52*
Environmental uncertainty → Communication willingness	-			0.05	(0.03)	1.44
Environmental uncertainty → Media modernity	-			0.01	(0.02)	0.31
Environmental uncertainty → Communication frequency	-			0.02	(0.03)	0.59
Environmental uncertainty → Multi-function staff involvement	-			0.04	(0.03)	1.17
Transaction specific investments → Trust	0.26	(0.09)	2.93**	0.26	(0.09)	2.93**
Transaction specific investments → Contractual governance	0.06	(0.08)	0.72	0.20	(0.09)	2.17*
Transaction specific investments → Communication willingness	-			0.12	(0.05)	1.88
Transaction specific investments → Media modernity	-			0.03	(0.03)	0.87
Transaction specific investments → Communication frequency	-			0.04	(0.04)	0.64
Transaction specific investments → Multi-function staff involvement	-			0.07	(0.05)	1.18
Trust → Contractual governance	0.55	(0.10)	5.89**	0.55	(0.10)	5.89**
Trust → Communication willingness	0.36	(0.09)	3.73**	0.41	(0.08)	4.99**
Trust → Media modernity	0.11	(0.10)	1.11	0.10	(0.08)	1.27
Trust → Communication frequency	0.05	(0.16)	0.28	0.09	(0.13)	0.68
Trust → Multi-function staff involvement	0.12	(0.12)	0.92	0.19	(0.10)	1.78
Contractual governance → Communication willingness	0.11	(0.11)	0.88	0.11	(0.11)	0.88
Contractual governance → Media modernity	-0.01	(0.09)	0.19	-0.01	(0.09)	0.19
Contractual governance → Communication frequency	0.08	(0.16)	0.46	0.08	(0.16)	0.46
Contractual governance → multi-function staff involvement	0.13	(0.13)	0.99	0.13	(0.13)	0.99

[1] A relationship is significant at * $P<0.05$, or ** $P<0.01$.
[2] Average $R^2 = 0.107$.

Appendix 4.3. Results of hypotheses testing of the Communication Antecedents Model for the company-customer sample (N=96)

Relationships	Path coefficient	(S.E.)	t-value[1,2]	Total effect	(S.E.)	t-value[1,2]
Environmental uncertainty → Contractual governance	0.12	(0.10)	0.98	0.12	(0.10)	0.98
Environmental uncertainty → Communication willingness	-			0.03	(0.03)	0.79
Environmental uncertainty → Media modernity	-			0.03	(0.03)	0.84
Environmental uncertainty → Communication frequency	-			0.04	(0.04)	0.80
Environmental uncertainty → Multi-function staff involvement	-			0.03	(0.03)	0.85
Transaction specific investments → Trust	0.34	(0.12)	2.87**	0.34	(0.12)	2.87**
Transaction specific investments → Contractual governance	0.32	(0.08)	3.98**	0.48	(0.08)	6.29**
Transaction specific investments → Communication willingness	-			0.25	(0.07)	3.39**
Transaction specific investments → Media modernity	-			0.13	(0.06)	2.19*
Transaction specific investments → Communication frequency	-			0.16	(0.05)	2.74**
Transaction specific investments → Multi-function staff involvement	-			0.21	(0.07)	2.75**
Trust → Contractual governance	0.46	(0.09)	5.27**	0.46	(0.09)	5.27**
Trust → Communication willingness	0.38	(0.10)	3.69**	0.49	(0.08)	6.32**
Trust → Media modernity	0.03	(0.10)	0.33	0.14	(0.09)	1.63
Trust → Communication frequency	-0.00	(0.14)	0.07	0.15	(0.12)	1.27
Trust → Multi-function staff involvement	0.19	(0.14)	1.37	0.31	(0.11)	2.82**
Contractual governance → Communication willingness	0.24	(0.10)	2.41*	0.24	(0.10)	2.41*
Contractual governance → Media modernity	0.24	(0.11)	2.13*	0.24	(0.11)	2.13*
Contractual governance → Communication frequency	0.33	(0.11)	2.75**	0.33	(0.11)	2.75**
Contractual governance → multi-function staff involvement	0.27	(0.10)	2.61**	0.27	(0.10)	2.61**

[1] A relationship is significant at * $P<0.05$, or ** $P<0.01$.

[2] Average $R^2 = 0.200$.

Appendix 4.4. Results of hypotheses testing of the revised Communication Antecedents Model for the company-customer sample (N=96)

Relationships	Path coefficient	(S.E.)	t-value[1,2]	Total effect	(S.E.)	t-value[1,2]
Environmental uncertainty → Contractual governance	0.10	(0.09)	1.00	0.25	(0.10)	2.56*
Environmental uncertainty → Transaction specific investments	0.34	(0.10)	3.04**	0.34	(0.10)	3.04**
Environmental uncertainty → Trust	-			0.11	(0.04)	2.39*
Environmental uncertainty → Communication willingness	-			0.11	(0.04)	2.29*
Environmental uncertainty → Media modernity	-			0.06	(0.03)	1.87
Environmental uncertainty → Communication frequency	-			0.08	(0.04)	1.88
Environmental uncertainty → Multi-function staff involvement	-			0.09	(0.04)	2.30*
Transaction specific investments → Trust	0.33	(0.12)	2.74**	0.33	(0.12)	2.74**
Transaction specific investments → Contractual governance	0.33	(0.08)	3.95**	0.48	(0.08)	5.71**
Transaction specific investments → Communication willingness	-			0.25	(0.08)	3.23**
Transaction specific investments → Media modernity	-			0.13	(0.05)	2.33*
Transaction specific investments → Communication frequency	-			0.16	(0.06)	2.42*
Transaction specific investments → Multi-function staff involvement	-			0.21	(0.07)	2.65**
Trust → Contractual governance	0.46	(0.09)	4.98**	0.56	(0.09)	4.98**
Trust → Communication willingness	0.38	(0.11)	3.53**	0.49	(0.08)	6.02**
Trust → Media modernity	0.03	(0.10)	0.34	0.14	(0.08)	1.78
Trust → Communication frequency	0.01	(0.15)	0.07	0.16	(0.12)	1.23
Trust → Multi-function staff involvement	0.19	(0.13)	1.39	0.31	(0.11)	2.93**
Contractual governance → Communication willingness	0.25	(0.10)	2.44*	0.25	(0.10)	2.44*
Contractual governance → Media modernity	0.24	(0.11)	2.20*	0.24	(0.11)	2.20*
Contractual governance → Communication frequency	0.32	(0.13)	2.38*	0.32	(0.13)	2.38*
Contractual governance → multi-function staff involvement	0.27	(0.10)	2.58**	0.27	(0.10)	2.58**

[1] A relationship is significant at *: $P<0.05$, or **: $P<0.01$.
[2] Average $R^2 = 0.185$.

Appendix 4.5. The influences of company characteristics on communication antecedents for the company-supplier sample

Relationships[1]	Path coefficient significant?[2,3]	Sign of coefficient
CV_1: Firm size → Transaction specific investments	No	+
CV_1: Firm size → Trust	No	+
CV_1: Firm size → Contractual governance	No	+
CV_2: Firm age → Transaction specific investments	No	+
CV_2: Firm age → Trust	No	+
CV_2: Firm age → Contractual governance	No	-
CV_3: Firm type → Transaction specific investments	**Yes***	-
CV_3: Firm type → Trust	No	-
CV_3: Firm type → Contractual governance	No	+
CV_4: Quality standard → Transaction specific investments	No	+
CV_4: Quality standard → Trust	No	+
CV_4: Quality standard → Contractual governance	No	+
CV_5: Administrative level of a location → Transaction specific investments	No	-
CV_5: Administrative level of a location → Trust	No	+
CV_5: Administrative level of a location → Contractual governance	No	-

[1] The five control variables are: company size, company age, company type, quality standard applied, and the administrative level of a location. Specifically, company type: 0 = production firms with lower market power; 1 = trading firms with higher market power. Administrative level of a location: 1 = town or county; 2 = medium-sized city; 3 = national.

[2] The same significant paths for both the company-supplier and the company-customer (see Appendix 4.6) samples are shown in **bold** and *italics*.

[3] * Significant at 5%; ** significant at 1%.

Appendix 4.6. The influences of company characteristics on communication antecedents for the company-customer sample

Relationships[1]	Path coefficient significant?[2,3]	Sign of coefficient
CV_1: Firm size → Transaction specific investments	No	+
CV_1: Firm size → Trust	No	-
CV_1: Firm size → Contractual governance	No	-
CV_2: Firm age → Transaction specific investments	No	-
CV_2: Firm age → Trust	No	-
CV_2: Firm age → Contractual governance	No	-
CV_3: Firm type → Transaction specific investments	**Yes****	**-**
CV_3: Firm type → Trust	No	+
CV_3: Firm type → Contractual governance	No	+
CV_4: Quality standard → Transaction specific investments	No	-
CV_4: Quality standard → Trust	No	+
CV_4: Quality standard → Contractual governance	No	+
CV_5: Administrative level of a location → Transaction specific investments	No	+
CV_5: Administrative level of a location → Trust	No	+
CV_5: Administrative level of a location → Contractual governance	No	-

[1] The five control variables are: company size, company age, company type, quality standard applied, and the administrative level of a location. Specifically, company type: 0 = production firms with lower market power; 1 = trading firms with higher market power. Administrative level of a location: 1 = town or county; 2 = medium-sized city; 3 = national or provincial capital city.

[2] The same significant paths for both the company-supplier and the company-customer (see Appendix 4.5) samples are shown in **bold** and *italics*.

[3] * Significant at 5%; ** significant at 1%.

Appendix 5.1. Results of hypotheses testing of the Communication Elements Model for the company-supplier sample (N=165)

Relationships	Path coefficient (S.E.)		t-value[1,2]	Total effect (S.E.)		t-value[1,2]
Communication willingness → Knowledge of each other's requirements and expectations	0.53	(0.08)	6.90**	0.53	(0.08)	6.90**
Communication willingness → Information quality	0.35	(0.10)	3.56**	0.47	(0.08)	5.92**
Communication willingness → Perceived communication benefits for the companies	-			0.30	(0.05)	5.51**
Communication willingness → Perceived communication benefits for suppliers	-			0.36	(0.06)	6.14**
Media modernity → Knowledge of each other's requirements and expectations	0.01	(0.06)	0.14	0.01	(0.06)	0.14
Media modernity → Information quality	-0.07	(0.05)	1.30	-0.07	(0.05)	1.25
Media modernity → Perceived communication benefits for the companies	-			-0.02	(0.03)	0.63
Media modernity → Perceived communication benefits for suppliers	-			-0.02	(0.03)	0.55
Communication frequency → Knowledge of each other's requirements and expectations	0.17	(0.06)	2.50*	0.17	(0.06)	2.50*
Communication frequency → Information quality	0.06	(0.09)	0.54	0.10	(0.09)	0.98
Communication frequency → Perceived communication benefits for the companies	-			0.08	(0.04)	1.92
Communication frequency → Perceived communication benefits for suppliers	-			0.10	(0.04)	2.28*
Multi-functional staff involvement → Knowledge on each other's requirements and expectations	0.10	(0.07)	1.51	0.10	(0.07)	1.51
Multi-functional staff involvement → Information quality	0.19	(0.06)	3.02**	0.22	(0.07)	3.35**
Multi-functional staff involvement → Perceived communication benefits for the companies	-			0.09	(0.03)	2.80**
Multi-functional staff involvement → Perceived communication benefits for suppliers	-			0.11	(0.04)	3.05**
Knowledge of each other's requirements and expectations → Perceived communication benefits for the companies	0.29	(0.07)	3.91**	0.37	(0.07)	5.07**
Knowledge of each other's requirements and expectations → Perceived communication benefits for suppliers	0.39	(0.07)	5.63**	0.47	(0.06)	7.30**
Information quality → Perceived communication benefits for the companies	0.30	(0.09)	3.35**	0.30	(0.09)	3.35**

Relationships	Path coefficient	(S.E.)	t-value[1,2]	Total effect	(S.E.)	t-value[1,2]
Information quality → Perceived communication benefits for suppliers	0.32	(0.08)	4.13**	0.32	(0.08)	4.13**
Knowledge of each other's requirements and expectations → Information quality	0.24	(0.09)	2.78**	0.24	(0.09)	2.78**

[1] A relationship is significant at * $P<0.05$, or ** $P<0.01$.
[2] Average $R^2 = 0.378$.

Appendix 5.2. Results of hypotheses testing of the Communication Elements Model for the company-customer sample (N = 96)

Relationships	Path coefficient	(S.E.)	t-value[1,2]	Total effect	(S.E.)	t-value[1,2]
Communication willingness → Knowledge of each other's requirements and expectations	0.52	(0.11)	4.82**	0.52	(0.11)	4.82**
Communication willingness → Information quality	0.10	(0.16)	.60	0.25	(0.14)	1.79
Communication willingness → Perceived communication benefits for customers	-			0.26	(0.08)	3.35**
Communication willingness → Perceived communication benefits for the companies	-			0.29	(0.09)	3.29**
Media modernity → Knowledge of each other's requirements and expectations	-0.02	(0.09)	0.27	-0.02	(0.09)	0.27
Media modernity → Information quality	-0.12	(0.09)	1.31	-0.13	(0.09)	1.41
Media modernity → Perceived communication benefits for customers	-			-0.04	(0.04)	0.96
Media modernity → Perceived communication benefits for the companies	-			-0.06	(0.05)	1.06
Communication frequency → Knowledge of each other's requirements and expectations	0.20	(0.09)	1.99*	0.20	(0.09)	1.99*
Communication frequency → Information quality	0.13	(0.13)	1.04	0.19	(0.11)	1.68
Communication frequency → Perceived communication benefits for customers	-			0.13	(0.05)	2.27*
Communication frequency → Perceived communication benefits for the companies	-			0.15	(0.06)	2.36*
Multi-functional staff involvement → Knowledge of each other's requirements and expectations	0.19	(0.09)	2.04*	0.19	(0.09)	2.04*
Multi-functional staff involvement → Information quality	0.31	(0.11)	2.75**	0.37	(0.11)	3.45**
Multi-functional staff involvement → Perceived communication benefits for customers	-			0.17	(0.06)	2.94**
Multi-functional staff involvement → Perceived communication benefits for the companies	-			0.21	(0.06)	3.28**
Knowledge of each other's requirements and expectations → Perceived communication benefits for customers	0.36	(0.10)	3.62**	0.44	(0.10)	4.35**
Knowledge of each other's requirements and expectations → Perceived communication benefits for the companies	0.36	(0.12)	3.14**	0.47	(0.12)	3.96**

Relationships

	Path coefficient	(S.E.)	t-value[1,2]	Total effect	(S.E.)	t-value[1,2]
Information quality → Perceived communication benefits for customers	0.28	(0.10)	2.65**	0.28	(0.10)	2.65**
Information quality → Perceived communication benefits for the companies	0.40	(0.11)	3.62**	0.40	(0.11)	3.62**
Knowledge of each other's requirements and expectations → Information quality	0.29	(0.17)	1.72	0.29	(0.17)	1.72

[1] A relationship is significant at * P<0.05, or ** P<0.01.
[2] Average R^2 = 0.411.

Appendix 5.3. The influences of company characteristics on communication for the company-supplier sample

Relationships[1]	Path coefficient significant?[2,3]	Sign of coefficient
CV_1: Firm size → Communication willingness	**Yes***	+
CV_1: Firm size → Media modernity	Yes*	+
CV_1: Firm size → Communication frequency	No	+
CV_1: Firm size → Multi-functional staff involvement	Yes**	+
CV_1: Firm size → Knowledge of each other's requirements and expectations	No	+
CV_1: Firm size → Information quality	Yes*	-
CV_1: Firm size → Perceived communication benefits for the companies	Yes*	+
CV_1: Firm size → Perceived communication benefits for suppliers	Yes*	+
CV_2: Firm age → Communication willingness	No	-
CV_2: Firm age → Media modernity	No	+
CV_2: Firm age → Communication frequency	No	+
CV_2: Firm age → Multi-functional staff involvement	No	+
CV_2: Firm age → Knowledge of each other's requirements and expectations	No	-
CV_2: Firm age → Information quality	No	+
CV_2: Firm age → Perceived communication benefits for the companies	No	-
CV_2: Firm age → Perceived communication benefits for suppliers	No	-
CV_3: Firm type → Communication willingness	No	-
CV_3: Firm type → Media modernity	No	-
CV_3: Firm type → Communication frequency	No	+
CV_3: Firm type → Multi-functional staff involvement	**Yes***	-
CV_3: Firm type → Knowledge of each other's requirements and expectations	No	+
CV_3: Firm type → Information quality	No	+
CV_3: Firm type → Perceived communication benefits for the companies	No	-
CV_3: Firm type → Perceived communication benefits for suppliers	No	-
CV_4: Quality standard → communication willingness	No	-
CV_4: Quality standard → Media modernity	No	+
CV_4: Quality standard → Communication frequency	No	+
CV_4: Quality standard → Multi-functional staff involvement	No	-
CV_4: Quality standard → Knowledge of each other's requirements and expectations	No	+
CV_4: Quality standard → Information quality	No	+
CV_4: Quality standard → Perceived communication benefits for the companies	No	-
CV_4: Quality standard → Perceived communication benefits for suppliers	No	-
CV_5: Administrative level of a location → Communication willingness	No	-
CV_5: Administrative level of a location → Media modernity	Yes**	-

Relationships[1]	Path coefficient significant?[2,3]	Sign of coefficient
CV$_5$: Administrative level of a location → Communication frequency	No	-
CV$_5$: Administrative level of a location→ Multi-functional staff involvement	Yes**	-
CV$_5$: Administrative level of a location → Knowledge of each other's requirements and expectations	No	-
CV$_5$: Administrative level of a location→ Information quality	No	+
CV$_5$: Administrative level of a location → Perceived communication benefits for the companies	No	-
CV$_5$: Administrative level of a location→ Perceived communication benefits for suppliers	No	-

[1] The five control variables are: company size, company age, company type, quality standard applied, and the administrative level of a location. Specifically, company type: 0 = production firms with lower market power; 1 = trading firms with higher market power. Administrative level of a location: 1 = town or county; 2 = medium-sized city; 3 = national or provincial capital city.

[2] The same significant paths for both the company-supplier and the company-customer (see Appendix 5.4) samples are shown in **bold** and *italics*.

[3] * Significant at 5%; ** significant at 1%.

Appendix 5.4. The influences of company characteristics on communication for the company-customer sample

Relationships[1]	Path coefficient significant?[2,3]	Sign of coefficient
CV[1]: Firm size → Communication willingness	**Yes****	+
CV[1]: Firm size → Media modernity	No	+
CV[1]: Firm size → Communication frequency.	No	-
CV[1]: Firm size → Multi-functional staff involvement	No	+
CV[1]: Firm size → Knowledge of each other's requirements and expectations	No	+
CV[1]: Firm size → Information quality	No	-
CV[1]: Firm size → Perceived communication benefits for customers	No	+
CV[1]: Firm size → Perceived benefits of communication for the companies	No	+
CV[2]: Firm age → Communication willingness	No	-
CV[2]: Firm age → Media modernity	No	+
CV[2]: Firm age → Communication frequency	No	-
CV[2]: Firm age → Multi-functional staff involvement	No	+
CV[2]: Firm age → Knowledge of each other's requirements and expectations	No	-
CV[2]: Firm age → Information quality	No	+
CV[2]: Firm age → Perceived communication benefits for customers	No	+
CV[2]: Firm age → Perceived communication benefits for the companies	No	-
CV[3]: Firm type → Communication willingness	No	-
CV[3]: Firm type → Media modernity	No	-
CV[3]: Firm type → Communication frequency	No	+
CV[3]: Firm type → Multi-functional staff involvement	**Yes****	-
CV[3]: Firm type → Knowledge of each other's requirements and expectations	No	+
CV[3]: Firm type → Information quality	No	+
CV[3]: Firm type → Perceived communication benefits for customers	No	-
CV[3]: Firm type → Perceived communication benefits for the companies	No	-
CV[4]: Quality standard → Communication willingness	No	-
CV[4]: Quality standard → Media modernity	Yes**	+
CV[4]: Quality standard → Communication frequency	No	-
CV[4]: Quality standard → Multi-functional staff involvement	No	-
CV[4]: Quality standard → Knowledge of each other's requirements and expectations	Yes*	+
CV[4]: Quality standard → Information quality	No	-
CV[4]: Quality standard → Perceived communication benefits for customers	No	-
CV[4]: Quality standard → Perceived communication benefits for the companies	Yes*	-
CV[5]: Administrative level of a location→ Communication willingness	No	-
CV[5]: Administrative level of a location → Media modernity	No	-
CV[5]: Administrative level of a location → Communication frequency	No	-

Relationships[1]

	Path coefficient significant?[2,3]	Sign of coefficient
CV_5: Administrative level of a location → Multi-functional staff involvement	No	-
CV_5: Administrative level of a location → Knowledge of each other's requirements and expectations	No	-
CV_5: Administrative level of a location → Information quality	No	+
CV_5: Administrative level of a location → Perceived communication benefits for customers	No	-
CV_5: Administrative level of a location → Perceived communication benefits for the companies	No	+

[1] The five control variables are: company size, company age, company type, quality standard applied, and the administrative level of a location. Specifically, company type: 0 = production firms with lower market power; 1 = trading firms with higher market power. Administrative level of a location: 1 = town or county; 2 = medium-sized city; 3 = national or provincial capital city.

[2] The same significant paths for both the company-supplier (see Appendix 5.3) and the company-customer samples are shown in **bold** and *italics*.

[3] * Significant at 5%; ** significant at 1%.

Appendix 6.1. Results of hypotheses testing of the Communication-Chain compliance-Performance Model for the company-supplier sample (N=165)

Relationships	Path coefficient	(S.E.)	t-value[1,2]	Total effect	(S.E.)	t-value[1,2]
Perceived communication benefits for the companies → Logistics compliance	0.11	(0.12)	0.75	0.11	(0.12)	0.75
Perceived communication benefits for the companies → Quality compliance	0.12	(0.10)	1.00	0.12	(0.10)	1.00
Perceived communication benefits for the companies → Satisfactory	-			0.08	(0.07)	1.00
Perceived communication benefits for the companies → Efficiency	-			0.06	(0.05)	1.01
Perceived communication benefits for the companies → Profit & competitive edge	-			0.06	(0.05)	0.95
Perceived communication benefits for suppliers → Logistics compliance	0.30	(0.13)	2.41*	0.30	(0.13)	2.41*
Perceived communication benefits for suppliers → Quality compliance	0.44	(0.10)	4.42*	0.44	(0.10)	4.42**
Perceived communication benefits for suppliers → Satisfactory	-			0.28	(0.07)	3.98**
Perceived communication benefits for suppliers → Efficiency	-			0.24	(0.07)	3.48**
Perceived communication benefits for suppliers → Profit & competitive edge	-			0.21	(0.06)	3.54**
Logistics compliance → Satisfactory	0.09	(0.10)	0.79	0.09	(0.10)	0.79
Logistics compliance → Efficiency	0.08	(0.09)	0.83	0.08	(0.09)	0.83
Logistics compliance → Profit & competitive edge	0.14	(0.10)	1.38	0.14	(0.10)	1.38
Quality compliance → Satisfactory	0.57	(0.09)	6.36**	0.57	(0.09)	6.36**
Quality compliance → Efficiency	0.47	(0.09)	5.34**	0.47	(0.09)	5.34**
Quality compliance → Profit & competitive edge	0.36	(0.09)	4.01**	0.36	(0.09)	4.01**

[1] * Significant at 5% level; ** significant at 1% level.
[2] Average $R^2 = 0.257$.

Appendix 6.2. Results of hypotheses testing of the Communication-Chain compliance-Performance Model for the company-customer sample (N = 96)

Relationships	Path coefficient	(S.E.)	t-value[1,2]	Total effect	(S.E.)	t-value[1,2]
Perceived communication benefits for customers → Logistics compliance	0.09	(0.14)	0.71	0.09	(0.14)	0.71
Perceived communication benefits for customers → Quality compliance	0.28	(0.12)	2.36*	0.28	(0.12)	2.36*
Perceived communication benefits for customers → Satisfactory	-			0.11	(0.06)	1.77
Perceived communication benefits for customers → Efficiency	-			0.11	(0.07)	1.54
Perceived communication benefits for customers → Profit & competitive edge	-			0.15	(0.08)	1.84
Perceived communication benefits for the companies → Logistics compliance	0.35	(0.12)	2.87**	0.35	(0.12)	2.87**
Perceived communication benefits for the companies → Quality compliance	0.35	(0.13)	2.60**	0.35	(0.13)	2.60**
Perceived communication benefits for the companies → Satisfactory	-			0.17	(0.07)	2.20*
Perceived communication benefits for the companies → Efficiency	-			0.12	(0.07)	1.53
Perceived communication benefits for the companies → Profit & competitive edge	-			0.17	(0.08)	1.93
Logistics compliance → Satisfactory	0.12	(0.10)	1.10	0.12	(0.10)	1.10
Logistics compliance → Efficiency	-0.06	(0.15)	0.39	-0.06	(0.15)	0.39
Logistics compliance → Profit & competitive edge	-0.05	(0.11)	0.41	-0.05	(0.11)	0.41
Quality compliance → Satisfactory	0.36	(0.13)	2.73**	0.36	(0.13)	2.73**
Quality compliance → Efficiency	0.39	(0.15)	2.45*	0.39	(0.15)	2.45*
Quality compliance → Profit & competitive edge	0.53	(0.13)	3.96**	0.53	(0.13)	3.96**

[1] * Significant at 5% level; ** significant at 1% level.
[2] Average R^2 = 0.209.

Appendix 6.3. The influences of company characteristics on supply chain compliance and company performance for the company-supplier sample

Relationships[1]	Path coefficient significant?[2,3]	Sign of coefficient
CV$_1$: Firm size → Logistics compliance	No	-
CV$_1$: Firm size →Quality compliance	No	+
CV$_1$: Firm size → Satisfaction	No	-
CV$_1$: Firm size → Efficiency	No	+
CV$_1$: Firm size → Profit & competitive edge	No	+
CV$_2$: Firm age → Logistics compliance	No	-
CV$_2$: Firm age →Quality compliance	No	-
CV$_2$: Firm age → Satisfaction	No	+
CV$_2$: Firm age → Efficiency	No	-
CV$_2$: Firm age → Profit & competitive edge	No	+
CV$_3$: Firm type → Logistics compliance	No	+
CV$_3$: Firm type →Quality compliance	No	-
CV$_3$: Firm type → Satisfaction	No	-
CV$_3$: Firm type → Efficiency	No	-
CV$_3$: Firm type → Profit & competitive edge	**Yes****	-
CV$_4$: Quality standard → Logistics compliance	No	+
CV$_4$: Quality standard →Quality compliance	Yes*	-
CV$_4$: Quality standard → Satisfaction	No	-
CV$_4$: Quality standard → Efficiency	No	+
CV$_4$: Quality standard → Profit & competitive edge	No	+
CV$_5$: Administrative level of a location → Logistics compliance	No	+
CV$_5$: Administrative level of a location →Quality compliance	No	+
CV$_5$: Administrative level of a location → Satisfaction	**Yes***	-
CV$_5$: Administrative level of a location → Efficiency	**Yes****	-
CV$_5$: Administrative level of a location → Profit & competitive edge	No	-

[1] The five control variables are: company size, company age, company type, quality standard applied, and the administrative level of a location. Specifically, company type: 0 = production firms with lower market power; 1 = trade firms with higher market power. Administrative level of a location: 1 = town or county; 2 = medium-sized city; 3 = national or provincial capital city.

[2] The same significant paths for both the company-supplier and the company-customer (see Appendix 6.4) samples are shown in bold and italics.

[3] * Significant at 5%; ** significant at 1%.

Appendix 6.4. The influences of company characteristics on supply chain compliance and company performance for the company-customer sample

Relationships[1]	Path coefficient significant?[2,3]	Sign of coefficient
CV_1: Firm size → Logistics compliance	No	+
CV_1: Firm size →Quality compliance	Yes*	+
CV_1: Firm size → Satisfaction	No	+
CV_1: Firm size → Efficiency	No	-
CV_1: Firm size → Profit & competitive edge	No	-
CV_2: Firm age → Logistics compliance	Yes*	-
CV_2: Firm age →Quality compliance	No	-
CV_2: Firm age → Satisfaction	No	+
CV_2: Firm age → Efficiency	No	-
CV_2: Firm age → Profit & competitive edge	No	+
CV_3: Firm type → Logistics compliance	Yes**	+
CV_3: Firm type →Quality compliance	No	+
CV_3: Firm type → Satisfaction	No	-
CV_3: Firm type → Efficiency	No	-
CV_3: Firm type → Profit & competitive edge	**Yes***	**-**
CV_4: Quality standard → Logistics compliance	No	+
CV_4: Quality standard →Quality compliance	No	-
CV_4: Quality standard → Satisfaction	Yes*	-
CV_4: Quality standard → Efficiency	Yes*	-
CV_4: Quality standard → Profit & competitive edge	No	+
CV_5: Administrative level of a location → Logistics compliance	No	+
CV_5: Administrative level of a location →Quality compliance	No	+
CV_5: Administrative level of a location → Satisfaction	**Yes***	**-**
CV_5: Administrative level of a location → Efficiency	**Yes***	**-**
CV_5: Administrative level of a location → Profit & competitive edge	No	-

[1] The five control variables are: company size, company age, company type, quality standard applied, and the administrative level of a location. Specifically, company type: 0 = production firms with lower market power; 1 = trading firms with higher market power. Administrative level of a location: 1 = town or county; 2 = medium-sized city; 3 = national or provincial capital city.

[2] The same significant paths for both the company-supplier (see Appendix 6.3) and the company-customer samples are shown in **bold** and *italics*.

[3] * Significant at 5%; ** significant at 1%.

Summary

As one of the most substantial changes of modern business management, today's companies no longer compete as solely autonomous entities, but rather as supply chains (Lambert *et al.*, 1998). Supply chain collaboration can bring with substantial benefits and advantages for companies. To strengthen supply chain collaboration, inter-organizational communication is an essential enabler.

Inter-organizational communication is a broad concept covering a wide range of aspects, such as communication willingness, communication frequency, communication media, information quality, and so on. However, previous studies have typically considered communication as an aspect of a broader construct, such as supply management (e.g. Chen and Paulraj, 2004), or just studied one or limited aspects of communication. How to describe communication between business partners comprehensively? What are the interrelationships of the important aspects of communication? These still remains more or less as in a 'black box'. Meanwhile, our research interest was also induced by the question, 'how inter-organizational communication can be used to improve company performance?'.

Research objective and research questions

The objective of this research is therefore to develop insights into effective ways, i.e. suitable governance structure, to improve inter-organizational communication and ultimately, to improve company performance. To fulfill this objective, this research addresses the following central research question:

> How inter-organizational communication can be improved and used to improve company performance?

In order to answer the central research question and to achieve the research objective, the following specific research questions are formulated:

Research question A: what are the impacts of transaction attributes and governance structure on inter-organizational communication?

Research question B: what are the main aspects of inter-organizational communication, and what are their interrelationships?

Research question C: what are the relationships between inter-organizational communication and company performance?

Research methodology

This research has integrated different schools of thought, including Transaction Cost Economics, the literature on Management Information Systems, and Supply Chain Management. These theories have their own focus, assumptions, and framework for studying the relationships between companies. Nevertheless, they also provided complementary theoretical foundation. This research has put extensive effort into developing a conceptual framework that integrates insights from these theories in one overall framework (Figure 1), which is helpful for understanding inter-organizational communication, its antecedents, and chain compliance and performance results.

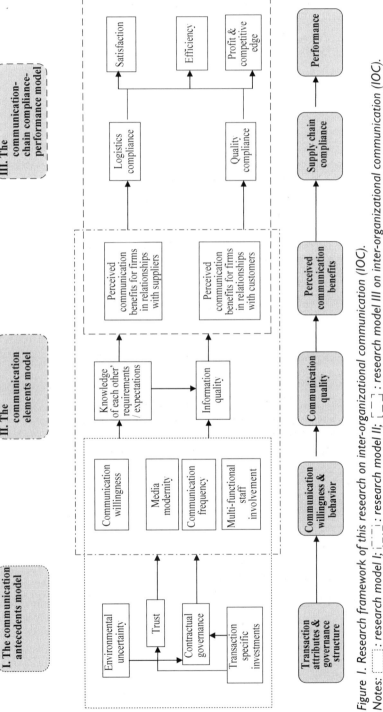

Figure 1. Research framework of this research on inter-organizational communication (IOC).
Notes: ⬜ : research model I; ⬚ : research model II; ⬚ : research model III on inter-organizational communication (IOC).

To answer the research questions, a 'mixed-methodology' approach combining literature study, pretest and survey was applied in this research, and turned out to be useful. The study domain is the poultry chain in China. Primary data were gathered from October 2008 to June 2009. Considering that China is a vast country, data were collected from two regions: the Eastern and Northern China with relatively higher and the Western China with relatively lower economic development level. This research focuses on two directly linked stages in the supply chain and has identified two sides of the 'coin' of the communication: the communication of companies with their most important suppliers and with their most important customers, respectively. After the examination of construct validity and reliability, partial least squares modeling technique was applied for data analysis.

Results and discussion

In order to achieve the research objective, three lines of researches were applied to answer the three research questions, respectively. Figure 2 and 3 illustrate the results of these three lines of researches. *The first line of research* (see the Communication Antecedents Model in Figure 1) focused on potential antecedents of inter-organizational communication with intention to answer the research question A, '*what are the impacts of transaction attributes and governance structure on inter-organizational communication?*' In general, the results of his research support positive and significant associations between transaction attributes and governance structure, and between governance structure and communication willingness and behavior. The results also support significant and positive association between 'environment uncertainty' and 'transaction specific investments', and between 'trust' and 'contractual governance' (pre-agreements).

Interestingly, when environmental uncertainty is higher, companies are likely to invest higher in specific transactions with their main suppliers and customers, to safeguard against uncertainty and risk. And when specific investments are higher, companies tend to build trust with their main suppliers and customers, to safeguard their investments. Differently, the association between specific investments and contractual governance is found for companies in relationships with their main suppliers, but not for companies with their main customers. A likely explanation is that, companies often have more negotiation power than their suppliers, but less than their customers in a buyer dominated market. Thus, in relationships with their main customers, they tend to invest in closer contractual relationship, and take use of trust and contractual governance to safeguard jointly their specific investments and markets.

This research supports that trust appears to be a reliable indicator for the level of communication willingness between companies and their main suppliers and customers, but not necessarily for communication behavior (focusing on media modernity, communication frequency, and multifunctional staff involvement). Meanwhile, this research finds that contractual governance do not necessarily indicate the level of communication willingness and behavior for companies in relationships with their main suppliers. Differently, companies tend to pay more attention to their contractual *customers* than non-contractual customers, and are likely to communicate with contractual customers more willingly and frequently, by employing more advanced information media, senior managers and staff from different functions.

The second line of research (see the Communication Elements Model in Figure 1) focused on the interrelationships of important aspects of communication, with intention to answer the research question B, '*what are the main aspects of inter-organizational communication, and what are their*

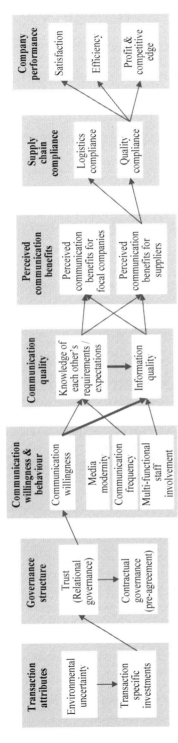

Figure 2. *The significant (and positive) relationships for the company-supplier sample.*
Thin arrows show path coefficients significant at 5% for both samples; thick arrows show path coefficients significant at 5% for only one sample.

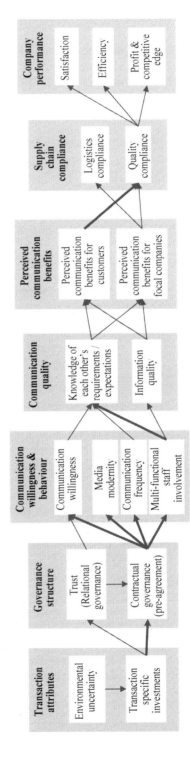

Figure 3. *The significant (and positive) relationships for the company-customer sample.*
Thin arrows show path coefficients significant at 5% for both samples; thick arrows show path coefficients significant at 5% for only one sample.

interrelationships?' In general, this research supports the significant and positive associations between communication willingness and communication quality, between certain aspects of communication behavior and communication quality, and between communication quality and perceived communication benefits. Thus, it is communication willingness and communication behavior that jointly lead to improved communication quality, whilst improved communication quality further contributes to greater communication benefits for companies.

The results support the critical role of *communication willingness* in improving communication quality and further providing benefits for companies. In contrast to our expectations, higher *media modernity* does not appear to lead to higher communication quality or greater communication benefits for companies in relationships with their suppliers or customers. A likely reason is the fact that there is only limited implementation of modern media in the Chinese poultry chain. Nevertheless, companies still reported that they had perceived major benefits from good communication with their customers and suppliers. Thus, companies should build a diverse communication system, which combines both traditional tools and modern media.

The results also support that, for companies in relationships with their main suppliers or customers, *communication frequency* is positively and significantly linked with knowledge of each other's requirements and expectations, but not with information quality. In addition, adopting *senior managers and staff from different functions* is positively and significantly linked with information quality. However, it is not significantly associated with knowledge of each other's requirements and expectations for companies in relationships with their main suppliers, but is for companies with their customers. A likely explanation is that, in a buyer dominant market, grasping markets is more complicated and challenging than safeguarding purchasing sources. Inputting senior managers and staff from different functions to communicate with their customers could help companies enrich their knowledge of their customers and grasp markets better.

Although the literature has typically take *communication quality* as being equal to information quality, this research supports that communication quality is composed of different dimensions. A new dimension found in this research is 'knowledge of each other's requirements and expectation'. Such knowledge might be valuable because it brings with opportunities for companies to grasp the changing events of business partners in the dynamic and challenging economy. The results also reveal that knowledge of each other's requirements and expectations is significantly linked with information quality for companies in relationships with their suppliers, but not for companies with their customers. Meanwhile, each dimension of communication quality is strongly linked with perceived communication benefits for companies, their suppliers and customers.

This research reveals that companies have perceived equal *communication benefits* for themselves, and for their important suppliers and customers. Moreover, communication benefits for companies and their suppliers are significantly linked with each other; and communication benefits for companies and their customers are as well. Thus, this research provided empirical support that it would be advantageous for both companies and their important business partners to invest greatly, and more or less equally in their mutual communication. In this way, it contributes to the important discussion on 'to what extent companies should invest in information exchange with their suppliers and customers'.

The third line of research (see the Communication-Chain compliance-Performance Model in Figure 1) focused on the potential influence of communication on supply chain collaboration and ultimately, on company performance, with intention to answer the research question C, '*what are the relationships between inter-organizational communication and company performance?*' In general, the empirical results supported the significant and positive associations between 'perceived communication benefits' for companies and 'supply chain compliance', between 'quality compliance' and each aspect of performance.

The results indicate that, when a company communicates with its main suppliers, it appears to be the communication benefits obtained by its main suppliers, rather than those obtained by itself, that help to improve the suppliers' supply chain compliance. In addition, when a company communicates with its main customers, it appears that both communication benefits obtained by itself and by its main customers help to improve its supply chain compliance.

The expected positive relationship between 'logistics compliance' and 'performance' was not supported here. This might reflect that there is still limited implementation of logistics compliance, and chain collaboration is still at an early stage in the Chinese poultry chain, as it was found with other meat chains in the Mainland China.

This research also examined the potential influence of companies' characteristics on the above constructs, by adding five company characteristics as five *control variables* into the research models. These control variables are: firm size, firm age, firm type sorted by market power, quality standard implemented, and economic level of a location (represented by administrative level of a location). The results indicate that companies' characteristics are likely to influence the level (i.e. magnitude) of these constructs in one way or the other. However, they do not necessarily influence the relationships between transaction attributes, governance structure, inter-organizational communication, supply chain compliance, and performance. Thus, the above findings and induced insights are likely to be tenable for different companies with different characteristics.

Theoretical contributions

First, this research has put extensive effort into integrating different theories in one comprehensive antecedents-communication-performance framework. These theories provide complementary theoretical foundation to reveal the communication relationships between companies. We have strong indications, both theoretical and empirical, that such an integrative research framework is needed to grasp the complexity of information exchange between business partners.

Second, this research is the extension of existing research on contractual governance and trust. No other study has been found to empirically test the relationship between contractual governance and communication, although the relationship is discussed in the literature. Moreover, this research for the first time empirically supported the complementary roles between contractual governance and trust in the process of improving communication (willingness).

Third, this research is the extension of existing research that has typically limited communication quality to information quality. The results strongly support the fact that communication quality has diverse dimensions, and each dimension is worth to be examined, respectively. The new dimension found in this research is 'knowledge of each other's requirements and expectations'. It appears to be a valid and complementary indicator to reveal the total quality of the communication between companies.

Fourth, this research is the extension of existing research on communication values. The literature has often examined communication values by the constructs of company performance. The results of this research support that communication benefits should be operationalized in a way to measure the direct benefits that a company obtains from the communication, whilst company performance might partly be an indirect and further result of communication. In addition, this research has distinguished between communication benefits for customers and for suppliers. The results support that inter-organizational communication is likely to provide significant and more or less equal (!) benefits for a company and its important suppliers, or for a company and its important customers. Moreover, it is the communication benefits obtained by a company and its main suppliers that jointly improve chain compliance, and furthermore, make the company stands out in each aspect of performance, compared to its main competitors. Thus, it appears to be advantageous for companies and their important business partners to invest in their own communication willingness, behavior and quality, and those of their important partners. In this way, this research contributes to the important discussion 'to what extent a company should invest in its communication with business partners?'

Fifth, this research is among the first to look at both sides of the 'coin' of communication: the communication of companies with their suppliers, and with their customers. Most extant studies are limited to collecting data on focal companies, or only take into account the customer or the supplier side of focal companies. However, this research has provided empirical support that important differences exist between relationships of companies with suppliers and relationships of companies with customers.' As such, this research has contributed to the adoption of such innovative method, which examining perceptions of both customers and suppliers.

Methodological contributions

First, the *'mixed-methodology' approach* was applied in this research and turned out to be useful. This research starts with an extensive literature study, which helped to identify the research topic, design the research, and draft a questionnaire. Then, a three-step procedure of the field research, which combined face-to-face interviews and site visits, a pre-test of the questionnaire and finally the survey, has proved to be beneficial by providing: (1) validated constructs and items for the questionnaire, and (2) valuable insights for the analysis and interpretation of the data results.

Second, partial least squares (PLS) modeling was applied in this research, and proved to be successful in examining the proposed relationships between the major constructs. To our knowledge, no study has made use of structural equation modeling techniques to examine inter-organizational communication in food chains in China. As such, we have contributed to the adoption of SEM techniques in social science research and in a new socio-economic context.

Managerial implications

This research has formulated several important managerial implications to answer the central research question, *'How inter-organizational communication can be improved and used to improve company performance?* Based on the research results, approaches to communication and performance were identified for companies in relationships with their main suppliers, and with their main customers, respectively (Figure 2 and 3).

Summary

For companies in relationships with their most important suppliers

First, although these companies prefer flexibility in purchasing sources, we would like to advise them to consider adopting certain types of contracts, if they intend to improve communication willingness and behavior of their important suppliers. Second, in order to realize more potential communication benefits, companies should invest to improve communication willingness of their own and their suppliers. In addition, special attention should be paid to understand the suppliers' changing requirements and expectations. This will substantially enhance their knowledge of their suppliers and information quality, and thus, help to realize more potential communication benefits. Indeed, it is the communication benefits obtained by their main suppliers, rather than those by themselves, that make them stand out from their main competitors.

For companies in relationships with their most important customers

First, these companies should focus on building mutual trust, if they intend to improve the communication willingness of their important customers. Although these companies are more interested in promoting contractual relationships with their main customers, it would be wise to bear in mind that, it is mutual trust built by companies with their customers, rather than contracts, that lead to long-term market opportunities. Second, these companies should adopt senior managers and staff from different functions to communicate with their important customers. This would help them obtain greater understanding of the customer's changing requirements and expectations, and ensure such knowledge is used by staff in the different functions. Third, in order to advance from realizing potential communication benefits to making themselves stand out from their main competitors, companies should not only commit to realizing more potential communication benefits for themselves, but also for their main customers.

For food policy makers

We advise food policy makers to pay explicit attention to facilitate food companies' *self-motivation* to implement quality standards. Food policy that encourages *retailers* to adopt high food quality standards is in particular critical as food production companies and food logistics companies are likely to comply with increased quality requirements of the retailers.

Limitations and future study

First, the main findings and conclusions of this research are based on the poultry chain in China, an emerging economy. It would be valuable to conduct a comparative study between poultry chains in developing countries or emerging economies and developed countries so as to investigate the impact of differences in governance mechanisms, technology applications and communication on performance of these chains. Such a study might provide unexpected valuable insights, such as unexpected disadvantages of integrated supply chain or unexpected advantages of non-integrated supply chain.

Second, this research focuses on the communication of companies with their most important suppliers and customers. However, it would be valuable also to address the communication of companies with less important suppliers and customers.

中文研究摘要 (summary in Chinese)[20]

作为现代工商管理界最重大的转变之一，今天的商业竞争不仅仅在独立的企业个体之间展开，更激烈存在于供应链与供应链之间 (Lambert *et al.*, 1998)。实施供应链合作 (supply chain collaboration) 可以为企业带来巨大的效益和竞争优势。为加强供应链合作，组织之间的信息交流 (inter-organizational communication) 是一个必不可少的推动器。

组织之间的信息交流是一个广泛的概念，涵盖多方面的内容，如：信息交流的意愿，信息交流的频率，信息交流的工具，信息的质量，等等。然而，现有的文献往往把信息交流当作一个较大的范畴(如供应管理)的一个方面来考察(例如 Chen and Paulraj, 2004)，或仅考察信息交流的一个或极少的几个方面。如何系统而全面地描述商业合作伙伴之间的信息交流？信息交流的各个重要方面之间存在着什么样的相互关系？企业应当如何运用组织之间的信息交流来实现企业绩效的提高？这些重要的问题仍然隐藏在"黑匣子"中，激发了作者开展本研究的兴趣。

研究目的和研究问题

本研究的目的旨在发展有效的途径，如适合的治理结构等，用以改善组织之间的信息交流，并进而实现提高公司绩效的最终目标。为实现此研究目的，提出了如下核心研究问题 (central research question)：

> 如何改善组织之间的信息交流，并利用信息交流来促进公司绩效的提高？

为回答此核心研究问题并实现前面所述的研究目的，提出了以下特定研究问题 (specific research questions)：
研究问题一：交易特征和治理结构对组织之间的信息交流有何影响？
研究问题二：组织之间的信息交流包括哪些重要的方面？这些方面之间存在着什么样的相互关系？
研究问题三：组织之间的信息交流与企业绩效之间存在着什么样的相互关系？

研究方法

为回答这些研究问题并实现前述研究目的，本研究整合了不同的思想流派，包括交易成本经济学理论 (Transaction Cost Economics)，管理信息系统 (Management Information Systems) 的理论和供应链管理 (Supply Chain Management) 理论。这些理论各有其侧重点，假设和理论框架。然而，它们为研究组织之间的相互关系提供了互补的理论基础。本研究努力整合这些不同但相关的理论，发展了一个概念框架（图1）。该概念框架有助于我们理解组织之间的信息交流的先决条件，以及信息交流对供应链协作和公司绩效的影响。

本研究采用了"混合研究法"(mixed-methodology)，即综合运用了文献研究、预测试、实地调研和问卷调查等研究方法。调查对象是中国大陆地区的家禽产业供应链。问卷调查的时间是2008年10月至2009年6月。考虑到中国地域广阔，数据收集主要在以下地区进

20　　彭广茜　　(2011)《组织之间的信息交流，供应链协作与企业绩效》，Wageningen学术出版社，Wageningen, the Netherlands. 2011. (英文著作)

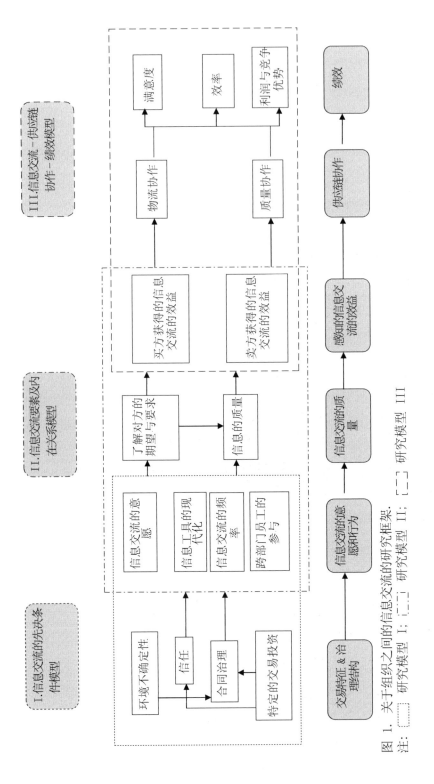

图 1. 关于组织之间的信息交流的研究框架.

注: [　] 研究模型 I; [┈] 研究模型 II; [┅] 研究模型 III

I. 信息交流的先决条件模型

II. 信息交流要素及内在关系模型

III. 信息交流－供应链协作－绩效模型

行：经济相对发达的华北地区（北京和河北）和华东地区（山东），以及经济欠发达的西南地区（贵州）。本研究侧重考察供应链上相邻的两个节点之间的关系，并区别分析了信息交流这枚"硬币"的两面：一面是公司与其重要供应商之间的信息交流，即本文中的"公司-供应商"样本；另一面是公司与其重要客户之间的信息交流，即本文中的"公司-客户"样本。本研究检查了结构变量的信度 (construct reliability) 和结构变量的效度 (construct validity)，并运用了先进的结构方程模型 (structural equation modeling) 中的一个重要分支方法（偏最小二乘模型技术 partial least squares modeling technique）来分析数据。

结果与讨论

为实现相关研究目的，本书通过三条研究主线来分别回答三个特定研究问题。图2和3展示了这三部份研究的结果。第一部份研究（见图1中的"信息交流的先决因子模型"）着重考察影响组织之间信息交流的潜在因素。此条研究主线旨在回答研究问题一："交易特征和治理结构对组织之间的信息交流有何影响？"概言之，研究结果支持"交易特征"和"治理结构"之间，"治理结构"和"信息交流的意愿和行为"之间存在着积极而显著的相互关系。研究结果也表明，"环境不确定性"和"特定交易投资"之间，以及"信任"与"合同治理"之间存在着积极而显著的相互关系。

有趣的是，当环境不确定性较高时，公司倾向于增加对其重要的供应商和客户的特定交易投资，目的可能是用以应对较高的不确定性和风险。进而，当特定交易投资的水平较高时，公司与其重要供应商和客户之间的信任程度也更高，这种更高的信任有助于保护他们的投资。值得注意的是，特定交易投资与合同治理之间的显著关系得到了"公司-供应商"样本的支持，但在"公司-客户"样本中则不显著。一种可能的解释是，在买方市场，公司通常比其供应商拥有较强的谈判权，而比其客户拥有较弱的谈判权。因而，在与其重要客户的关系管理中，他们倾向于建立密切的合同关系，并利用信任和合同治理来一起保护他们对于重要客户的特定交易投资，并进而保卫其市场。

研究结果表明，"信任"似乎是影响公司与其重要供应商和重要客户之间信息交流意愿高低的一个可靠指标。但信任程度似乎并能不影响信息交流的行为（包括信息工具的现代化，信息交流的频率和跨部门员工的参与）。与此同时，研究结果也表明，合同治理的水平不一定反映公司与重要供应商之间信息交流的意愿的高低，但似乎反映公司与重要客户之间信息交流的意愿的高低。数据表明，与非合同客户相比，公司更加重视其合同客户，与合同客户进行信息交流的意愿更高，交流频率也更高，且在交流中往往采用更加先进的信息交流工具，并有更多高级经理和跨部门的员工投入交流。

第二部份的研究（见图1中的"信息交流的要素和内在关系模型"）着重考察了信息交流的要素和这些要素之间的相互关系。此条研究主线旨在回答研究问题二：组织之间的信息交流包括哪些重要的方面？这些方面之间存在着什么样的相互关系？概言之，研究结果支持"信息交流的意愿"与"信息交流的质量"，某些"信息交流的行为"与"信息交流的质量"，以及"信息交流的质量"与"感知的信息交流的效益"之间存在着积极而显著关系。信息交流的意愿与信息交流的行为协同作用提高了信息交流的质量，更高的信息交流的质量进而帮助公司实现了更高的信息交流的效益。

研究结果显示，"信息交流的意愿"对提高"信息交流的质量"和进而实现更高的"信息交流的效益"起着关键性的作用。值得注意的是，预期的"信息交流工具的现代化"

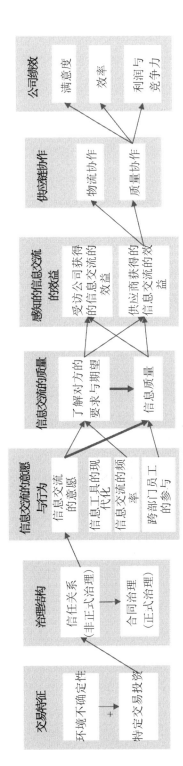

图 2. "公司-供应商"样本支持的显著（且积极）的相互关系。中的细线显示在"公司-供应商"和"公司-客户"两个样本中都显著存在的关系；粗线显示仅在其中一个样本中显著存在的关系（P<0.05）。

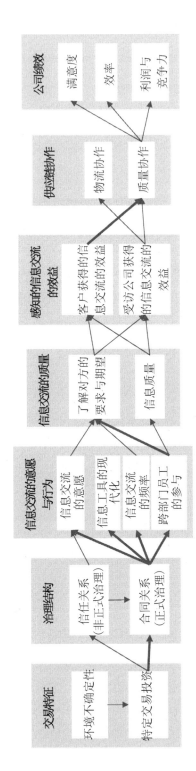

图 3. "公司-客户"样本在的显著（且积极）的相互关系。中的细线显示在"公司-供应商"和"公司-客户"两个样本中都显著存在的关系；粗线显示仅在其中一个样本中显著存在的关系（P<0.05）。

水平与"信息交流的质量"之间，以及与实现更多的"信息交流的效益"之间的关系并不显著。这可能是由于中国家禽供应链中现代化的信息工具的使用并不普及。即使如此，受访公司普遍认为他们在与重要供应商和客户的信息交流过程中受益匪浅。因此，即使在所谓的现代信息时代，公司应当综合利用传统和现代的信息交流工具，建立多样化的信息交流系统。

研究结果还显示，"企业-供应商"和"企业-客户"两样本都支持"信息交流的频率"与"了解双方的期望与要求"之间存在着积极而显著的关系，与"信息的质量"之间则不存在显著的关系。此外，"跨部门员工的参与"与"信息的质量"之间也存在着积极而显著的相互关系。但是"跨部门员工的参与"与"了解双方的期望与要求"之间积极的相互关系只在"公司-供应商"样本中显著存在，而在"公司-客户"样本中却并不显著。一个可能的解释是，在买方市场中，占领与保持市场比保证采购来源的活动更加复杂且更具有挑战性。在与重要客户的信息交流中投入高级经理和跨部门的员工有助于公司更好地了解客户的期望与要求，从而更好地占领与保持市场。

现有的研究文献往往把"信息交流的质量"等同于"信息的质量"。然而，本研究提出信息交流的质量是一个多维的概念。在本研究中首次发现的另一维是"了解双方的期望与要求"。了解商业伙伴的期望与要求之所以重要，可能在于它有助于一个公司迅速察知商业伙伴的变化，而此点在这个动态而富有竞争性的经济中尤为重要。研究结果还显示，"了解双方的期望与要求"与"信息质量"之间的关系在"企业-供应商"样本中显著存在，但在"企业-客户"样本中却并不显著。与此同时，两个样本都支持"信息交流的质量"与"感知的信息交流的效益"之间存在着积极而显著的关系。

研究结果还显示，公司与其重要供应商，以及公司与其重要的客户获得了相等（！）的信息交流的效益。进而，公司获得的信息交流的效益和其重要供应商获得的信息交流的效益之间，以及公司获得的信息交流的效益和其重要客户获得的信息交流的效益之间都存在着积极而显著的关系。因此，本研究进行的实证检验支持公司与重要合作伙伴之间大力开展信息交流不但对交流双方都有利，并且为双方带来的效益几乎是相等的。因而，本研究对"关于公司应当在多大程度上投入与商业伙伴之间的信息交流"这一重要的讨论作出了贡献。

第三部份研究（见图1中的"信息交流-供应链协作-公司绩效模型"）着重考察信息交流对供应链协作和公司绩效的影响。此条研究主线旨在回答研究问题三：组织之间的信息交流与企业绩效之间存在着什么样的关系？概言之，本实证研究的结果显示，"察知的信息交流的效益"与"供应链协作"之间，以及"质量协作"与"公司绩效"的各个方面之间存在着积极而显著的关系。

研究结果表明，在公司与其重要供应商的相互关系中，其供应商获得的"信息交流的效益"有助于显著地提高"供应链协作"的水平，而公司自身获得的"信息交流的效益"与"供应链协作水平"之间的关系却并不显著。此外，在公司与其重要客户的相互关系中，公司和其客户获得的信息交流的效益都有助于显著提高供应链的协作水平。

值得注意的是，预期的"物流协作"与"公司绩效"之间的关系并不显著。这可能反映了中国家禽供应链的各个节点之间开展物流协作的水平很低。与中国的猪肉供应链相似（Han, 2009），其物流协作尚处于早期发展阶段。

本研究也考察了公司特征对上述结构变量(construct)的潜在影响。五个方面的公司特征被作为控制变量 (control variable) 加入了研究模型中。这五个控制变量是：公司规模，公司年龄，公司类型（按市场谈判力大小分类），产品质量（按公司执行的最高质量标准来分类）和所在地区的经济发展水平。研究结构表明，公司特征倾向于影响这些结构变量的大小，然而，公司特征似乎并不影响交易特征，治理结构，组织之间的信息交流，供应链协作和公司绩效这些结构变量之间的相互关系。因此，本研究的上述发现和相关结论很可能对各种类型的公司都成立。

理论贡献

首先，如前所述，本研究整合了不同的思想流派，包括交易成本经济学理论，管理信息系统理论和供应链管理理论，发展了一个综合反映组织之间信息交流的概念框架："先决因素-信息交流-组织绩效"框架（图1）。理论和实证研究结果都有力地支持，这样一个整合的研究框架有助于我们全面地认识和把握商业合作伙伴之间的信息交流这一复杂事物。

第二，本研究拓展了关于"合同治理"和"信任"的现有研究。现有文献中对于合同治理与信息交流之间的关系有理论上的讨论，但尚未发现对两者之间关系的实证研究。此外，本研究首次提供了实证检验，支持合同治理和信任在提高信息交流（意愿）的过程中起着互补的作用。

第三，本研究拓展了关于"信息交流的质量"的现有研究。现有的文献把"信息交流的质量"等同于"信息的质量"。本研究的结果有力地支持信息交流的质量是一个多维而不是一维的概念，应当对其各维加以区别考察。本研究中发现的能反映"信息交流的质量"的一个新的显变量是"了解双方的期望与要求"。研究结果支持这是一个与"信息的质量"互补，从而有助于全面反映"信息交流的质量"的全貌的有效变量。

第四，本研究拓展了关于"信息交流的价值"的现有研究。相关文献通常使用"公司绩效"这一变量来反映"信息交流的价值"。本研究认为公司绩效当是信息交流的间接和进一步的结果，且本研究结果支持应当构建"信息交流的效益"这一结构变量，用以反映信息交流为公司带来的直接的效益。此外，本研究区分了信息交流对客户和对供应商的效益。研究结果表明，信息交流有助于为公司和其重要供应商，以及公司和其重要客户带来显著且相等(!)的效益。进一步地，是公司及其重要供应商获得的信息交流的效益共同提高了供应链协作的水平，并进而使得该公司在各方面绩效指标的表现比其主要竞争对手更加卓越。因此，公司及其重要的合作伙伴不但应当作出相应投资，以努力提高自身的信息交流的意愿，信息交流的行为和信息交流的质量，且应当投资以努力提高其重要合作伙伴的信息交流的意愿，信息交流的行为和信息交流的质量。基于此，本研究对"关于公司应当在多大程度上投入与商业伙伴之间的信息交流"这一重要的讨论作出了贡献。

第五，本研究是现有的考察信息交流这一枚"硬币"的两面的为数极少的研究之一：一面是公司与其重要供应商之间的信息交流；另一面是公司与其重要客户之间的信息交流。现有的文献通常只考察受访公司的情况，或受访公司与供应商之间的情况，或受访公司与客户之间的情况。然而，本研究的实证检验显示，公司与供应商之间的关系和公司与客户之间的关系存在着重要的区别。由此，本研究的一个贡献是采用了该创新性的研究方法，区别地考察了买方和卖方的观点。

研究方法上的贡献

第一，本研究有效地采用了"混合研究法"。在研究设计阶段，广泛研究了大量的相关文献，并在此基础上提出了研究题目和研究问题，开展了研究设计，并草拟了调查问卷。之后，在实证研究阶段采用了三步研究步骤，包括面对面访谈和实地调查、预测试和正式的问卷调查。这一阶段的研究有助于为设计出有效的结构变量和观测变量，并为后来的数据分析和解释提供有价值的相关行业知识。

第二，本研究运用了结构方程模型中的一个重要分支（偏最小二乘模型技术），并成功地检查了相关研究假设。目前，尚未发现其它研究采用结构方程模型来考察中国食品供应链中的信息交流。在此意义上，本研究为推动该技术在社会科学领域和一个新的社会经济环境中的应用作出了贡献。

管理实践上的意义

本研究对管理实践提出了一些重要的建议，用以回答中心研究问题："如何改善组织之间的信息交流，并利用信息交流来促进公司绩效的提高？"。在该研究结果的基础上，分别提出了买方和卖方实现促进信息交流和提高公司绩效的路径（如图2和3）。

对买方的建言

首先，虽然公司倾向于对采购来源的选择保持更大的自由度，本研究建议公司在与重要供应商的关系中采用适当形式的合同，因为合同有助于提高供应商的信息交流的意愿和改善其信息交流的行为。此外，公司还应当注意考察供应商变化的期望与要求。这将极大地提高公司对供应商的了解和信息的质量，并进而实现更多的潜在的信息交流的价值。事实上，是其重要供应商获得的信息交流的效益而不是公司自身获得的信息交流的效益使得公司比他们的竞争对手在各方面表现得更加卓越。

对卖方的建言

首先，公司应当注意建立与重要客户之间的相互信任，这将有助于提高其客户的信息交流的意愿。虽然公司通常热衷于加强与客户之间的合同关系，但是，睿智的经理人应当记住，为公司带来长期的市场机会的不是合同关系，而是他们与客户之间建立的相互信任。第二，建议公司采用高级别的经理和跨部门员工与重要客户进行信息交流。这将有助于他们了解客户的期望与要求，确保这些知识被不同部门的员工掌握和运用，并及时把握快速变化的市场。第三，为了现实更多的潜在的信息交流的效益，并进而比其主要竞争对手表现得更加卓越，建议公司不但要努力使自己获得更多的信息交流的效益，也应当努力帮助其重要的客户获得更多的信息交流的效益。

关于食品政策的建言

建议食品政策的制订和调整应着力于提高食品公司执行相关质量标准的内在动力。进而，刺激食品零售商采用更高的质量标准的食品政策尤其重要，因为，在买方市场经济条件下，零售商具有强大的谈判能力，食品生产商和物流公司都倾向于服从零售商提出的相关质量要求。

局限性与未来的研究

首先，本研究在对中国大陆的家禽供应链进行调研的基础上提了上述发现和结论。将来可考虑对发展中国家和发达国家的家禽供应链开展比较研究，从而进一步考察公司治理机制、技术运用和信息交流对这些供应链的绩效可能产生的不同影响。这样的比较研究有可能产生意料之外的有价值的认识，如高整合水平的供应链的缺点或低整合水平供应链的优点。

第二，本研究侧重考察公司与其最重要的供应商之间，以及与最重要的客户之间的信息交流。未来，可考虑对公司与次重要的商业合作伙伴之间的信息交流开展有价值的研究。

About the author

Guangqian Peng (彭广茜) was born in 1972 in P.R. China. She obtained a BSc degree from Nanjing Agricultural University in Plant Protection Sciences in 1993. From 1993 to 2000, she worked as a teacher and researcher in Guizhou University and became an assistant professor in 1999. She received her MSc degree in *Economics, Management and Consumer Studies* at Wageningen University with a specialization in business administration in 2004. Her MSc thesis is on "strategic use of E-commerce by SMEs". Thereafter, she worked as a junior researcher at Chinese Center of Agricultural Policy (CCAP), Chinese Academy of Sciences. In 2006, she was appointed as a PhD researcher at Business Administration Department of Wageningen University. Her PhD research project is on "inter-organizational information exchange, supply chain compliance and company performance". The results of this research are described in the present book. In 2010, she also worked as the guest lecture for the international master course of 'Case Study' at Wageningen University. She has presented her works in countries in Europe, Asia and North America. In addition, her works have contributed to book chapters and a number of (inter)national journals. Her research interests are in the interdisciplinary areas involving management information systems, supply chain management, consumer study, and company innovation and strategy management.

Her e-mail adresses for comments and contact are gqpeng@gmail.com and gqpeng@hotmail.com.

The research described in this book was financially supported by Wageningen University and Nuffic Fund (project nr. 2100842400, contract nr. CF4661)

Financial support from Wageningen University and Nuffic Fund for publishing this book is gratefully acknowledged as well.

Printed in the United States
by Baker & Taylor Publisher Services